# The Peoples Multicultural Almanac

## America from the 1400s to Present

### 365 Days of Contributions by

African Americans

Asian Americans

Hispanic Americans

Native Americans

European Americans

**The Peoples Publishing Group, Inc.**

*Free to Learn, to Grow, to Change*

## Credits

*Contributing writers:* Earl J. Taylor, Jr., Gabriela Enser and Linda Zierdt-Warshaw
*Editing by* Diane Tapp, Daniel Ortiz, Jr. and Sharen Levine
*Copyediting by* Salvatore Allocco
*Design by* Margarita T. Giammanco and Fernando J. Camacho
*Desktop Publishing Assistance and Graphics by* James E. Duck and Sharen Levine
*Photo Research by* Judith M. Kerns and Daniel Ortiz, Jr.
*Cover Design by* Westchester Graphic Group
*Logo Design by* Wendy E. Kury
*Electronic Publishing Consultant:* James Fee Langendoen

ISBN 1-56256-199-5

© 1994 by The Peoples Publishing Group, Inc.,
230 West Passaic St.
Maywood, NJ 07607

Printed in the United States of America.

9

## The Peoples Multicultural Almanac is the perfect daily reference for people interested & concerned with sharing multicultural information.

**K**nowledge about different cultures increases sensitivity and understanding, and, besides, almanacs are fun (and fast) to read every day! You'll find that you look forward to increasing your multicultural literacy by reading about these five groups each day in *The Peoples Multicultural Almanac*:

African Americans   Hispanic Americans   Asian Americans   Native Americans   European Americans

## The Peoples Multicultural Almanac was designed for:

- TEACHERS
- STUDENTS
- PARENTS & FAMILIES
- SUPERINTENDENTS, PRINCIPALS, & MULTICULTURAL COORDINATORS
- CHURCH & COMMUNITY LEADERS
- HUMAN RESOURCE DIRECTORS & BUSINESS PEOPLE

IN SHORT, *ALL OF US* WHO ARE CONCERNED & INTERESTED IN ENHANCING SENSITIVITY TO MULTICULTURAL ISSUES.

## How is The Peoples Multicultural Almanac organized?

- **5** entries for each day in the school year, September through May:
  - ● African Americans,
  - ▲ Asian Americans,
  - ❖ European Americans,
  - ◆ Hispanic Americans, and
  - ■ Native Americans;
- A concise calendar with 1-2 entries each day for the summer months;
- Entries highlight significant social, political, historical, cultural, artistic, literary, and popular people and events as they have impacted the United States within the global community;
- The time period covers 1400 to the present in the United States;
- Entries give background information to shed light on the significance and context for the reader;
- Gender balance is roughly half-female, half-male;
- Photos & quotations present the faces & voices of America;
- Authentic ethnic motifs on each page show a textile or fabric design from one of the five cultural or ethnic groups. (See next page.)

Each month in the school year opens with a photograph, quotation and more extensive information about a significant person(s) or event(s) from one of the five cultural groups represented. The motif matches the ethnic heritage of the person or event presented in the opening page of the month.

Some artificial limits were necessary to keep the size of the *Almanac* manageable, so you will find the Asian American entries limited to persons of color with Japanese and Chinese heritage, and the Hispanic American entries limited to persons of color with Puerto Rican, Cuban and Mexican heritage. European Americans vary greatly, but the majority are of English, Irish, French, Spanish, Italian, German, Scandinavian, Polish, Dutch or Russian heritage. Native Americans are from several different nations.

Why did we create The Peoples Multicultural Almanac?
We at The Peoples Publishing Group, Inc. hope you enjoy using The Peoples Multicultural Almanac each day of the year, and that you come to realize, as we did, that the complex character of America can never be fully appreciated without a deep understanding of the many different cultures, peoples and events that have formed our country. We like to think that our Almanac is reflective of the changes that must occur in America, heralding the increasing demand for quality, easily accessible information on all peoples in our public libraries, universities, public school curriculums, and in our definition of cultural literacy. We encourage you to share your sources, documents and knowledge with us to make future Almanacs even more inclusive.

*The Peoples Publishing Group, Inc.*

**1-800-822-1080**

## AFRICAN AMERICAN MOTIF

## ASIAN AMERICAN MOTIF

## EUROPEAN AMERICAN MOTIF

## HISPANIC AMERICAN MOTIF

## NATIVE AMERICAN MOTIF

Constance Baker Motley is an African American woman whose achievements have taken her near the top of both the legal profession and the political arena in the state of New York. While in Columbia University Law School in New York City, she worked with the NAACP (National Association for the Advancement of Colored People) Legal Defense Fund, Inc. Graduating with a law degree in 1946, Motley became an associate counsel of the fund. She participated in almost every major civil rights case involving the NAACP before the New York State Supreme Court.

In 1964, Motley left the NAACP and won a seat in the New York State Senate. A year later, she was elected Manhattan borough president by the unanimous vote of the city council. She was the first African American woman to serve in both positions.

In 1966, Motley was appointed United States district judge for the Southern District of New York State. With this appointment by President Lyndon B. Johnson, Motley achieved another historic first by becoming the first African American woman appointed to the federal bench.

Constance Baker Motley's date of birth is September 14, 1921. In 1992, she still worked in the US Southern District Court of New York.

> *"America is about to make good on its promise of equal opportunity for all."*
>
> Constance Baker Motley,
> 1966

◄ Constance Baker Motley, US district judge for the Southern District of New York State

● General Daniel "Chappie" James, Jr., was promoted to the rank of four-star general and was named commander-in-chief of NORAD (**Nor**th American **A**ir **D**efense command) in 1975.

**SEPTEMBER**

■ James H. Wilbur was appointed as superintendent of the Yakima Agency Boarding School in 1860. The boarding school, the first to be located on a reservation, was created for the Yakima Nation as a result of a treaty between the Yakima and the US government in 1855. The school was located in the buildings of Fort Simco on the Yakima reservation in Washington.

▲ On this day in 1980, Chun Doo Hwan was sworn in as the Republic of Korea's new president.

◆ Beginning in 1969, California's San Jose College began offering a graduate program in Mexican American studies. The program was offered by the Mexican American Graduate Studies Department.

❖ The first college in the United States founded by Norwegians, Luther College, was founded on this day in 1861. The college is located in Decorah, Iowa. The college focused on educational and religious teachings of the children of Norwegian immigrants. Laur Laisen was the first president of the college.

**SEPTEMBER**

● Alabama Governor George Wallace in 1963 violated a US Supreme Court ruling against segregation in schools by preventing the integration of Tuskegee High School in Alabama. Wallace enforced his decision by surrounding the school building with state troopers.

■ In September 1969, Louis W. Ballard, of Cherokee-Sioux descent, was awarded the first Marion Nevins MacDowell Award for a chamber-ensemble composition. Ballard won the award for *Ritro Indio.* The composition was performed the following month in New London, Connecticut.

▲ On this day in 1899, two Buddhist missionaries, Kukuyro Nishijima and Shuyei Sonada, arrived in San Francisco, California. The Buddhist Churches of America use this date to mark their beginning.

*"Walk softly and carry a big stick."*

President Theodore Roosevelt, 1901

◆ The Bronx, New York City-based anticrime group known as the *Magnificent 13* changed its name to the *Guardian Angels* during this month in 1979. The group was formed in 1978 by Puerto Rican American Curtis Sliwa to help patrol the city's subway system and neighborhoods as a deterrent to crime. With its new name, the group began to wear a uniform consisting of red berets and red-and-white T-shirts so people would recognize its members. Within four years of its origin, the group, which was frequently described as a "vigilante force" by law-enforcement officials, claimed a membership of more than 2,000 volunteers in 33 major US cities.

❖ A few weeks after becoming president in 1901, Theodore Roosevelt said, "Walk softly and carry a big stick." In saying this, the president was emphasizing the need for a strong foreign policy. The saying caught the fancy of the nation, and the "big stick" became the favorite prop of political cartoonists of the era.

● After an eight-year struggle, the schools of St. Louis, Missouri, were peacefully desegregated in 1980.

■ During this month in 1831, Major Francis W. Armstrong was appointed as an agent to the "Choctaw West Movement." Armstrong's duties were to assist in removing the Choctaw people to the West and to ensure that the terms of the *Treaty of Rabbit Creek* were met.

▲ During this week in 1883, an official goodwill visit led by Korean Min Yong Ik arrived in the United States. This marked the beginning of Korean migration to the United States. Min Yong Ik remained in the United States. He became the first Korean student in the US. Later, Min Yong Ik returned to Korea. He wrote of his visit to the United States in *Soya Kyun Mun,* which translated means, *What I Saw and Heard During My Visit to the West.*

◆ During this month in 1972, Secretary of Labor of the Commonwealth of Puerto Rico Julia Rivera de Vincente was appointed as a member of the US Mission to the United Nations. De Vincente was the first woman appointed to this position.

❖ During this week in 1921, Margaret Gorman became the winner of the first beauty contest ever held in the US. Gorman, who was from the state of Washington, won the *Miss America* beauty contest. The contest was held in Atlantic City, New Jersey.

**4**

SEPTEMBER

● Arkansas Governor Orval Faubus called in the National Guard to prevent nine African American students from entering Central High School in Little Rock, Arkansas, in 1957. The Governor's actions went against the US Supreme Court ruling in the 1954 *Brown v Board of Education of Topeka, Kansas,* case.

■ Apache Chief Geronimo surrendered for the last time to General Miles at Bowie Station in 1886. During the 1870s and 1880s, Geronimo fought in the Apache Wars under the great leader Cochise. Geronimo had been captured before, only to escape from a reservation and flee to Mexico. After his surrender, he was sent to a reservation in Florida. Ten years later, he was sent to Fort Sill, Oklahoma. Geronimo remained at Fort Sill as a prisoner of war until his death.

▲ Alex Kimura became the first mainland person of Japanese descent to serve as a page in the US House of Representatives in 1973.

◆ On the final day of the founding convention of *La Raza Unida* (The United Race), an independent Chicano political party, 28-year-old party founder Jose-Angel Gutierrez was elected chairman of the organization. Gutierrez, a Texan, defeated Rudolfo Gonzalez in the election. Gonzalez was a militant leader of the Crusade for Justice in Denver, Colorado.

❖ Mark Spitz of the US swimming team was awarded his seventh gold medal at the 1972 Olympic Summer Games in Munich, West Germany. Spitz won his seventh medal as a member of the winning 400-meter relay team. The seven gold medals were an all-time record for an individual Olympic athlete.

● The first published novel written by an African American was issued in Boston, Massachusetts, in 1859. The novel, titled *Our Nig; or Sketches from the Life of a Free Black,* was written by Harriet Wilson. Little is known about the author who apparently was a free African. What is known is that the novel is an autobiography and was written to raise money to care for her son. The novel was published privately by the Boston firm of George C. Rand and Avery.

■ Chief Frank Fools Crow, an Oglala Sioux holy man, delivered a prayer for peace and understanding on the floor of the US Senate chamber in Washington, DC, in 1975. Fools Crow was a guest Senate chaplain for the day. Senator James Abourezk, Democrat of South Dakota and a Native American, arranged for the appearance of Chief Fools Crow. The prayer was translated by fellow Oglala Sioux, Virgil Kills Straight.

▲ In 1973, UNCURK, the United Nations Commission for the Unification and Rehabilitation of Korea, announced that it had recommended that UNCURK be dissolved in its annual report to the UN General Assembly .

◆ During this month in 1499, a revolution on the island of Hispaniola was finally suppressed. The revolt had begun because of Columbus's poor administration of the island. Detractors of Columbus reported that he had been cruel to both Spanish immigrants and the natives of the island. Often this cruelty took the form of withholding food and supplies.

❖ Jack Kerouac's book, *On the Road,* was published in 1957 in New York City by Viking Press. His book gave a voice to the "Beat Generation" of the 1950s and early 1960s. The Beat Generation was made up of young people who searched for an alternative life-style and meaning of life. Kerouac wrote of his travels throughout North America, Mexico and Europe. These writings were mostly autobiographical. This book and others emphasized human sexuality, drugs and the Asian religion called Zen. Kerouac criticized what he felt was negative about US life, most notably its commercialism, conformity, and stiff conventionality.

● Governor A. B. "Happy" Chandler of Kentucky sent the Kentucky National Guard to Surgis, Kentucky, after angry mobs demonstrated against the admission of African American students to the local high school (1956).

■ During this week, the Reverend Dr. Roe B. Lewis, a Presbyterian minister of Phoenix, Arizona, was chosen to receive the 1968 Indian Achievement Award presented by the Indian Council of Fire. Dr. Lewis, of Pima and Papago ancestry, was chosen because of his excellent work in education counselling and for helping Native American high school graduates get through college and graduate school.

▲ Korean Park Tong Sun was indicted by the US Department of Justice as the key person involved in the alleged "Korean influence-buying on Capitol Hill." The indictment was made in 1977.

◆ Thirty-seven-year-old Mexican Speranza del Valle Vasquez was released from Methodist Hospital in Houston, Texas, on this day in 1966. Vasquez, who underwent surgery on August 7, became the first person to survive a heart-pump implantation. The surgery was performed by Dr. Michael E. DeBakey.

❖ Humanitarian and social reformer Jane Addams was born in 1860 in Cedarville, Illinois. The most famous legacy of Addams is the US settlement-house movement, the best example being Hull House in Chicago. While visiting Europe in 1883 and 1888 Addams saw the prototype of what she wanted to build in the US in London's Toynbee Hall. Along with Ellen Gates Starr, Addams founded the Hull settlement house in Chicago in 1889. Settlement houses provided many services to the community from day care to college courses. They were built with the idea of assisting new European immigrants and African American immigrants to adjust to urban life. Jane Addams's concerns ranged from child-labor laws to the relationship between poverty and crime, fair housing, public health and international peace. She wrote and lectured extensively on these and many other social concerns. In 1931, she received and shared the *Nobel Peace Prize* with Nicholas Murray Butler.

● During this week in 1967, President Lyndon B. Johnson announced that he would nominate Walter E. Washington to head the newly reorganized government of the city of Washington, DC. Washington became the first African American to govern a major US city.

■ Chief Crazy Horse of the Oglala Sioux Nation was placed under arrest in 1877. Crazy Horse was arrested by General Mackenzie. Crazy Horse fought with Chief Sitting Bull in the Battle of Little Bighorn in which General Custer was defeated.

## SEPTEMBER

▲ During this week in 1973, more than one thousand people, both US residents and Chinese, attended the dedication ceremony of the Sun Yat Sen Memorial Hall on the campus of St. John's University in the New York City borough of Queens. The Oriental-style hall would house the university's Center of Asian Studies. The director of the center was Dr. Paul K. T. Sih, professor of history and assistant to the president of the university.

◆ Beginning on this day in 1960 and ending on the 12th, the American Conference on Economic Aid met in Bogota, Colombia. A United States program for liberal aid had been revealed by US Undersecretary Douglas C. Dillon. At the end of the conference, 19 American republics voted in support of the Act of Bogota, an aid plan for social and economic development.

❖ The Clara Barton commemorative stamp went on sale on this day in 1948 in Oxford, Massachusetts, the birthplace of Barton. Barton is credited as being the founder of the Red Cross in the United States.

> "The first is the period of military government; the second, the period of tutelage; and the third, the period of constitutional government."
>
> Sun Yat Sen,
> The Three Phases of National Reconstruction, 1918

## SEPTEMBER
**Independence Day**
Brazil

● During this month in 1950, Gregory Swanson became the first African American student admitted to the University of Virginia. Swanson was admitted into the university's law school under a court order.

■ At a battle near Lake George, New York, in 1755, Mohawk Chief Hendrick was killed. Chief Hendrick is sometimes called King Hendrick. He fought with the British against the French during the French and Indian Wars.

▲ On this day in 1941, the US government had Los Angeles-born Japanese American Iva Togori arrested. Togori, who was known to American GIs as "Tokyo Rose," was arrested in Yokohama, Japan, and charged with treason. Togori had gone to Japan in 1941 to "visit a sick aunt." While there, she was recruited by Tokyo radio, where she broadcast information to GIs for propaganda purposes in an attempt to demoralize US troops.

◆ In 1565, a Spanish expedition led by Don Pedro Menendez de Aviles landed at what is now St. Augustine, Florida. The group founded the first permanent settlement of Europeans on the continent of North America.

❖ Edmund Muskie (Marciszewski) was elected as the first Democratic US senator from Maine and the first Polish American US senator anywhere in the United States in 1958. His father changed the family surname in 1903 after emigrating to the US.

> *"The mere imparting of information is not education. Above all, the effort must make a man (person) think and do for himself (herself)."*
>
> Carter G. Woodson
> *The Mis-Education of the Negro*
> 1990

## SEPTEMBER 9

● Dr. Carter G. Woodson, called by many "the father of Negro history," established the Association for the Study of Negro Life and History in 1915. The organization was dedicated to the scholarly pursuit of collecting documents of historic and social importance and to promoting the study of all things connected with "Negro life."

■ Around this date in 1797, the mission of San Fernando was established. The mission was established in Achois, a Native American village in the Encino Valley of southern California.

**Chrysanthemum Day**
Japan

▲ Kim Il Sung declared the establishment of the Korean People's Democratic Republic in 1948. The republic claimed authority over all of Korea.

◆ Haiti became a protectorate of the United States later in this month in 1915. On February 28, 1916, the US Senate approved a treaty that allowed the United States to maintain Haiti's protectorate status for a period of one year.

❖ In 1964, leading East German nuclear physicist Heinz Barwich defected to the United States while attending an Atoms for Peace conference that was being sponsored by the United Nations. While in Europe, Barwich was director of the Central Institute for Nuclear Research in Russendorf, East Germany.

## SEPTEMBER 10

● Following a standoff between Governor George Wallace of Alabama and federal authorities in 1963, 20 African American students entered the public schools in Mobile and Tuskegee, Alabama.

■ During this week in 1957, the Chilkat "Indian" village near Klukwan, Canada, acquired the rights to the minerals on its land, which it had once lost.

▲ During this week in 1990, President George Bush issued a formal public apology to Japanese Americans who were placed in internment camps, or had friends or relatives placed in those camps, by the US government during World War II (1941-1945). Many Japanese Americans were placed in the camps because the US was at war with Japan and was biased against those of Japanese descent in the US.

◆ During this month in 1962, President John F. Kennedy signed the Migrant Health Act of 1962. The legislation has since helped improve the quality of life for Mexican American and other migrant workers in the US.

❖ During this week in 1850, P.T. Barnum, showperson and entrepreneur, brought Swedish singer Jenny Lind to the United States. Lind, who was known as the "Swedish Nightingale," made her US debut in New York City at Castle Garden.

**Key:** ● African Americans ■ Native Americans ▲ Asian Americans ◆ Hispanic Americans ❖ European Americans

● George Jackson, African American social and political militant and a former inmate at California's San Quentin Prison, was posthumously awarded the first annual Black Academy of Arts and Letters Award in the nonfiction book category in 1971. Jackson's book, *Soledad Brothers: Prison Letters of George Jackson,* is an autobiography telling of his youth, his imprisonment and his growing militancy during his ten years in San Quentin.

**SEPTEMBER**

■ Chief Big Bill of the Paiute joined forces in 1857 with the Mormon leader, John D. Lee, in the Mountain Meadow Massacre. Emigrants known as the Fancher Party were attacked by "Indians" as they made their way through Utah heading for California.

▲ The United States passed the Refugee Escape Act in 1957. This act was created to protect many "paper sons" (males born in China who claimed US citizenship because their fathers had become naturalized citizens of the US) who were threatened with deportation due to illegal entry into the US.

◆ In this month, the USSR accused the United States of preparing aggression against Cuba and warned that it would go to war over the issue. During the month that followed, the Cuban missile crisis would come to a head in the US-USSR confrontation over the installation in Cuba of Soviet offensive missile and bomber bases in 1962.

◆ Pete Rose, baseball player for the Cincinnati Reds, broke the major league record for the most "safe" hits in a career when he hit a double in a home game against the San Diego Padres in 1985. The hit was the 4,192nd in Rose's career, breaking the record formerly held by Ty Cobb of the Detroit Tigers by one hit.

● Prince Hall established the first Masonic Lodge for Africans and African Americans in Boston, Massachusetts, in 1787. Hall, who served in the Revolutionary War, was inducted into a British Lodge by British soldiers stationed in Boston. When the the British fled near the end of the war, Hall organized his now-famous Lodge. A Masonic Lodge is a fraternal organization that raises money for various charities, uses symbols of masonry or other building professions to promote its moral view of the world and often holds secret ceremonies at their meetings.

**SEPTEMBER**

■ During the 1723 school year of the College of William and Mary, the campus included a new addition--the Brafferton Building. The building was constructed for use by Native American students whose enrollment in the college had increased in such numbers as to require an additional structure.

▲ ● ◆ A survey conducted by the National Council of Negro Women reported in 1991 that 60 percent of women in the US of Asian, African and Hispanic descent as well as Native American women believed that they had no chance of contracting the AIDS virus.

◆ The University of Havana was founded in Cuba on this day in 1721.

◆ Former social worker Alice J. Stebbins Wells joined the Los Angeles Police Department in 1910, becoming the first policewoman in the US with full powers of arrest. By necessity, she designed her own police uniform. Her primary duties included supervising and enforcing the laws of public recreation areas, searching for missing persons and "maintaining a general information bureau for women seeking advice within the scope of police departments." Wells was an excellent police officer who traveled widely to drum up support for policewomen in other areas of the country. Because of Wells's efforts, 17 other US police departments were employing women by 1916.

● African American inventor Lewis Latimer and associate Joseph V. Nichols were granted a patent for an electric lamp that featured a new, more cost-effective type of filament in 1881.

■ In an ongoing battle between the US Cavalry and the Nez Perce, who refused to be removed to a reservation in Idaho, the Nez Perce held off the cavalry at Canyon Creek in Montana on this day in 1877.

▲ On this day in 1888, a bill banning the immigration of working-class Chinese for 20 years was approved by Congress. The ban did not include, however, Chinese officials, students, merchants or travelers.

◆ President Jimmy Carter made two historic appointments in 1979. First, he appointed Edward Hidalgo as secretary of the navy. Second, he appointed Abelardo Lopez Valdez as chief of protocol. This is the first time either of these positions was held by an Hispanic American.

❖ Jane Cahill Pfeiffer became the highest ranking woman executive in the broadcasting industry in 1978. Pfeiffer was named chairman of the board and director of the Radio Corporation of America, the parent company of NBC.

● The Twenty-Fourth Amendment to the Constitution was proposed by Congress in 1962. The amendment, which forbids the use of a poll tax as a prerequisite to voting in federal elections, was ratified on January 20, 1964. One reason for the creation of this amendment was to ensure that African Americans and other "minorities" who were in lower income brackets retained their voting rights. Many states had instituted poll taxes to prohibit "minorities" from voting.

■ While visiting the United States in 1987, Pope John Paul II addressed a conference of about 1,600 Native American leaders in Phoenix, Arizona. The Pope urged the leaders to forget past "mistakes and wrongs" in Catholic-church dealings with Native Americans and, instead, focus on furthering Native American rights in the present.

▲ Zubin Mehta officially took over as music director and conductor of the New York Philharmonic orchestra in 1978. Mehta, who was born in India, previously directed and conducted symphony orchestras in Israel, Montreal and Los Angeles, where, in 1962, he became the youngest major symphony orchestra conductor in US history.

◆ In 1847, US forces under the orders of President Polk occupied the Mexican capital, completing their conquest of Mexico. Polk's intent was to write a treaty of peace with the Mexicans which would later be called the *Treaty of Guadalupe Hidalgo*.

❖ Elizabeth Ann Seton in 1975 became the first person born in the US to be canonized (made a saint) by the Roman Catholic Church. Born in New York City in 1774, Mother Seton, as she was called, was the founder of the first US Catholic religious community, the Sisters of Charity. In Baltimore, MD, she established the first Catholic elementary school in the US (1808), the Paca Street School, and in Philadelphia (1814) she established the first Catholic child-care institution, the Orphan Asylum of Philadelphia. She took her religious vows in 1809. The feast day of Elizabeth Ann Seton is January 4th.

● The Sixteenth Street Baptist Church, an African American church in Birmingham, Alabama, was bombed in 1963. Four teenage girls were killed in the explosion. This was one of the most cold-blooded acts of violence against African Americans during the early years of the civil rights movement.

■ In 1893, land in the northern part of Oklahoma, called the "Cherokee Strip," was opened for white residence. Prior to 1893, this fertile land was closed to whites; however, in 1892, Congress paid the Cherokee Nation $1.40 per acre for their hunting grounds. On this day in 1893, a crowd of 100,000 gathered at the Kansas border to begin a race across the region to claim the 40,000 160-acre homesteads made available by the government.

▲ Japanese Americans celebrate Respect for the Aged Day.

◆ In 1982, Richard Rodriguez, whose parents are Mexican immigrants, published his autobiography, *Hunger of Memory*. In his book, Rodriguez spoke of his educational experience as a child and argued against bilingual education.

❖ The first female minister of religion in the US was the Reverend Antoinette Brown who was ordained minister of the South Butler Congregational Church, NY, in 1853 at a salary of $300 per year. Previously she was the first female divinity student at the Oberlin College Theological Seminary. In 1848, she preached her first sermon in New York City while still a seminary student. She was not always well received and once was booed while attending a temperance convention.

> "I hoarded the pleasures of learning. Alone for hours. Enthralled. Nervous. I rarely looked away from my books--or back on my memories."
>
> Richard Rodriguez, *Hunger of Memory*, 1982

● The Missionaries of Divine Word dedicated the first Catholic seminary for the education of African American priests in 1923. The seminary was located in Bay St. Louis, Mississippi.

■ Congress approved a bill in 1976 that authorized $480 million to be spent in fiscal years 1978 through 1980 for the health care of Native Americans. The bill allotted monies for the recruitment and training of Native Americans in the health-care profession, for patient care, for the construction and renovation of medical facilities and for health care for Native Americans living in urban areas. The bill was signed by the President Gerald Ford on September 30.

▲ The Korean Youth Corps, established in Hastings, Nebraska, under the leadership of Pak Yong-man, graduated its first class of 13 students in 1912.

◆ Father Miguel Hidalgo y Costillo of Dolores, Mexico, met with the townspeople of Dolores in 1810 to discuss their desire for independence from Spain. This date is celebrated as Independence Day in Mexico.

❖ In 1974, Mary Louise Smith, originally from Eddysville, Iowa, became the first woman "chairman" of the Republican National Committee. Smith was 60 when she took the job and held the position through the presidential campaign of Gerald Ford. She resigned from the post following the 1976 presidential election.

● In 1957, musician Louis Armstrong confirmed reports that he had canceled a US government-sponsored tour of the Soviet Union in protest of the social and political conditions of African Americans in the South.

■ One of the earliest treaties ever made between Native Americans and the United States was signed by the Delawares on this day in 1778 at Fort Pitt. The treaty allowed US troops to pass through their country to attack the British posts on the Great Lakes. The treaty also said that the Delaware would sell corn, horses, meat and other supplies to the US troops.

▲ On this day in 1987, a bill (HR442) passed in the US House of Representatives. This bill, along with its companion bill in the Senate (SR1009), outlined a proposal for restitution and apology to those Japanese inmates of internment camps of the World War II era who were still alive. The Senate version passed on April 20, 1988, and was signed into law by President Reagan on August 10, 1988. Under the terms of the bill, each individual who was imprisoned under Executive Order 9006 was to receive payment of $20,000.

◆ César Chávez, leader of the United Farm Workers of California (UFWOC), many of whom were"minorities," organized and began a nationwide boycott of lettuce in an attempt to settle a wage dispute with California lettuce growers in 1970.

❖ In 1782, a formal treaty was made between the United States and the republics of the Netherlands. The treaty called for friendship and trade between the two groups.

● Booker T. Washington delivered his famous "Atlanta Compromise" speech at the Atlanta, Georgia, Cotton Exposition in 1895. This speech outlined, for the first time to a wide US audience, Washington's views on race relations. Through his words, he supported the concept of peaceful coexistence between African Americans and whites.

■ Harriet Maxwell Converse became the first non-Native American woman to become chief of a Native American tribe in 1891. Converse, as chief of the Six Nations Tribe, represented the Seneca, Onondaga, Cayuga, Oneida, Mohawk and Tuscarora Nations.

▲ The head of the Evangelical Unification Church, Reverend Sun Myung Moon, presided over a "God Bless America" rally in Washington, DC, in 1976. Moon, an advocate of US defense in South Korea, attracted a crowd of about 50,000 people.

◆ Independence Day is celebrated by Hispanic Americans of Chilean descent on both the 18th and the 19th. The day marks the liberation of Chile from Spanish rule in 1810.

❖ Sonja Henie, a Norwegian-born United States championship figure skater, took the US citizenship oath of allegiance to become a US citizen in 1941. Sonja Henie won the world amateur skating championship, women's division, for ten consecutive years (1927-1936). She also won a gold medal in the Winter Olympic Games of 1928, 1932 and 1936. Sonja Henie achieved financial success as a professional ice skater and as a motion picture actress.

"No race can prosper until it learns that there is as much dignity in tilling a field as in writing a poem."

Booker T. Washington, *Up From Slavery,* 1907

● Booker T. Washington opened the world famous Tuskegee Institute in Alabama in 1881. This institute of higher learning was built by Washington with his own hands. The mission of Tuskegee was to train African Americans to be of service to the social and economic concerns of America through careers in agriculture and domestic service. Instead of destroying the European-based system and rebuilding it in favor of African Americans, as many more radical African leaders wanted to do, Washington, through Tuskegee, wanted to work within the system and rise to the top through it.

■ On this day in 1661, Governor Philip Calvert of Maryland held a peace conference with Chief Pinoa of the Delaware at Appoquinimink (what is now Odessa, Delaware). The meeting was called to help bring an end to recent confrontations between the Delaware and European Americans living in the region. This meeting resulted in the first treaty negotiated between Native Americans and European American colonists.

▲ Philippine President Corazon Aquino addressed Congress on this day in 1986. In her address, Aquino requested economic aid for her country from the United States. The address was hailed as being very strong and effective. In record time, Congress voted to send economic aid to the struggling Filipino community to help in its fight against poverty, disease, malnutrition and high infant-mortality rate.

*Corazon Aquino*

❖ The film *Goodfellas* was released on this day in 1990 to critical acclaim. The film, which was directed by Italian American Martin Scorsese, had its premiere in New York City. The story of the film was the life of an Irish American from Brooklyn who joins the mob and later became an informant for the FBI.

● The first African American female director of a full-length film for a major United States movie studio, Euzhan Palcy, received high praise for her movie, *A Dry White Season*, when it opened in 1989. The movie, set in South Africa, looked at a case involving the deaths of a black South African gardener and his son while in police custody and their white boss's efforts to find out the truth. Palcy was originally from Martinique.

■ The Haskell Institute of Lawrence, Kansas, was opened in 1884. The institute was designed as a vocational educational facility for the benefit of Native Americans. Students attending the school came from the Arapaho, Cheyenne, Ottawa, Ponca and Pawnee nations.

▲ Early this month in 1946, 21,000 workers in 33 plantations in Hawaii walked off their jobs to strike. The strike lasted nine days, and 6,000 Filipino laborers had to be imported to take the Hawaiians' place. The dispute finally ended when Castle and Cooke, one of the "Big Five" (the five major corporations in Hawaii), decided to settle its differences with the unions, and the other companies followed suit.

◆ On this day in 1985, a second earthquake, measuring 7.3 on the Richter scale, struck Mexico City. The earthquake killed an estimated 9,000 people and left about 30,000 homeless. The United States government donated $1 million in emergency aid to the Mexican city and pledged to help in "any way possible."

❖ Former men's tennis champion, Bobby Riggs, challenged women's champion, Billie Jean King, to what was billed as the "Match of the Century" at the Houston Astrodome in 1973. Riggs, who was labeled as a "male chauvinist pig," had great disdain for women tennis players and believed women could not play as well as men. King beat him in three straight sets with scores of 6-4, 6-3 and 6-3.

● On this day in 1989, army general Colin Powell was confirmed by the Senate as chairman of Joint Chiefs of Staff. With this appointment, General Powell became the highest-ranking African American in the military.

## 21
## SEPTEMBER

■ Native American Recognition Week, usually celebrated during the last weeks in September each year in Tucson, Arizona, includes the sale and display of Native American crafts, food and art. The celebration generates funds for schooling, emergency assistance, community recreation, staff training and other social-service needs on reservations.

▲ During this week in 1912, US troops began occupation of Tientsin (China) for the protection of US interests in the Chinese Revolution. The revolution began in October of the previous year.

◆ An English fort in Baton Rouge fell to Spanish troops on this day in 1779. Louisiana Governor Bernardo de Galvez announced that 375 English prisoners had been taken and that no Spaniards were wounded in the battle. The successful attack on Baton Rouge was the first major battle to take place after the Spanish declared war on England in June.

❖ The Peace Corps, a brainchild of President John F. Kennedy, was established in 1961. The corps was designed as a voluntary government agency whereby young, skilled US volunteers brought their skills, such as farming or medicine, to growing countries in Asia, South America and Africa for a specified length of time. This agency greatly helped many newly emerging African nations during the 1960s.

## 22
## SEPTEMBER

● Judge James Benton Parsons was sworn in as a US district judge for the Northern District of Illinois in 1961. Judge Parsons became the first African American judge of a US district court within the continental United States.

■ When Adam Nordwall, a chief of the Chippewa Nation and a professor at California State University, stepped off a plane in Rome, Italy, in 1973, he was dressed in full tribal regalia. Nordall announced that he was "taking possession of Italy by right of discovery," the same way that Christopher Columbus took possession of the "New World" in 1492.

▲ During this year in 1965, a Senate committee voted on a liberal bill that would replace the restrictive McCarran-Walter Act of 1952. This act was particularly discriminatory to Asians, and it had long been recognized that an amendment was needed. The bill that was finally passed into law in October of 1965 became the Immigration Act of October 3, 1965. The new law was based on the principle of equality, not on the basis of racial orgin, and it also repealed the national origins-quota system.

> "What right did Columbus have to discover America when it had already been inhabited for thousands of years?"
>
> Adam Nordwall, 1973

◆ The trial of Reies Lopez Tijerina, Mexican American founder and director of the Alianza de los Pueblos Libres (Alliance of Free City-states), began on this day in 1969. Tijerina was charged with destruction of federal property and the assault of two officers. The Alliance was organized to open the question of Spanish and Mexican land grants. Tijerina was found guilty of the crimes for which he was accused and sentenced to prison.

❖ In 1656, the first jury composed entirely of women was ordered by the General Provincial Court in Patuxtent, Maryland. The court required an all-woman jury to hear the case of Judith Catchpole, who was on trial for the murder of her child. The jury found Cathpole not guilty of the crime.

● Thurgood Marshall was appointed as a judge of the US Court of Appeals by President John F. Kennedy in 1961. Marshall later became solicitor general of the US, and in 1967 he became the first African American to sit on the Supreme Court of the United States.

■ During this month in 1978, the American Indian Commission awarded $800 million to Native Americans. The money was to be used to pay more than 500 claims Native Americans had made against the federal government for violation of treaties.

**23**

**SEPTEMBER**

▲ A Japanese fisherman named Aikiahi Kuboyama died on this day in 1954. Kuboyama became the world's first H-bomb fatality as a result of being dusted by radioactive debris during a US H-bomb explosion that took place on March 1st of that year.

◆ On this day in 1868, the town of Lares, Puerto Rico, was attacked by 400 Puerto Rican patriots. The attack was planned in cooperation with revolutionary leaders who lived in Cuba and the United States. Within a few hours, the revolutionaries had taken the town. Following the revolution, Francisco Ramirez Medina was named president of the new Republic of Puerto Rico.

❖ In 1806, Meriwether Lewis and William Clark arrived in St. Louis in Missouri Territory, to a hero's welcome. The two former army officers had just completed a combined 15,400-mile journey from St. Louis northwest up the Missouri River to the Pacific Northwest seacoast and back again to St. Louis. President Thomas Jefferson planned the route Lewis and Clark took soon after he became president in 1801. Jefferson wanted to explore the as-yet-uncharted northwestern wilderness of North America in order to establish relations with the Native American population who lived along the route. Lewis and Clark's journey began in 1804 with 45 additional men, 3 boats and tons of provisions. Along the way there were violent encounters with bears, peaceful and violent encounters with Native Americans and dangerous Rocky Mountain climbings.

**24**

**SEPTEMBER**

● President Dwight D. Eisenhower ordered troops to Little Rock, Arkansas, in 1957 to enforce court-ordered desegregation of public schools. The act followed the use of troops by Governor Faubus earlier in the month to prevent school desegregation.

■ In 1861, 12 women and children were among those killed after Colonel Manual Chaves of Fort Fauntleroy in New Mexico ordered soldiers to open fire on a group of Navaho who had come to the fort to get food rations. The rations were to be given to the Navaho as part of the terms of a treaty signed by the US government and the Navaho earlier that year. The order was given following a dispute in which US soldiers were accused of cheating the Navaho of bets won during a horse-race competition.

▲ In 1971, Japanese Emperor Hirohito was greeted by President Nixon in Anchorage, Alaska. This event marked the first meeeting between a US president and Japanese monarch.

◆ In 1965, an agreement in principle on a new Panama Canal treaty that would supersede the 1903 pact that gave the United States sole control over the canal was announced by President Johnson. The new treaty would provide for joint administration of the canal between Panama and the United States.

❖ Marathon swimmer Diana Nyad, a 25-year-old from New York, attempted to swim around the island of Manhattan in New York. Nyad, whose name *naiad* means "water nymph" in Greek, was unsuccessful in her swim; however she made a second successful attempt 11 days later on October 5, 1975.

*Diana Nyad*

● In 1957 nine African American children successfully integrated Central High School in Little Rock, Arkansas, under escort from federal troops. This would not have been possible without the help of Daisy Bates, a state NAACP official and concerned citizen. When the Arkansas NAACP sought to challenge the state's policy of gradual integration, Bates, as part of the challenge, publicly tried to enroll a group of eligible African American children into the high school with unsuccessful results. This strategy began in 1955 under threats of mob violence and verbal and physical intimidation but had a successful result. Daisy Bates became known nationally as a champion of human rights, particularly where children are concerned.

■ The Commissioner of Indian Affairs, Louis R. Bruce (a Mohawk), reported this week in 1969 that income from Native American timber had doubled over the last two-year period.

*Evita Peron*

▲ John F. Aiso became the first mainland Nisei, a Japanese person born and living in the 48 contiguous states, to be named to a judicial post in 1953. He was appointed to the Municipal Court of Los Angeles by then California Governor Earl Warren.

◆ The musical *Evita,* about the rise of Evita Peron from a life of poverty to the powerful position as wife of Argentine dictator Juan Peron, opened in 1979 at the Broadway Theater in New York City. The musical was written by Andrew Lloyd Webber and Tim Rice and starred Patti Lupone, Mandy Patinkin, and Bob Gunton.

❖ Sandra Day O'Connor was sworn in as associate justice of the US Supreme Court in 1981. Chosen by President Ronald Reagan, O'Connor was the first woman to become a Supreme Court justice.

● The tenth anniversary of the Congressional Black Caucus was celebrated in 1980 during the annual legislative weekend of the caucus members.

■ On this day in 1862, Colonel H. H. Sibley of the militia marched into the Santee camp of Little Crow and declared that all Santees in the camp should consider themselves prisoners of war until those responsible for recent slayings of US militia members could be found. Several of Sibley's soldiers had been killed in a battle near the old Yellow Medicine Agency by Santee warriors four days earlier. Sibley's intention was to have those guilty of the attack hanged.

▲ On this day in 1975, Foreign Minister Yeshwantrao Bawantrao Claran of India addressed the Association of Indians in America. Claran told the group that "Democracy has not only not suffered a demise in India, but is more living and throbbing than ever."

◆ Fidel Castro, prime minister of Cuba, addressed the United Nations in 1960 in a speech that took more than four hours. The goal of the speech was to gain international support for Cuba's "struggle."

❖ John Jay of New York City became the first candidate for chief justice of the US Supreme Court when he was appointed by President George Washington. Jay was confirmed by the Senate on this day in 1789.

● Edmonia Lewis became the first woman and the first African American woman to receive national recognition as a sculptor in 1873. In order to finance her training in Europe, she sold a bust that she had sculpted of Colonel Robert Gould Shaw. Colonel Shaw was the commander of the first voluntary African American regiment in the Civil War. Her most famous work is entitled *Forever Free*(1867).

■ Choctaw chiefs Greenwood Leflore Nitakechi and Mushulatubbe, representing three districts of Choctaw, signed a treaty in 1830 with the US government. In the treaty, the chiefs agreed to the removal of the Choctaw to western lands that the government had set aside for them on a reservation.

▲ In the fall of 1919, the American Loyalty Club was established by a small group of Nisei. Nisei are native-born US citizens of Japanese descent. The club, which was based in San Francisco, set two goals: (1) to provide the US public with a speaker's bureau so that the concerns of Japanese Americans would be known, and (2) to review political candidates for the upcoming election and to encourage Japanese American voters to vote.

◆ On this day in 1821, Mexico declared its independence from Spain.

◆ In 1964, the Warren Commission issued its findings in its probe into the assassination of President John F. Kennedy. In its findings, the commission stated that Lee Harvey Oswald, a former defector to Russia, acted alone in the shooting death of the president. Following his arrest in 1963, Oswald was shot to death by Jack Ruby while he was being escorted from a Texas jail.

**28**

SEPTEMBE**R**

● *David Walker's Appeal*, or more precisely titled *Walker's Appeal in Four Articles Together with a Preamble to the Colored Citizens of the World, but in Particular and Very Expressly to Those of the United States,* was discovered in various parts of the country in 1829. This pamphlet was a militant call for the overthrow of the slave system. David Walker was a free African American born in North Carolina. He finally settled in Boston where his appeal was published. His call for mass slave uprisings spread concern throughout the white community.

■ In 1864, Cheyenne and Arapaho chiefs held a council meeting at Camp Weld near Denver, Colorado. The meeting was organized by US Army Major Edward W. Wynkoop and the chiefs of the two nations to prevent war between the army and the Cheyenne and Arapaho. Black Kettle (Motavato), a Cheyenne, and Notanee, an Arapaho, were among the eight Native American leaders who met with John Evans, governor of the Colorado Territory, and Army Colonel John M. Chivington. These two men wanted to drive the Plains Indians out of Colorado.

▲ Asian Americans from Taiwan celebrate Confucius's birthday.

◆ During this month in 1877, conflict on the US-Mexican border came to a head in a struggle that has come to be called the Salt War. This conflict began in the 1860s when salt deposits at the Guadalupe Lakes about 100 miles from El Paso were being freely used by both Mexicans and Americans. Several groups tried to control the use of the salt beds by laying claims to the land. Missouri Democrat Charles Howard resolved the Salt War by requiring all parties to pay for the salt they used.

◆ On this day in 1781, troops under the command of General George Washington began a siege of Yorktown. This battle, which resulted in the surrender of British General Cornwallis, ended the Revolutionary War.

● The first US merchant ship with an African American captain, Hugh Mulzac, was launched in 1942. The ship was christened the *Booker T. Washington*.

■ The Oglala Sioux Chief American Horse was killed at Slim Buttes in South Dakota on this day in 1875. American Horse fought with Chief Sitting Bull in the Sioux War. He also was a signer of the treaty made between the Sioux and the Crook Commission.

▲ On this day in 1950, General MacArthur returned to Seoul, Korea, in triumph as United Nations troops recaptured the South Korean capital. The capital had fallen to the communists three months earlier.

◆ The United States assumed military control of Cuba in 1906 under the terms of the Platt Amendment. William Howard Taft, who was secretary of war at the time, was made provisional governor of the island.

❖ On this day in 1965, President Lyndon B. Johnson signed a bill that established the National Foundation on the Arts and Humanities.

## 29
### SEPTEMBER

## 30
### SEPTEMBER

● The attempted enrollment of African American student James Meredith at the University of Mississippi in 1962 led to rioting among a group of angry whites. More than 200 people were arrested and another two were killed in the ruckus that quickly became dubbed "the Battle of Ole Miss."

■ Seven Cherokee chiefs and headmen entered into an alliance called "The Articles of Agreement" with the Lords Commissioners of the British Court at London in 1730. The agreement was a result of negotiations in which Sir Alexander Cummings convinced the Cherokee to accept Montoy as Emperor of Nequese (what is today Georgia).

▲ On this day, the House and the Senate agreed to pass bill HR2580. The bill liberalized US immigration procedures by eliminating the national-origins quota system and setting new immigration ceilings. The bill also repealed the "Asia-Pacific Triangle" stipulation present in earlier legislation. This stipulation required that Asian emigration be charged against the country of the person's ancestry, even when the person was born outside the triangular area that was formed by the boundaries of Pakistan, India, Japan and the Pacific islands. President Johnson signed the bill into law on October 3.

◆ In 1959, Brazil, Colombia, Argentina, Bolivia, Chile, Paraguay, Peru and Uruguay agreed on a draft for a South American free trade agreement.

❖ President Dwight Eisenhower announced his choice for appointment to the US Supreme Court as chief justice in 1953. His choice was California Governor Earl Warren. Warren would later be confirmed by the Senate and sworn in. Earl Warren's tenure as chief justice (1953 - 1969) began what many historians have called a period of judicial activism because the "Warren Court" actively impacted the American social fabric. The many liberal Warren Court landmark decisions, such as *Brown v Board of Education of Topeka, Kansas* (1954), *Gideon v Wainwright* (1963) and the *Miranda v Arizona* (1966), secured rights for equal education of African American students and of people arrested for crimes. Warren later headed a commission in 1964 that investigated the assassination of President John F. Kennedy.

**Key:** ● African Americans ■ Native Americans ▲ Asian Americans ◆ Hispanic Americans ❖ European Americans

# MY PERSONAL LIST

# OCTOBER

One of the most moving stories of Native American resistance to white domination is that of Chief Joseph and the Nez Perce Nation, once settled in what is now the Wallowa Valley of Oregon. The US government wanted the Nez Perce to settle on an Idaho reservation and leave their homeland in the 1870s.

Chief Joseph met with government officials hoping to reach a compromise, but his hopes were dashed by a violent conflict. A small group of Nez Perce warriors attacked and killed 12 white people who had taken the land from the Nez Perce. The conflict grew into a major battle with the US Army. At first, Chief Joseph and his warriors held their own, but Chief Joseph knew that, in the long run, the US Army would most likely dominate the Nez Perce. Chief Joseph planned to take his tribal members to Canada to join a group of Sioux. While fighting off pursuing army soldiers, Joseph led about 800 Native Americans 1,000 miles southeast through Montana and then across the Yellowstone Park area. Resting 40 miles from the Canadian border, the Nez Perce thought they had eluded the US Army. Suddenly, the Nez Perce people were attacked by the US Army led by General O. O. Howard and Colonel Nelson Miles. The brutal battle lasted five days, and the US Army killed many of the Nez Perce. Like other Native Americans doomed to lose their land to the US government, the Nez Perce had no choices left.

Following the fierce battle, a beaten but dignified Chief Joseph surrendered to US Army forces on October 5, 1877, delivering a speech with grace and eloquence. After his surrender, Chief Joseph and his people were shipped to Kansas and to the so-called "Indian Territory" in Oklahoma.

---

After his surrender, Chief Joseph said to his people:

" I am tired of fighting. Our chiefs are killed. Looking Glass is dead.... The old men are all dead.... He [Ollokot, Joseph's brother] who led the young men is dead. It is cold and we have no blankets. The little children are freezing to death. My people have run away to the hills...no one knows where they are--perhaps freezing to death. I want to have time to look for my children and see how many of them I can find. Maybe I shall find them among the dead. Hear me, my chiefs. I am tired; my heart is sick and sad. From where the sun now stands, I will fight no more forever."

◀ *Chief Joseph*

■ In 1969, parents of Native American school children in Ridgeville, South Carolina, were confronted by federal marshals and threatened with contempt-of-court charges when they tried to enroll their children in the public schools. The Native Americans were backed by African American civil rights workers who vowed to continue a drive to close down segregated county Native American schools.

# 1

## OCTOBER

▲ A report issued by the Office of Civil Rights of the US Department of Education disclosed that the University of California at Los Angeles had discriminated against Asian American students seeking admission into the graduate mathematics program in 1990. The Education Department ordered the university to admit five Asian American students who had been denied entrance into the program due to discriminatory practices, but the university had not agreed to these terms as of 1992.

◆ During this month in 1944, the California District Court of Appeals reversed the decision of a lower court in the "Sleepy Lagoon" case of Los Angeles and dismissed all charges in the case due to lack of evidence. The case resulted from the arrest of 23 Chicano youths and one European American for the murder of alleged Chicano gang member José Diáz, who had been beaten to death. The youths were arrested because they were members of Chicano gangs.

❖ Albert Einstein, a German physicist, was sworn in as a US citizen in Trenton, New Jersey, on this day in 1940. Einstein won international acclaim for his recognition of the relationship between matter and energy, which he explained in his formula $E = mc^2$. Einstein's daughter, Margot, and his secretary, Helene Dukas, were naturalized in the same ceremony.

● At the age of 137, Charlie Smith, who claimed to be the last surviving enslaved African in the United States, died in 1979.

# 2

## OCTOBER

■ The *Cherokee Phoenix*, a newspaper that began publication in February 1828, published its last issue during this month in 1835. The newspaper was edited by Elias Boudinot and was published in New Echota, Georgia. It was the first newspaper to be printed using the Cherokee alphabet created by Sequoya.

▲ During this month in 1854, Chief Justice Hugh Campbell Murray of the Supreme Court of the state of California ruled in the case of *People* (respondent) *v George W. Hall* (appellant) that a person of Chinese descent could not testify against a white person.

◆ In 1968, a large student protest took place in *La Plaza de las Tres Culturas* (The Plaza of Three Cultures) in Mexico City. The students opposed the government's high spending on the Olympic Games and wanted the government to increase financial aid and improve conditions for students attending universities. Hundreds of students were fired upon and killed by Mexican soldiers.

❖ The first German immigrants, called Mennonites, arrived in the United States from Krefeld, Germany, in 1663. The group first lived in Philadelphia, Pennsylvania, but later moved to the area called Germantown at the request of William Penn. The leader of the Mennonites, Francis Daniel Pastorius, was considered by some to be the most learned man in the US at the time the settlement was established.

● Thurgood Marshall was sworn in as a justice of the US Supreme Court in 1967. Marshall became the first African American to sit on the Supreme Court.

**Key:** ■ Native Americans ▲ Asian Americans ◆ Hispanic Americans ❖ European Americans ● African Americans

● ■ Black Hawk, Sauk tribal warrior and chief, died at the Sauk and Fox Reservation in 1838. Black Hawk was famous as a result of the Black Hawk War of 1832. At the age of 65, he surrendered to US soldiers and was sent to prison in Fort Monroe.

▲ In a ceremony at Ellis Island in New York (1965), President Johnson signed into law an act that revised quotas that had prevented Asian-Pacific peoples from migrating to the United States. The act placed all unused national quotas into a common pool.

◆ During this month in 1968, Mexican American Alicia Escalante was arrested during a sit-in at the Los Angeles Board of Education. She was later sentenced to three years probation. Escalante is credited with being the founder of the first Mexican American welfare rights group--the East Los Angeles Welfare Rights Organization. Escalante also was a part of the successful "Save Cal-Med" campaign of 1967, a campaign to preserve health and welfare programs in California.

❖ Rebecca Felton became the first woman senator in the United States when she was appointed to that position by Governor Hardwick of Georgia in 1922.

● In 1904, in Daytona, Florida, Mary McLeod Bethune began a school for African American girls with only $1.50 and five students in a rented house. The school would become the Bethune-Cookman College in 1923. Mary McLeod Bethune was president of the college until 1947. She became one of the country's leading educators. She was later part of President Franklin Roosevelt's "Black Cabinet," advising him on African American educational needs. Bethune was also the first African American woman to run a federal office as director of the Negro Affairs Division of the National Youth Administration.

*Mary McLeod Bethune*

**3**

OCTOBER

■ Ground-breaking ceremonies for the new $8 million Albuquerque Vocational Technical School for Indians were held during this week in 1969. The school was designed to attract Native American students from all over the US. The curriculum focused on the educational needs of Native Americans. Evening and weekend courses were available to students who were working or married. It was described as "... a place to which the Indian can return when he [or she] feels the need to update or up-grade his [or her] skills." Five hundred students opened the school.

**4**

OCTOBER ▲ The Chinese Embassy in Washington, DC, was established on this day in 1878. Chen Lan-Pin served as the envoy extraordinary and minister plenipotentiary for the embassy. Yung Wing served as associate minister.

◆ Cristina Saralegui, the Spanish talk show host of *Cristina,* became host of the English-speaking version of her television show on CBS in 1992. *Hispanic Magazine* described her as "...the one-woman media industry...."

❖ A postage stamp featuring a portion of an oil painting by Frederick Remington called *The Smoke Signal* was placed on sale by the US Post Office in 1961. Remington was known for his artistic representations of scenes from the American West.

● A former sheriff and three law-enforcement officers in Philadelphia, Mississippi, were arrested by the FBI in connection with the murder of three civil rights workers in 1964. Two of the civil rights workers were white (both were Jewish), and the third was African American. The murder of the civil rights workers and the investigation that led to the arrest of the law-enforcement officials became the story line for the movie *Mississippi Burning* in 1990.

> *"When literature becomes overly erudite, it means that interest in the art has gone and curiosity about the artist is what's most important. It becomes a kind of idolatry."*
>
> Isaac Bashevis Singer, November 26, 1978

# 5
## O C T O B E R

■ After battling and eluding the US Cavalry with some of the best military strategy ever seen, Chief Joseph of the Nez Perce Nation surrendered in despair at Eagle Creek, Montana, in 1877 to General O.O. Howard and Colonel Nelson Miles. His classic words tell the story of a people trying to survive against all odds: "Our chiefs are killed. Looking Glass is dead. . . . The children are freezing to death. . . . Hear me, my chiefs. I am tired; my heart is sick and sad. From where the sun now stands, I will fight no more forever."

▲ During this month in 1942, the Manzanar War Relocation Center, an internment camp for persons of Japanese descent, was set up as the US became involved in World War II. It was reported that the number of Japanese Americans there grew to a population of more than 10,270 people.

◆ During this month in 1885, Cuban immigrant Vincente Martinez Ybor moved his cigar business from Cuba to the Hillsborough section of Tampa, Florida. The area in which Ybor settled became known as *Ybor City*. The region quickly grew to become the major cigar-producing region of the United States.

❖ Isaac Bashevis Singer won the *Nobel Prize for Literature* in 1978. Singer was a naturalized Polish American citizen who wrote in Yiddish, a language used by some Jewish people. His award was given because of his "impassioned narrative art." Among the books written by Singer are *Enemies: A Love Story* (1972) and *The Magician of Lublin* (1960).

● Actor James Earl Jones opened on Broadway in *The Great White Hope*, a play about boxing great Jack Johnson, in 1968. Jones received rave reviews and a *Tony Award* for his performance.

# 6
## O C T O B E R

■ In 1774, the Shawnee, led by Chief Cornstalk, fought area residents led by Andrew Lewis at the Battle of Point Pleasant in what is now Virginia. After several hours of fighting, the Shawnee were defeated.

▲ During this month in 1990, the Japanese American classical violinist Midori made her debut recital in the famous Carnegie Hall of New York City. She was only 18 at the time of the recital.

◆ The motion picture *Old Gringo* was released on this day in 1989. The movie, starring Latino actor Jimmy Smits of *LA Law* fame, Jane Fonda and Gregory Peck, told the story of a young Mexican revolutionary and an old US writer who fell in love with the same woman during the Mexican Revolution. The movie was based on the novel *El Gringo Viejo* by Carlos Fuentes.

❖ The University of Chicago inaugurated Hannah H. Gray as its president in 1978. Upon accepting the position, Gray became the first woman university president in the history of the United States.

● Patricia Roberts Harris assumed her duties as ambassador to Luxembourg in 1965. She was the first African American woman to be chosen as a foreign ambassador. Harris was selected for the position by President Lyndon Johnson.

**Key:** ■ Native Americans ▲ Asian Americans ◆ Hispanic Americans ❖ European Americans ● African Americans

■ The 26th annual convention of the National Congress of American Indians was held during this week in 1969 in Albuquerque, New Mexico. The event, drawing Native Americans from almost every part of the US, was used as a forum to acknowledge Native American frustration with the federal government. The event also expressed hope for future improvement. The president of the Congress, Wendell Chino, in an evening address before 1,000 delegates, denounced White House plans to redirect, onto the state level, federal money meant for Native Americans. Chino wanted any such money to be given directly to the various Native American tribes.

**O C T O B E R**

▲ While actively campaigning for the 1980 presidential election, Democratic Governor of Georgia, Jimmy Carter met with an Asian American group on this day in 1976. Carter addressed the group at a fund-raising dinner that was held in Los Angeles.

◆ Republican vice presidential nominee William E. Miller said in 1964 that if Barry Goldwater was elected president, the Republican administration would provide arms to those exiled from Cuba to "let them fight to take back their own homeland."

❖ During the Battle of Saratoga in 1777, the colonists were victorious over the British. The victory was due in part to the efforts of Irish American sharpshooter Timothy Murphy. Murphy, who was a member of Morgan's Rifle Corps, was credited as being the best marksman of the Revolutionary War.

● In 1954, Marian Anderson became the first African American singer to be hired by the New York Metropolitan Opera Company.

**8**

**O C T O B E R**

■ In the tribal council room on the Red Lake (Minnesota) Indian Reservation in 1966, a call for unity of Midwestern Native American nations went forth. Roger Jourdian spoke of the many problems facing Native Americans. He then urged that the nations unite to support the strategies of BIA Commissioner Robert L. Bennett of the Oneida tribe.

▲ Ting Ying, president of the South China Institute of Agricultural Science in Canton, died later in this month in 1964 in Peking. Ying was praised for his implementation of Communist party agricultural policies and contributions to the improvement of rice production in China.

◆ In 1969, Professor Ralph Guzman of the University of California at Santa Cruz presented his article to Congress asserting that people of low-income backgrounds, in particular Mexican Americans, were at greater risk while involved in military service in Vietnam as a result of a selective service system that favored persons of middle- and upper-income backgrounds.

❖ Sergeant Alvin C. York of Tennessee, a US Army infantryman, single-handedly captured an entire German machine-gun battalion while under heavy fire during World War I in 1918. York's religious belief initially kept him from engaging in active battle, but he later changed his mind after being convinced by a superior officer that he would be doing a greater good by fighting. French Marshall Ferdinand Foch called his actions,"the greatest thing accomplished by any private soldier of all the armies of Europe." Sergeant York was later awarded a *Congressional Medal of Honor.*

● Roland Hayes, who had been developing his singing career in Europe, returned to the US on this day in 1923. While in Europe, Hayes met with great success and even sang before King George of England at Buckingham Palace. Hayes began his professional singing career in the US in recital at Symphony Hall in Boston in 1918.

> *"...it is good for the wife to ... assert her freedom as a woman ... as a wife and as a mother."*
>
> Ms. Kim,
> *The Lives of Korean Women in America*,
> 1973

■ Robert L. Bennett, a member of the Oneida tribe in Wisconsin and former commissioner of Indian Affairs under President Lyndon Johnson, was appointed director of the American Indian Law Center at the University of New Mexico School of Law in 1969.

▲ In 1973, Ms. Kim published her book, *The Lives of Korean Women in America*. Kim addressed the differences between Korean women in Korea and in the US. She singles out the differences in their domestic and working lives.

◆ A musical celebration of the tango called *Tango Argentino* opened in New York City at the Mark Hellinger Theater in 1985. The show was created by Claudio Segovia and Hector Orezzoli.

◆ Songwriter Gus Kahn (German American) died at the age of 54 in 1941. Kahn collaborated with many composers, among them Rudolph Friml, Walter Jurman and Sigmund Romberg. Kahn, who grew up in Chicago and later moved to Hollywood, California, is remembered as one of Tin Pan Alley's greatest songwriters. Some familiar songs he wrote include "Mammy," "Toot, Toot, Tootsie, Goodbye," and "Yes, Sir, That's My Baby."

● Joan Martin became the first African American woman ordained as a United Presbyterian Minister during this month in 1976. She was also the first African American woman to attend Princeton Theological Seminary in Princeton, New Jersey.

10

OCTOBER

**Kruger Day**
South Africa

■ John C. Rainer, a member of the Taos Nation of southwestern California, was elected vice-president of the National Congress of American Indians in 1969.

▲ The Chinatown section of New York City celebrated the 55th anniversary of the founding of the Republic of China in 1966. New York Governor Nelson Rockefeller paid a visit to the celebration. The governor said, "I am greatly inspired by the record you have made as Americans, while maintaining strong family ties. . . . You have many problems, including many newcomers from Hong Kong, job problems and health problems. I promise to do everything in my power to help you."

◆ Landowners in the town of Yara, Cuba, declared war against Spain in 1868. The revolt of the landowners became known as the *Revolt of Yara*.

◆ Barbara McClintock, a botanist at the Cold Spring Harbor Laboratory in Cold Spring Harbor, New York, was awarded the *Nobel Prize in Physiology or Medicine* in 1983. McClintock won the Nobel Prize for her studies of how shifting genes in plant chromosomes, which she called "jumping genes," affected the hereditary factors in plants.

● The St. Francis Xavier Church in Baltimore, Maryland, was purchased on this day in 1863. The church, which was dedicated on February 21, 1864, became the first Catholic parish for African Americans in the United States.

■ During this week in 1918, the first American Indian Church was incorporated in El Reno, Oklahoma, by Mack Hoag of the Cheyenne Nation. Other nations who participated were the Otto, Ponca, Commanche, Kiowa and Apache.

▲ In 1906, the San Francisco, California, Board of Education issued an order prohibiting persons of Chinese, Korean and Japanese heritage from attending neighborhood schools. The students were to be segregated and sent to the established Oriental School instead.

# O c t o b e R

◆ In 1992, former Secretary of Labor for the Commonwealth of Puerto Rico and member of the US Mission to the United Nations Julia Rivera de Vincente addressed a General Assembly to refute attacks made about Puerto Rico by the Cuban representative. The Cuban representative asserted that Puerto Rico owed all of its growth to the United States and that its government was, in essence, a puppet of the US government. De Vincente pointed out in her response to the Cuban representative that it was Puerto Rico itself, and not the United States, that was responsible for improvements in its employment and agricultural status.

◆ During the 6th flight of the space shuttle *Challenger*, Dr. Kathryn D. Sullivan became the first US woman astronaut to walk in space in 1984. The *Challenger* mission lasted from October 5 through October 13. Crew member Marc Garneau was the first Canadian to fly in a US space mission.

*Kathryn D. Sullivan*

● A. Phillip Randolph, the only African American member of the Executive Council of the AFL-CIO labor union, was censured for publicly accusing the AFL-CIO of bias in 1961. Randolph was a frequent critic of discriminatory practices by white labor unions and their leadership as they related to African American union members in particular and African American employment in general.

# O c t o b e R

■ During this month in 1969, Vice President Spiro T. Agnew promised Native Americans that the Nixon administration would work with Native Americans on a "community by community, and tribe-by-tribe basis. . . to urge greater local leadership on the part of the Indian."

▲ The Orphan Foundation Fund was incorporated in the US on this day in 1956. The fund was founded by Harry Holt, who brought eight children to the US from Korea and adopted them. In 1956, Holt established an office in Seoul, Korea where work was officially begun in March 1956. The work grew rapidly and, today, there are national and international branches of Holt International Children's Services. Since its establishment, the agency has brought more than 30,000 children to the US for adoption by US families.

◆ Hispanic and Italian Americans celebrate Columbus Day. Christopher Columbus and his three ships reached land in the Western Hemisphere in 1492. His native Italy would not finance his voyage, but Spain did. Columbus was seeking a route to Asia, expecting to find gold, spices and other treasures. Spain funded the voyage hoping to share in the wealth and to expand its empire. Columbus and his ships landed on an island called *Santo Domingo* by Spain, the present-day Dominican Republic and Haiti. The voyage of Columbus brought two worlds together and forever changed their relationship with one another.

◆ During this month in 1991, Linda J. Wachner, chair, chief executive officer and president of Warnaco Group, Incorporated, took the company public and raised an additional $140 million in revenue . Wachner holds the distinction of being one of the first women to run a Fortune 500 company. She had run the company since 1986.

● President Grant issued a proclamation against the Ku Klux Klan (KKK) in 1871.

■ Forest Gerard of the Blackfoot Nation of Montana was sworn in as the assistant secretary of the interior for Indian Affairs in 1977. With the position, Gerard held the highest public office ever served by a Native American since Charles Curtis of the Kaw Nation was elected vice-president with Herbert Hoover in 1928. "The greatest challenge for Indians is the development of their resources while preserving their cultural heritage," said Gerard.

**O C T O B E R**

▲ During this week in 1910, Syngman Rhee returned to Korea after receiving a Ph.D. from Princeton University. Rhee was the first Korean to receive such a degree from a US educational institution.

◆ The Texas border at El Paso was opened to Mexican laborers for a five-day period in 1948. The opening of the border resulted from a notification to the Immigration Service by farmers in Texas that the cotton crop of the region would be lost if laborers were not available to pick the crop.

❖ Jewish American Henry Jones and others founded the first Jewish fraternal society, the B'nai B'rith, in 1843. The B'nai B'rith, which means "Sons of the Covenant," was founded in New York City. Jones served as the group's chairman.

● In 1914, African American Garret A. Morgan was granted a patent for a breathing device that was created to make work safer in the mines.

---

**14**

**O C T O B E R**

■ In the 1964 Summer Olympics in Tokyo, Japan, US Marine Corps First Lieutenant, William M. (Billy) Mills was awarded the gold medal for his upset win in the 10,000 meter race. Mills, a Sioux from Pine Ridge, South Dakota, set an Olympic record with a time of 28 minutes, 24.4 seconds. The race was filled with drama as Mills, who came from behind, dueled a runner from Tunisia to win. He had never won a major race and had been given little or no chance to win this one. No American had ever before won the gold medal in the Olympic 10,000 meter race.

▲ During this week in 1959, Severo Ochoa of the New York University College of Medicine was awarded the *Noble Prize in Medicine or Physiology* along with Arthur Kornberg of Stanford University Medical School.

◆ The Swedish Academy of Letters awarded the *Nobel Prize in Literature* to Mexican Octavio Paz during this week in 1990. Paz is a novelist, essayist and poet and the first Mexican writer to receive the Nobel Prize. The academy granted the award to Paz because of his "impassioned writing with wide horizons, characterized by sensuous intelligence and humanistic integrity." Paz is well known for his poetry.

❖ In 1976, Martha Graham, world famous choreographer and a driving force behind modern dance, received the *Presidential Medal of Freedom Award*. This is the highest award given to a US civilian.

● While resting in a hospital room awaiting a physical examination, the Reverend Dr. Martin Luther King, Jr., was informed by telephone that he would be the recipient of the 1964 *Nobel Peace Prize*. The Nobel Peace Prize was awarded to King for his leadership during the nine-year struggle for civil rights, beginning with his leadership in the Montgomery, Alabama, bus boycott in 1955. The people of the US were greatly moved by his *I Have a Dream* speech at the 1963 march on Washington, DC. He was present at President Johnson's signing of the 1964 Civil Rights Bill, which was almost certainly inspired by Dr. King's hard work and dedication.

---

Key: ■ Native Americans ▲ Asian Americans ◆ Hispanic Americans ❖ European Americans ● African Americans

■ A six-cent stamp in recognition of the seventy-fifth anniversary of the rush through the Cherokee Strip of northern Oklahoma was issued by the US Post Office on October 15, 1968, in Ponca City, Oklahoma.

▲ In 1906, the US government claimed that segregating Japanese students in San Francisco, CA, in "Oriental" schools was in violation of the *Treaty of 1894*. The school segregation program had been passed by the Board of Education in San Francisco earlier in the week.

◆ On this evening in 1951, the first episode of the *I Love Lucy* show aired on CBS. It starred the husband-and-wife team of Cuban American Desi Arnaz and Lucille Ball. In the show, Desi Arnaz played the part of Cuban bandleader Ricky Ricardo, a character similar to Arnaz in real life. The show, which was produced by Arnaz and Ball's production company, Desilu Productions, came to be one of the most significant sitcoms in the history of television.

◆ Biochemist Konrad E. Bloch of Harvard University shared the *Nobel Prize in Medicine* for his research on cholesterol in 1964.

● The Civil Rights Act of 1875, which forbade racial discrimination and separation in public accommodations, was very much weakened in a US Supreme Court decision on this day in 1883. The court held that only state-imposed discrimination was forbidden. This court decision, in effect, made discrimination by individuals or corporations legal in the US.

*Lucy and Desi Arnaz*

■ About this day in 1948, the Indian Centennial Commemorative stamp honoring the "five civilized tribes" was placed on sale in Muskogee, Oklahoma. The stamp commemorated the Chickasaw, Choctaw, Muskogee, Cherokee and Seminole nations.

▲ Dr. Choh-Hao Li, a Chinese American biochemist, endocrinologist and director of the Hormone Research Laboratory at the University of California-Berkeley, won the $10,000 *Albert Lasker Medical Research Award* in 1962. Dr. Li isolated and identified six pituitary-gland hormones that control everything from skin color to body shape. He also isolated part of the ACTH hormone, which he was then able to synthesize.

◆ Mexican American folk singer Joan Baez was arrested on this day in 1967 for her participation in an antiwar protest in front of the Northern California Draft Induction Center. Arrested along with Baez were her mother, her sister Mimi Feriani, and about 120 other protesters. On the day following their arrests, a judge at the Oakland Municipal Court sentenced Baez and the other protesters to a ten-day prison term.

◆ The US Arsenal at Harper's Ferry, West Virginia, was raided in 1859. The leader of the raiding party was John Brown, a white man who was a fierce, longtime abolitionist. His plan seems to have been to raid the arsenal, give out the weapons to nearby slaves and encourage the slaves to revolt. After a battle with the local militia, Brown and his 18 men were surrounded and captured on October 18th by Colonel Robert E. Lee. Lee delivered Brown to the state for trial. He was found guilty of treason and hanged on December 2nd.

● When Maynard Jackson was elected mayor of Atlanta, Georgia, in 1973, he became the first African American mayor of a major city in the South.

■ Author Sarah Winnemucca Hopkins died on this day in 1891. Her autobiography *Life Among the Piautes* (1883), describing the early interactions between the Northern Paiute and whites, was one of the earliest works published in the US by a Native American woman. In addition to writing, Winnemucca worked as a translator, educator and lecturer. She was also an activist for Native American rights.

**O**CTOB**R**

▲ A four-day discussion during this week in 1940 between Japanese and Dutch East Indies authorities were held. The British government tried to block the resulting agreement which supplied Japan with 40 percent of Dutch East Indies oil production for six months.

◆ President Aries of Panama conferred with US President Roosevelt in Washington, DC, regarding treaty relations between the two countries. The result was a declaration that Panama should be given all the commercial rights of a sovereign nation in the Canal Zone, and that the US would not engage in economic enterprise detrimental to Panama in the Canal Zone.

❖ Jewish American Isidor Kalisch, who preached reform Judaism, held the first Jewish Rabbinical Conference in Cleveland, Ohio, in 1855. The main purpose of the meeting was to "better the spiritual conditions of the Jews in America."

● Dr. Clifton R. Wharton was elected president of Michigan State University in 1969. Dr. Wharton, an economist from New York City, became the first African American to run a major university that was public and predominantly white.

*18*

**O**CTOB**R**

■ The play *Indians* opened in New York City, New York, in this month in 1969. The play is a study of the mistreatment of Native Americans by European Americans at the end of the nineteenth century. *Indians* was written by Arthur Kopit. It included performances by actors Stacy Keach and Manu Topou.

▲ US Senator Hiram L. Fong of Hawaii, the first Chinese American senator, was selected to become a member of New York University's College of Electors Hall of Fame for Prominent Americans in 1959.

◆ Asian Hispanic American astronaut Franklin Chang-Díaz aboard the space shuttle *Atlantis* in 1989 made his second trip into space. This space mission was the first US mission after the explosion of the space shuttle *Challenger* on January 24, 1986.

❖ *The Amerikai Magyar Nepszava*, a Hungarian newspaper founded by Hungarian American Geza David Burko in March 1899, began publication as a daily newspaper in New York City. This was the first Hungarian daily newspaper in the states.

● Actor-singer Paul Robeson was awarded a *Springarn Award* in 1945. The award, issued by the NAACP, was given to Robeson for his "distinguished achievement in the theater and on the concert stage."

> "Negro action can be decisive. I say that we ourselves have the power to end the terror and to win for ourselves peace and security throughout the land."
>
> Paul Robeson,
> 1945

**19**

**O C T O B E R**

■ During this month in 1940, the Haskell Institute unit of the Kansas National Guard was mobilized. This unit of Native Americans entered into active duty for a period of one year.

▲ On this day in 1984, President Reagan signed a bill into law that created the National Academy of Peace. The bill for the National Academy of Peace advocated nuclear-arms control and was proposed by Hawaiian Senator Spark Masayuke Matsunaga.

◆ In October of 1977, the courts of Texas handed down a decision on the case of *Doc v Tyler*. A case had been filed against the Tyler School District by the Mexican American Legal Fund to prohibit the district from charging tuition to undocumented children. When the district court ruled that such an action was unconstitutional, the state of Texas appealed the verdict. A federal appeals court upheld the lower court ruling, reinforcing that discrimination against undocumented children was in violation of the Fourteenth Amendment's equal-protection clause.

◆ British troops led by General Cornwallis were defeated by American revolutionary forces at the last battle of the Revolutionary War in Yorktown, Virginia, in 1781. More than 8,000 British soldiers laid down their arms in surrender. The war did not end at once but left the British army with no alternatives. Major General Benjamin Lincoln of the revolutionary forces accepted the sword of British Brigadier General Charles O'Hara, who took the place of General Cornwallis.

● Two days of racial violence that had disrupted the Boston public school system came to an end on this day in 1979. The violence was initiated by whites attacking a school bus that carried African American students. As a result of the attacks, fights broke out between African American and white students in the school system.

**20**

**O C T O B E R**

■ The San Arcs made peace with the United States at Fort Sully, South Dakota, in 1865. The San Arcs were a division of the Hunkpapa and Teton Sioux. The tribe lived in the Dakotas.

▲ Early this month in 1890, President Benjamin Harrison signed into law the McKinley Act. Under its provisions, foreign sugar was allowed to come into the US duty free, and a bonus of two cents per pound was paid on US-produced sugar. This spelled economic disaster for Hawaii, who had enjoyed since 1875 the differential advantage for one of its main industries. The loss of this economic advantage was an added incentive for some key business people to press for the annexation of Hawaii to the US.

◆ In 1946, the pro-independence group PIP, the *Partide Independenista Puertoriquenno* (the Independence Party of Puerto Rico), was organized in Bayarow, Puerto Rico.

◆ The World's Columbian Exposition was opened on this day in 1892 in Chicago, Illinois. The exhibition was the result of public demand for an appropriate commemoration of the "discovery" of America by Europeans. The opening ceremonies included an address by the exposition's vice president, Levi Morton. The exposition included 50 acres of concession stands and 55 acres of state, transportation, electric and liberal-arts exhibits.

● *Raisin*, a musical adaptation of Lorraine Hansberry's play *A Raisin in the Sun*, opened this week at the 46th Street Theater in New York City, New York (1973).

> "... things were happening in this world that directly concerned me -- and nobody asked me, consulted me -- they just went out and did things -- and changed my life."
>
> Lorraine Hansberry, *"A Raisin in the Sun,"* 1973

*Saul Bellow*

**21**

O C T O B E R

■ In 1940, Native Americans were registered for the draft for the first time in US history. By the end of World War II in 1945, more than 25,000 Native American men and women had been involved in the defense of the US.

▲ Earlier this month in 1941, Japan's Prime Minister Konoye resigned from his position. In his place, war minister Tojo took over. Many thought that Tojo took the position of home afairs minister to prevent violence in Japan if a decision for peace was reached.

◆ After an agreement between the US and the Dominican Republic, US rule ended on this day in 1922. The last US Marines withdrew in September 1924, and a provisional government was set up under President Horacio Vasquez.

◆ Saul Bellow, professor of English at the University of Chicago, won the *Nobel Prize for Literature* in 1976. Bellow was the first American to win the award in this category since John Steinbeck in 1962. The year that Bellow won his award also marked the first time US citizens had won seven Nobel Prizes in the same year. Bellow was cited for "the human understanding and subtle analysis of contemporary culture that are combined in his work." Among his books are *Humbolt's Gift* (1975), *The Adventures of Augie March* (1954) and *Mr. Sammler's Planet* (1971).

● During this month, Charles R. Johnson won the 1990 *National Book Award* in the fiction category for his third novel, *Middle Passage*. The last African American to win this award had been Ralph Ellison in 1953 for *The Invisible Man*. Johnson described his book as a "philosophical sea adventure, a genre-crossing novel which is itself a kind of genre." The title of Johnson's book refers to the route taken by slave ships leaving Africa and heading for the Caribbean and the US, fully loaded with enslaved Africans, and the horror of that trip.

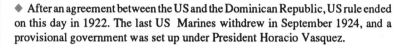

**22**

O C T O B E R

■ Late in this month in 1969, the AMERIND organization was founded. The organization was created to improve working conditions and protect the rights of Native American employees. The organization was formed as a result of the bad treatment received by some Native Americans who worked for the Bureau of Indian Affairs (BIA).

▲ The United Federation published its first newspaper, the *United Korean News*, in 1907.

◆ President John F. Kennedy announced a naval quarantine of Cuba in 1962. The action took place at the height of the Cuban missile crisis, a major cold-war confrontation between the United States, and Cuba and the Soviet Union. A tense week followed during which the US prepared for war. War was averted when Soviet Premier Khrushchev informed Kennedy that the missiles in Cuba would be removed from that country and returned to the Soviet Union.

◆ Kathy Kusner was awarded a jockey license by the Maryland Racing Commission in 1968. Kusner, one of the best Olympic equestrian sports figures in the United States at the time, became the first woman to gain permission to ride on a thoroughbred race track in the US.

● In 1970, the Council of Churches of New York City issued the *Annual Family of Man Award for Excellence* to Dr. Ralph C. Bunche. Bunche became the eighth recipient of the award.

■ *The Squaw Man,* a play by Edwin Milton Royle, opened at Wallack's Theater in New York City on this day in 1905. The play tells the story of a British nobleman's love for a Native American woman.

▲ Dr. Leo Esaki, a Japanese citizen living in New York City since 1959, was awarded part of the *Nobel Prize in Physics* in 1973. Dr. Esaki's theories on electron tunneling led to his development of the tunnel diode, enabling electric current to do the "impossible" because "electrons can behave whether like separate particles or like part of a wavelike chain in order to pass through normally impassable electronic barriers." In Japan, he had headed advanced development groups at Sony, doing the research for which he won the Nobel Prize.

◆ In this month in 1933, a cotton strike broke out in San Joaquin, Texas. It began with workers walking off the fields in Corcorcu, but the strike soon spread to other cities until 12,000 to 18,000 workers were on strike. This strike is considered to be the prototype for the grape strike that would occur in Delano 30 years later.

◆ Dr. Selman A. Waksman of Rutgers University was named as one winner of the *Nobel Prize in Physiology or Medicine* in 1952 for the discovery of the antibiotic streptomycin, which was used to treat tuberculosis and other bacterial infections after its discovery in 1943.

● Juanita Kidd Stout was sworn in as a judge in the Philadelphia, Pennsylvania, Municipal Court system in 1959. With this appointment, Stout became the first African American woman to serve as a judge in the history of Pennsylvania.

## 23
## OCTOBER

## 24
## OCTOBER

United Nations Day

■ The serpent is the totem for people born between October 24 and November 21 according to Sun Bear's Earth Astrology. In most Native American cultures, the serpent is respected as having special powers. Some Native American tribes have snake clans that carry out special functions.

▲ In a New York ceremony, the Japanese American Citizens League (JACL) paid tribute to 80-year-old Yoneo Arai in 1970. Arai was honored for his many contributions to Japanese American life, among which were graduating *cum laude* from Harvard University in 1912, his receipt of the *Order of the Sacred Treasure, Third Class* award by the Japanese government in 1969 and his helping to improve American-Japanese relations.

◆ The first major conference uniting Hispanic American groups voted in 1971 to set up a Washington, DC, office. The conference, sponsored by four of the six Hispanic Americans who held congressional seats, included Joseph Montoya and Manuel Lujan both of New Mexico, and Herman Badillo of New York.

◆ In 1859, Annie Taylor, a school teacher from Bay City, Michigan, became the first person to go over Niagara Falls in a barrel. After completing the trip with only slight injuries, Taylor told reporters, "Nobody ought ever do that again. . . ."

● Jackie Robinson became the first African American player in the 20th century to be permitted to play professional baseball outside the "Negro Leagues." He signed a contract with the Montreal Royals of the International League during this week in 1945.

> "My paintings are well painted, not with speed, but with patience ....I think that at least [they] will interest a few people."
>
> Frida Kahlo, 1938

**25** OCTOBER

■ During this week in 1991, *The New York Times* announced that it would move the book *The Education of Little Tree* by Forrest Carter from the nonfiction best-seller list to the fiction list. The book was moved from the list after it was discovered that the book's author was KKK member Asa Earl Carter and not Forrest Carter as the "autobiographical" text claimed. Under the pseudonym, the book's author had claimed to be a Native American orphan about whom the book was supposedly written.

▲ The headquarters of the International Ladies Garment Workers Union (ILGWU) was picketed by the New York Asian American Group in 1972. This was in response to the union display posters throughout New York City and elsewhere with the slogan, "Don't Buy 'Made in Japan'."

◆ Frida Kahlo, Mexican artist and wife of muralist Diego Rivera, had her first one-woman exhibit at the Julian Levy Gallery in New York City in 1938. The exhibit lasted from October 25th through November 14th. Kahlo, who was born and raised in Russia, moved to Mexico after she married Diego Rivera.

◆ John Steinbeck was awarded the *Nobel Prize in Literature* in 1962. The award was given primarily for his 1961 novel *The Winter of Our Discontent*.

● Colonel Benjamin O. Davis became the first African American army officer to be promoted to the rank of brigadier general in 1940. At this time, however, the US Army was still organized into separate, segregated African American units.

**26** OCTOBER

■ This day in 1956 marks the extinction of the language spoken by Native Americans of the Delaware Nation. The language ceased to exist when Jane Mountour Battice, the last-known person to be fluent in the language, died.

▲ During this week in 1871, one of the worst riots in Chinese American history took place in Los Angeles. The rioting started as an argument between two Chinese, then rapidly developed into utter chaos, with shootings and non-Asians venting their resentment against the Chinese. By the end of the riot, 19 were dead. The event sparked world outrage, but nothing was ever done to identify the Chinese Americans who suffered losses of life and property as a result of the rioting.

◆ During this month in 1979, Patrick Flores was appointed archbishop of San Antonio, Texas. Archbishop Flores, a Mexican American, was noted for his support of the Chicano struggle for social justice and especially for his support of Cesar Chavez and Mexican American migrant farm workers.

◆ The Erie Canal opened for business in 1825. The canal, which runs from Lake Erie to Albany, New York, was the idea of New York Governor DeWitt Clinton. First proposed in 1812 by Clinton, the concept of the canal was not very popular.

● The movie *Five on the Black Hand Side* opened on this day in 1973. The movie focuses on the domestic views of an African American middle-class family. The movie featured actors Clarice Taylor and Leonard Jackson.

■ John and Burton Pretty of Top of the Crow Nation in what is now Montana were among the 150 religious leaders to take part in a day-long pray-in for peace in Assisi, Italy, in 1986. The assemblage had been called for by Pope John Paul II.

▲ During this month in 1928, the case of *V.T. Tashiro v Secretary of State* was being heard by the Supreme Court. The case involved Dr. Tashiro, a resident of California, who proposed the building of a Japanese Hospital in Los Angeles, California. The state, however, refused to allow Dr. Tashiro to file the articles needed in order to incorporate the hospital on the grounds that, under the California Land Law, Japanese citizens could not incorporate. The decision handed down by the US Supreme Court was an important one, ruling in favor of Dr. Tashiro.

## O CTOBE R

◆ In 1492, Columbus left the island of San Salvador of the Dominican Republic and sailed toward Cuba.

❖ The movie *The New Land* opened on this day in 1973. The movie was a sequel to an earlier movie entitled *The Emigrants*. Both *The New Land* and *The Emigrants* followed the lives of a Swedish family as it made its new home in the United States. The movie was based on a novel by Vilhelm Moberg.

● Dr. Clifton R. Wharton was appointed president of the State University of New York (SUNY) in 1977. Prior to holding this position at New York State's largest university, Wharton served as president of Michigan State University.

■ The first tribal constitution of Native Americans, written as part of the Indian Reorganization Act of June 18, 1934, was signed on this day in 1935. The constitution was signed in the office of Secretary of the Interior Harold Le Claire Ickes.

▲ In October 1983, Chun Doo Hwan, the first president of the fifth Republic of Korea, went on a goodwill visit to Burma. While in Burma, a bomb was set off by North Korean agents, killing 13 South Korean officials and 4 cabinet ministers. The bombing clearly expressed the tensions between North and South Korea.

## O CTOBE R

◆ In 1967, El Chomizal, a 437-acre border area was officially returned to Mexico during ceremonies in El Paso, Texas. The ceremonies were attended by President Johnson of the United States and President Gustavo Diaz Ordaz of Mexico. El Chomizal was taken by the US in the 1850s.

❖ The Statue of Liberty was officially dedicated on this day in 1886 in Upper New York Bay. President Grover Cleveland presided over the dedication which included a large parade in New York City, fireworks, and a boat-filled New York Harbor. Also present at the ceremony were Frederic Auguste Bartholdi, the French sculptor and designer of the statue, and representatives of the French government. The statue symbolized the alliance between America and France during the Revolutionary War in the US and was a memorial to the people of France and America who died during that struggle.

● The First Kansas Volunteers, an army unit composed of soldiers of African descent, held off a Confederate Army force at the Battle of Island Mount in Missouri in 1862. The First Kansas Colored Volunteer Unit had been organized by the Union Army in August of the same year.

■ On this day in 1813, US Colonel Dyer burned down the town of Littlefutchi. The town was located at the head of Canoe Creek in St. Cloud County, Alabama. The town had served as the home for the Upper Creek Nation.

▲ In 1870, Chinese merchants in Honolulu, Hawaii, sent a letter to a public meeting to point out the bad aspects of contract labor and to encourage free immigration of Chinese to Hawaii.

◆ In 1982, Filipe Gonzalez of the Socialist party became the new prime minister of Spain. With his election victory, Gonzalez became the youngest leader of a European country.

◆ A special postage stamp honoring Juliette Gordon Low, founder of the Girl Scouts of the United States, was issued by the US Post Office in 1948. The three-cent stamp first went on sale in Savannah, Georgia, the birthplace of Low.

● In 1949, Alonzo G. Moron of the Virgin Islands became the first person of African descent to become president of the Hampton Institute in Virginia. The institute was founded in 1868 to help educate "freed slaves."

O CTOBE R

■ On this day in 1937, the Stockbridge-Munsie Community of Wisconsin (a division of the Delaware) ratified a constitution and bylaws organizing their group. The constitution and bylaws were subsequently approved by the secretary of the interior.

▲ General Li Hung, commander of the 38th Division of the Chinese Army, received the *American Silver Star Medal* from Lieutenant General Daniel E. Sultan, commander-in-chief of US forces in the Burma-Indian war theater in 1944. General Hung was awarded the medal for "gallantry in action during the Hukawng campaign . . ." that helped allied war interests.

◆ In 1950, five armed Puerto Rican nationalists attacked the governor's mansion in Puerto Rico. Other violence followed as Puerto Ricans continued to fight for self-government.

◆ Orson Welles and his Mercury Radio Theatreplayers performed the radio play *The War of the Worlds* this evening in 1938. Based on the H.G. Wells's novel about an invasion of Earth by aliens from Mars, the radio play caused nationwide panic. People listening to the broadcast believed that the Martian invasion was real. Many fled their homes, while others armed and barricaded themselves in their homes against the nonexistent threat. The incident demonstrated the influential effect of the relatively new medium of radio.

● The famous revolt organized by enslaved African American Nat Turner ended in 1831 when he surrendered to Virginia authorities and was later hanged. When Turner began the uprising against slavery, he was a literate preacher who was inspired by spiritual conviction and heavenly signs. After seeing what he regarded as a sign in the heavens, he began his revolt by killing his white master's entire family with the help of six other enslaved persons. During the two-month revolt, local authorities killed many African Americans in retaliation. The immediate effects of *Nat Turner's Revolt* were more laws that further hurt the enslaved people, and the realization by whites that people could and would rebel against enslavement.

■ Big Snake, brother of Ponca Chief Standing Bear, felt empowered to take advantage of Federal Judge Elmer Dundy's ruling that "Indians" were people with legal rights--in particular, the right not to be held in custody without just cause and the right to freedom of movement. Big Snake tested this ruling by moving himself 100 miles within "Indian Territory" to a Cheyenne reservation. There, he was captured by US soldiers and returned without incident to the Ponca reservation. However, in 1879 William H. Whiteman, a Ponca "Indian" agent, wanted to make an example of Big Snake, and sent a group of soldiers to the reservation to arrest Big Snake. When the soldiers tried to arrest Big Snake, he resisted and was shot to death.

▲ In 1984, many Asian American businesses closed the day after four-time Prime Minister of India, Indira Ghandi, was shot by two members of her personal security squad. Ghandi underwent four hours of surgery before dying from her wounds.

◆ On this day in 1989, the House Ethics Committee announced that it was about to begin an inquiry to determine whether the recent conviction of Representative Robert Garcia on extortion charges in New York warranted congressional punishment.

◆ Fifty-three Norwegians arrived at a site called the Kendall Settlement near Rochester, New York, in 1825. The Norwegians, known as the "sloop party," were permitted to purchase land in 40-acre tracts at the price of $5 per acre. The land had to be purchased from a Pultway land agent, a representative of a group that had control of much of the land in western New York State.

● Booker T. Washington, educator and founder of Tuskegee Institute in Alabama, became the first African American elected to the New York University Hall of Fame in 1945.

*Indira Ghandi*

# MY PERSONAL LIST

VERSTRAETE
KIMBER L HALL
LAMMERS
BALLANCE
BARNES
BRYANT
MASDEN
BILLY RAY COFFEY · HOWARD
WILL R DANTZLER
ARCHIE T LUCY · GEORGE P MARTIN
STEVEN J McDONALD
OSCAR PAULLEY Jr · BRINSLEY B
THOMPSON · CARL L THORNTON
ROBERT L WYNN · STEPHEN
JOE S BURCHFIELD · THOMAS
KENNETH R PERRY · WILLIAM T
THOMAS E FIKE · RONALD P REMBOLDT
LEWIS A WALTON
GALLAGHER III · ISADORE
LLOYD S RAINEY
GREGG N HOLLINGER
PETER C
LEO T THOMAS Jr · RONALD
COLEMAN · WILLIAM R FINN
DALE F KOONS
ROBERT L DENMARK · WILLIAM Y
DOUGLAS E TROTTER · HARVEY W BAKER
RAUL LOSOYA · STANLEY

# NOVEMBER

In 1973, US troops finally left Vietnam, but there was no hero's welcome upon their return. The reasons for US involvement in this war were never clear to many people. A decade elapsed before plans for a national monument to the men and women who served in Vietnam were finalized. Washington, DC, was chosen as the site for the memorial. Now all that was needed was a design.

In 1981, a national contest was held to select a design. After reviewing all entries, the award winner selected was Maya Ying Lin, an architecture student from Yale University. The actual structure of the memorial would consist of two black granite walls, each about 250 feet long, sloping down into the ground and meeting to form an inverted V that would point toward the Washington and Lincoln memorials. Lin worked as a consultant, overseeing and making final decisions on most aspects. She said, "I decided on everything from the lettering to the sandblasting to the alphabet style of the inscription."

Henry Hyde, a member of Congress from Illinois, referred to the design as "...a political statement of shame and dishonor." Some, such as James Watt, secretary of the Interior under President Reagan, whose approval of the design was necessary for it to be built, wanted a more traditional monument, such as a flag or a statue of a soldier and an inscription honoring the Vietnam War veterans. These changes were eventually added to Lin's design, and the monument was built. It is a moving experience to walk through this unique national monument, past row after row of names of those who served and died in Vietnam.

> Maya Ying Lin described her Vietnam War memorial design as follows:
>
> "...a rift in the earth, a long polished black stone wall, emerging from and receding into the earth."

◀ *Maya Ying Lin and the Vietnam War Memorial*

▲ Cyrus S. Ching, director of industrial and public relations for the United States Rubber Company, was elected chairman of the board of the China-American Council of Commerce and Industry in 1944. The organization existed to promote positive economic relations between China and the United States, especially during World War II.

◆ President George Bush formally chose Dr. Antonia C. Novello to replace the retiring Dr. C. Everett Koop as surgeon general of the United States in 1989. Dr. Novello, a Puerto Rican native, would later be officially confirmed and sworn in by the US Senate. With her appointment, Dr. Novello became both the first woman and the first Hispanic American to become surgeon general. Dr. Novello, a pediatrician and specialist in AIDS research, also served as deputy director of the National Institute of Child Health and Human Development.

❖ On this day in 1911, Swiss American Louis Chevrolet and his partner William Durant announced the incorporation of the new Chevrolet Motor Company. The company planned to establish its headquarters in Detroit, Michigan. Chevrolet, who had emigrated to the US from Switzerland only 11 years earlier, had already established himself as an automotive giant by the time the announcement of the new company was made.

● The first issue of *Ebony* magazine was published in 1945. After gaining success in 1942 with *Negro Digest*, publisher John J. Johnson decided to create a second magazine for the African American market. The new magazine would make creative use of photographs and would be patterned after its European American based competitor, *Life*. *Ebony* sold out its 25,000 copy press run and became the foundation upon which Johnson built his publishing empire. The magazine's market was middle-class African Americans who were presented as successful and glamorous.

# NOVEMBER 1

▲ Branch No. 4 of the Filipino Labor Union, located in Guadalupe, Mexico, held a meeting for Filipino agricultural workers in 1934. This meeting was held to pass a resolution protesting against a wage cut of five cents.

◆ Gloria Molina was elected to the California State Assembly in 1982. Molina was the first Mexican American to hold that office. Prior to her election, Molina was a community activist in Los Angeles. Later, in 1987, she was elected to the Los Angeles City Council.

# NOVEMBER 2

*Gloria Molina*

❖ Margaret Chase Smith became the first female US senator to be elected to office without having been previously appointed in 1948. When she won her Senate seat, she became the only woman to ever serve in both the Senate and the US House of Representatives (1940-1948). Among other honors, she was the first elected public official to speak out against Senator Joseph McCarthy (her *Declaration of Conscience, 1950*), the first woman senator elected to a position of leadership (chairperson of the Senate Republican Conference in 1967), and the first woman to seek the presidential nomination of a major political party. Margaret Chase Smith also holds the distinction of being the longest-serving female senator (1948-1972).

● President Ronald Reagan signed into law a federal holiday honoring slain civil rights leader, Dr. Martin Luther King, Jr., in 1983. The holiday, observed on the third Monday in January, was the first to be named for an individual since the birthday of Abraham Lincoln was designated a holiday.

■ Approximately 500 Native Americans, mostly young, arrived in Washington, DC, (1972) after a "Trail of Broken Treaties" march across the country to protest the federal government's policies toward them. Upon their arrival, they proceeded to go to the Bureau of Indian Affairs (BIA) building, where they staged an occupation that lasted for six days.

**Key:** ▲ Asian American ◆ Hispanic American ❖ European American ● African American ■ Native American

▲ Dr. Hideki Yukawa was awarded the *Nobel Prize in Physics* in 1949 for his successful prediction of the existence of an elementary particle, the meson, in 1935. Dr. Yukawa, a professor at Kyoto University in Japan, was a visiting professor at Columbia University in New York City when the award was announced. He was the first person of Japanese ancestry ever to win the award.

◆ Herman Badillo became the first Puerto Rican American to be elected to the US House of Representatives in 1970. His congressional district was the borough of the Bronx, New York City. Badillo was president of the Bronx from 1966-1970.

◆ In 1992, Democrat Governor Bill Clinton of Arkansas was elected by the people of the United States to be the forty-second president, defeating President George Bush. This victory marked the end of a 12-year era of Republicans in the White House.

● Irvin Mollison, a Republican from Chicago, was sworn in as a United States Customs Court judge in New York City in 1945. Judge Mollison became the first African American to sit on the federal bench within the continental United States.

■ The Sioux of North Dakota gained what many considered to be the "greatest political victory in (American) Indian history" when, in 1964, they held onto the right to police their own reservations. They needed and received support from many other North Dakotans. In a final referendum, a law that would have extended the jurisdiction of state civil and criminal laws to the reservation was voted down by a four-to-one margin.

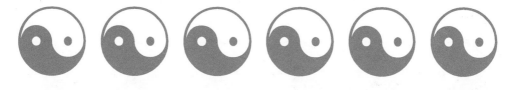

▲ William Mo Marumoto was appointed to the position of presidential assistant on executive manpower in 1970. Marumoto became the first Nisei (US-born Japanese) person to be placed on the White House staff.

◆ After a long trek through the jungle, Hernando Cortes arrived in Mexico City with 500 soldiers this week in 1519. Montezuma, the emperor of the Aztecs, addressed the Spaniards as gods and generously gave them gifts. Within days of their arrival, however, cordial relations between the two groups ceased as Cortes attempted to conquer the Aztecs.

❖ In 1924, Miriam Ferguson was elected governor of Texas. Ferguson, who was more commonly known as "Ma," became the first woman in the United States to be elected to this office. Ferguson ran for the office to vindicate her husband James, who had been impeached as governor for diverting funds for personal use.

● In 1953, African American Hulan Jack was elected to the position of president of the borough of Manhattan in New York.

■ Will Rogers, part-Cherokee, was born on this day in 1879 in the Cherokee area that would later become the state of Oklahoma. An internationally-famous entertainer and social commentator, Rogers starred in rodeos, vaudeville, movies and the radio for many years. At one time, he was the top male box office star in the first talking movies.

> *"My family didn't come over on the Mayflower but they met the boat."*
>
> Will Rogers

▲ In 1946 Wing F. Ong became the first Chinese American elected to a state legislature. Ong was elected to the state of Arizona legislature.

◆ Dennis Chavez was elected US senator from New Mexico in his own right in 1936. Chavez, a Mexican American, was first appointed to the position following the death of the previous senator in an airplane crash. Chavez, who served his state since the 1920s, was elected to Congress in 1930. As a Democrat, Chavez supported President Roosevelt's New Deal programs, particularly the fair-employment laws. He also worked on behalf of Hispanic American rights. His statue represents New Mexico in the US Capitol Building in Washington, DC.

> *"Woman must not depend upon the protection of man, but must be taught to protect herself."*
>
> Susan B. Anthony
> Speech in San Francisco
> 1871

❖ Leading women's rights agitator Susan B. Anthony was arrested on this day in 1871. Anthony was arrested in Rochester, New York, for attempting to vote. Other women's rights leaders were arrested at the same time as Anthony. Anthony was fined $100, which she never paid.

● Dr. Carter G. Woodson, a pioneer in the study and writing of African American history, established "Negro History Week" in 1926. This was one of the earliest attempts at getting the nation to recognize the history and achievements of African Americans.

■ During this month in 1883, the US Supreme Court declared that Native Americans are by birth aliens and dependents of the United States.

6

NOVEMBER

▲ When Dalip Singh Saund was elected to the eighty-fifth Congress (House of Representatives) in 1956, he became the first congressional member of Asian ancestry. Born in Amritsar, India, Saund, a Democrat representing the twenty-ninth district of California, served until 1962.

◆ Octavio A. Larrazolo, a Mexican American, was elected as one of the earliest senators from the state of New Mexico in 1928. His election capped a long and distinguished career in public service. After receiving a law degree, Larrazolo entered politics. When New Mexico became a state in 1912, he was among a group of Hispanic leaders who made sure that the state constitution assured Hispanics of their right to vote and to hold elected office. Later, Larrazolo was elected governor of New Mexico. As governor, he supported the teaching of Mexican American culture in the public schools, as well as the use of both English and Spanish there.

❖ German American Victor Berger was elected as the new mayor of Milwaukee, Wisconsin, in 1900. Berger ran for the mayoralty on the Socialist ticket.

● Shirley Chisholm became the first African American woman to serve in the US Congress when she was elected in 1968. Chisholm, a Democrat from Brooklyn, New York, served in Congress until 1983. She also became the first African American woman from a major political party to run for the presidency in 1972. While in Congress, Chisholm fought to reform US political parties and legislatures and make them more accountable to the people. She also fought against the seniority system in Congress in terms of committee assignments.

■ Charles Curtis, US senator from Kansas (Republican) and a member of the Kaw Nation, became the first Native American to serve as vice president of the United States as he and President-elect Herbert Hoover won the national election in 1928. Curtis had previously been a member of Congress and had served in the Senate for 25 years.

▲ In 1974, the people of Hawaii, particularly the Japanese community, reflected upon their history-making decision on the previous day. The Hawaiians had just elected their first governor of Japanese descent, George Ariyoshi. Before his election as governor, Ariyoshi, a Democrat was lieutenant governor.

◆ On this day in 1978, 12 members of the *La Raza Unida* Party won elections held in Zavola County Texas. *La Raza Unida,* which means "the United People," was formed in 1970 to organize the masses of unregistered Mexican voters into a united independent political block that could elect candidates to office in areas where Chicanos could be a voting majority.

◆ Abolitionist Elijah P. Lovejoy was killed by proslavery rioters in Alton, Illinois, in 1837. Lovejoy printed many antislavery documents on his printing press. Opponents of Lovejoy destroyed his printing press many times; however, each time, it was replaced by the Ohio Anti-Slavery Society. Following his death, Elijah P. Lovejoy became known as the "martyr abolitionist."

● Douglas Wilder became the first African American since the Reconstruction period (1865 - 1877) to be elected governor of a state when he won the Virginia gubernatorial election in 1989. The event was significant because Virginia, up until the Civil War, was the "Cradle of the Confederacy." Wilder later announced his intention to seek the Democratic party nomination for the 1992 presidential election; however, he dropped out of the election before the primaries.

■ The Potawatomi and the Miami were defeated by General Harrison in the Battle of Tippecanoe in 1811. The slogan, "Tippecanoe and Tyler Too," resulted from this battle and was used as the rally cry against the election of Tyler as president. The Native Americans who were defeated in this battle were under the direction of Chief Tecumseh and his brother, The Prophet.

▲ During this week in 1946, the Anti-Discrimination Committee of the Japanese American Citizens League (JACL) tried to defeat California's Proposition 15, titled "Validation of Legislative Amendments to Alien Land Law." This bill tried to reestablish the legal authority of the Alien Land Law of 1913. This law, directed mostly at Japanese Americans, prohibited the ownership of land by and the leasing of land to "aliens ineligible to citizenship." Despite their citizenship, Japanese Americans had been included in this group of "aliens."

◆ Governor Munoz Márin of Puerto Rico and his popular Democratic party won all but one precinct in the 1960 election. The Republican Statehood party increased its share of the vote by 32 percent, while the Independence party was reduced to 3.1 percent of the votes cast.

◆ Hattie Caraway was reelected Democratic senator from the state of Arkansas in 1932. She first became senator in a specially-held election in order to complete her deceased husband's term as senator from Arkansas, in 1931. During her career in the Senate, which lasted until 1945, she became both the first woman to chair a Senate committee and the first to preside over a session of the Senate.

● Attorney General of the state of Massachusetts Edward Brooke became the first African American to be elected to the US Senate by popular vote in 1966. Senator Brooke was a member of the Republican party.

■ A book about Native American problems, titled *Our Brother's Keeper: The Indian in White America,* was published in this month in 1969. The book was written by task-force workers and the Citizens Advocate Center. One of the main themes of the book was the role of the Bureau of Indian Affairs (BIA) in dealing with Native American concerns. The book describes the BIA as "the only agency that stands between the Indian and extinction as a racial and cultural entity."

▲ The Vietnam Memorial was opened on this day in 1982 in Washinton, DC. The memorial was designed by Maya Ying Lin, a Chinese American architecture student from Yale University. It was the first major tribute to US soldiers who fought in Vietnam.

◆ The Ford Foundation announced that it would fund a six-year $100-million program to aid "minority" education. About $40 million of the grant was to be used to support scholarships and fellowships of Puerto Rican, Mexican, Native and African American students at the college and graduate levels.

❖ Oveta Culp Hobby was named to the presidency of the Southern Newspaper Publishers' Association in 1948. Hobby was the wartime director of the Women's Army Corps (WAC). She was the first woman to be named to the presidency of this association.

● Heavyweight boxer Larry Holmes knocked out James "Bonecrusher" Smith in the twelfth round of a boxing match in Las Vegas, Nevada, in 1984. With this victory, Holmes became the first boxer to win a match under the auspices of the International Boxing Federation (IBF).

■ At a Miwok Native American village site near the northern tip of San Francisco, California, an Elizabethan coin was unearthed in 1974. The coin is believed to be further evidence that explorer Sir Francis Drake came to the area via San Francisco Bay in 1579 and not via the northern coast of the state as some historians have suggested.

**10**

**NOVEMBER**

▲ Emperor Hirohito ascended to the throne of Japan in 1928 to become the new ruler of that country.

◆ During this month in 1968, the Hispanic membership of the New York State Assembly grew by four members. Elected to the state office were Puerto Rican Americans Luis Nino, Manuel Ramos, Armando Montana and Roberto Garcia.

*Emperor Hirohito*

❖ In 1917, 41 women from 15 states were arrested outside the White House in Washington, DC, for suffragette demonstrations. The women did nothing more than picket the White House with signs demanding voting rights. The arrested women drew sentences that ranged from six days' to six months' imprisonment.

● Charles Sifford of Philadelphia became the first African American golfer to win a major US professional tournament when he won the Long Beach (California) Open for $1,200 in 1957. From 1947 to 1953, Sifford worked as a private golf instructor and part-time chauffeur and valet to singer Billy Eckstine when he wasn't playing in matches. Eckstine gave Sifford the financial support he needed to continue playing professional golf. Starting in the early 1950s, he won the Negro National six times. In 1967, he earned $20,000 at the Hartford Open and in 1968, he earned $20,000 at the Los Angeles Open.

■ Harry White Wolf, a Cheyenne six-month-old baby, was the first reported death in 1884 at the Haskell campus for "Indians." Many "Indian" children died of diseases such as pneumonia and tuberculosis due to the conditions at the school. An investigative report on the Haskell campus was submitted to the US government, leading to improved conditions for these Native Americans.

▲ In 1972, the Social Security amendment was passed. As reinterpreted by Congress in 1973, the amendment allowed Americans of Japanese ancestry to be eligible for wage coverage for the period covering World War II.

◆ In 1854, Alejandro Tapia y Rivera published the *Historical Library of Puerto Rico*. This was a collection of valuable documents from the fifteenth to the eighteenth centuries. Alejandro Tapia y Rivera is known for giving birth to Puerto Rican literature.

## NOVEMBER

❖ Assistant US Army surgeon Dr. Mary E. Walker, in a citation from President Andrew Johnson in 1865, became the only woman to have received the *Congressional Medal of Honor*. She was held as a prisoner of war by the South from April to August of 1864 in Richmond, Virginia. Dr. Walker gave her medical services to women prisoners in Louisville, Kentucky. She was generally recognized for the care she provided to numerous wounded and sick soldiers in hospitals and, at great risk to her own life, on the battlefield. In 1917, the Board of Medal Awards revoked her award along with 910 others. However, her award was later posthumously restored to her by Army Secretary Clifford Alexander.

● In 1925, musician and trumpeter Louis Armstrong recorded the first of his *Hot Five* and *Hot Seven* recordings. Armstrong came to be known and respected as one of the greatest jazz musicians of all time.

■ The Osage Nation held its first public auction sale for oil leases on their reservation in 1912. Located in Oklahoma, the land was sold in 160-acre tracts from beneath an elm tree which was later dubbed the "Million-Dollar Elm."

▲ Sun Yat-sen's birthday is celebrated in Taiwan. Sun Yat-sen became the ruler of the country after he successfully overthrew the Manchu ruler who was in power.

◆ The United States-Puerto Rico Commission on the Status of Puerto Rico met during November and December of 1965 in San Juan, Puerto Rico. During its meeting, the commission solicited information about the economic status of the commonwealth. The findings of the commission were published in 1966 in *The Report of the United States-Puerto Rico Commission on the Status of Puerto Rico*.

## NOVEMBER

❖ William O. Douglas, associate justice of the US Supreme Court, announced his retirement from the court in 1975. Douglas served for 36 years, the longest term of service of any Supreme Court justice through the year 1992. He retired due to illness. Justice Douglas earned a reputation during his service as a civil libertarian, broadly interpreting the Constitution for the benefit of the rights of individuals, including civil rights.

● For the first time in history, a delegation of African American members of the Baptist faith met with white members of the Baptist faith in Georgia in 1946. This was part of a goodwill session of the General Missionary Baptists Convention held in Savannah, Georgia.

■ A Senate subcommittee reported in 1969 on the educational condition of Native Americans. The committee had been in existence for two years and was started by Senator Robert Kennedy. Following his death, the committee was chaired by Robert Kennedy's brother, Senator Edward Kennedy. The two-year study concluded that national policies regarding the education of Native Americans had not provided Native American children with "an education opportunity equal to that offered the great bulk of American children." The report also suggested that one solution to the problem would be to give Native Americans a greater voice in running their children's schools.

▲ The Corporation Asian, Inc. was awarded $61,000 by the Federal Equal Employment Opportunity Commission (EEOC) in 1973 for its research on job discrimination against Japanese.

# NOVEMBER

◆ In a run-off election for the mayoral seat in Miami, Florida (1985), Cuban American Xavier Suarez became the new mayor of the city. In the mayoral election, held on the 5th of this month, a close count of ballots determined that incumbent mayor Maurice Ferre, who came from a well-known Puerto Rican family, would not be elected to another term. A run-off election was held to determine whether Cuban American Xavier Suarez or Cuban American Raul Masvidal would hold the mayoral seat. Suarez won the election. He was reelected to the position in the 1987 mayoral election.

❖ Eudora Welty won the *O. Henry Memorial Prize* for her short story, *The Wide Net,* published by Harper's Magazine in 1942. Welty wrote mostly about small-town life in the US South. Themes such as loneliness, growing pains and the need for understanding were the foundation of her writing. Other stories she has written include *The Ponder Heart, The Bridge of the Innisfallen,* and her *Pulitzer Prize*-winning, *The Optimist's Daughter*.

● Carl Stokes was sworn in as mayor of Cleveland, Ohio, in 1967. Stokes became the first African American mayor of a major US city. Twenty years later on this same date, Carrie Saxon Perry was elected mayor of Hartford, Connecticut. Perry became the first African American woman to hold a mayoral seat in a major northeastern city.

■ Creeks and Seminoles began a journey together northward from Florida to Kansas in order to escape the Civil War fighting and to seek refuge with the Union Army in 1861. Earlier, the Seminoles had done the Creeks a great favor by giving them refuge in Florida when they fled the armed forces of then US Cavalry officer Andrew Jackson.

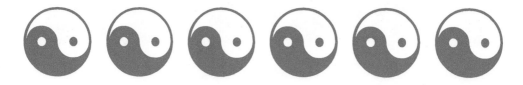

# NOVEMBER

▲ On this day in 1947, the UN General Assembly adopted a resolution which stipulated that general elections were to be held on the entire Korean peninsula. The goal of the resolution was to establish a unified government and a temporary commission to observe the general elections.

◆ Francisco Pizarro sailed from Panama for Peru in 1524. Pizarro had been commissioned to explore Peru for Spain.

❖ In 1952 later in this month, George Meany was appointed president of the AFL labor union. Meany was to fill the remainder of the term of William Geer who died in this month.

● At age 71, Rosa Parks was presented with the first *Eleanor Roosevelt Woman of Courage Award* from the Wonder Woman Foundation (1984). The award, established three years earlier, was given to Parks in recognition of her defiance of a segregationist law in Alabama that prohibited African Americans from sitting anywhere except in the back of buses.

■ Sometime during this month, Leonard Crow Dog, a Sioux medicine man and the recognized medicine man for more than 80 Native American tribes, was imprisoned by the US government for political activities. Crow Dog remained imprisoned until March 1977. In 1992, Crow Dog was serving as a peyote priest, or roadman, of the Native American church.

"I stand before you full of courage and determination not to retire, as long as I feel I can be of some assistance to troubled people...."

Rosa Parks,
1955

▲ On this day in 1969, Asian Americans living in California held a Vietnam Peace March. The march was held in San Francisco, California.

◆ In 1946, the US Department of State notified the Mexican government that it wished to terminate the *Bracero* (Mexican contract laborer) *Agreement* it had made in 1942. The wish to terminate the agreement resulted from the government's determination that it no longer needed the contracted laborers because World War II had ended.

## 15
### NOVEMBER

◆ The highly popular play *Sunday*, starring Ethel Barrymore, sister of John and Lionel Barrymore, opened at the Hudson Theater on this day in 1904. In this play, Barrymore improvised the famous line, "That's all there is, there ain't no more!"

● On this day in 1791, free African Lucy Arbuckle paid the first installment needed to buy the freedom of her enslaved daughter, Nancy. Arbuckle was one of a small group of Africans living in Petersburg, Virginia. Her daughter, Nancy, was a slave of the Reverend William Harrison. Through an intermediary named Lewis Lanier, Lucy Arbuckle was able to buy the freedom of her daughter in time to have her home for the Christmas holidays.

■ In November 1973, the first American Indian Bank opened in Washington, DC. The officers of the bank were W.W. Keeler (chairman), Barney Old Coyote (president) and Charles W. Swallow (senior vice president). In addition to their prestigious roles in the newly formed bank, each had achieved success in other areas. Keeler formerly served as chief of the Cherokee Nation. Coyote, of the Crow Nation, was also economics professor at Montana State University. Swallow, an Oglala Sioux, was chief of credit and finance for the Bureau of Indian Affairs.

## 16
### NOVEMBER

▲ Doctors Min Chen and Y. Y. Lee were among a team of four doctors headed by Dr. Samuel C. C. Ting who announced the discovery of a new type of atomic particle in 1974. These doctors conducted their experiments at the Brookhaven National Laboratory, Brookhaven, Long Island. This particle, later to be called "J" by the Brookhaven scientists, is one of the heaviest ever known. The new particle may be the "long sought manifestation of so-called weak force, one of four basic forces in nature...that binds together atomic nucleus." Similar experiments were conducted at the same time at Stanford University using different methodology but with the same results.

◆ Congressman Jose E. Serrano, a Puerto Rican American representing New York, sponsored the Public Law 101-600 bill that was signed into law on this day in 1990 by President Bush. The law provided funding for a successful school drop-outs program.

◆ Convinced that Confederate General John B. Hood had abandoned Georgia, General William T. Sherman and his Union Army of 60,000 began their famous "March to the Sea" on this day in 1864, devastating everything in their path.

● Clarence Pendleton was appointed chairperson of the US Civil Rights Commission in 1981, becoming the first African American to hold this post. Appointed by President Ronald Reagan, Pendleton, a Republican since the late 1970s, took opposing views on civil rights issues from those of the traditional members of the Civil Rights Coalition. Pendleton was opposed to busing to integrate schools and was against the concept of affirmative action.

■ The US Postal Service issued a stamp honoring the life of Chief Joseph of the Nez Perce Nation in 1968. The stamp featured a reproduction of a painting made by artist Cyrenius Hall of Chief Joseph, which hangs in the National Portrait Gallery in Washington, DC.

> "It does not require many words to speak the truth."
>
> Chief Joseph
> of the Nez Perce

▲ In 1966, the first episode of the television show *Star Trek*, called "The Menagerie,"was aired. The show, which had the exploration of space as one of its themes, also called for peace and unity among peoples of all cultures. The show featured a crew made up of persons of varied cultures, aboard a United States space vehicle, the *USS Enterprise*. The cast included Japanese American actor George Takei (Sulu), African American actor Nichelle Nichols (Uhura), Canadian American actor William Shatner (Captain Kirk), European American Leonard Nimoy (Mr. Spock), James Doohan (Scotty), a native of Scotland, and Irish American actor DeForest Kelley as the ship's doctor, "Bones" McCoy.

NOVEMBER

◆ During this week in 1953, Luis Munoz Marin of the Migration Division of the Department of Labor in the Commonwealth of Puerto Rico wrote a document summarizing the changes that had occurred in Puerto Rico since its "discovery" by Columbus. The article, titled *Puerto Rico Since Columbus*, was released on November 19, 1953--the anniversary of Columbus's second visit to the island 460 years earlier.

❖ British American Anne Hutchinson, founder of the Antinomian Party in New England, was banished from the colony of Massachusetts in 1637 following a trial held in Cambridge. Hutchinson was banished as a result of her influence over women in the area who gathered at her home to discuss secular and theological questions that were not part of the Puritan philosphy.

● African American writer Gloria Naylor was awarded the 1989 *Lillian Smith Award* for her third novel, entitled *Mama Day*. The book is about the trials and tribulations of an African American community on South Carolina Sea Islands. The award is named for the late Georgia civil rights activist who wrote a book titled *Strange Fruit*. The award recognizes outstanding writing about the South.

■ In 1990, President Bush signed a bill that protected the gravesites of Native Americans and required the return of remains and artifacts from such sites to the Native American tribes to which they belonged. A specific bill that would deal only with artifacts contained within the Smithsonian Institution was also proposed.

▲ In an attempt to regain her US citizenship, Iva Toguri D'Aquino AKA Tokyo Rose petitioned the US for a presidential pardon during this week in 1976. Toguri, in 1949, was convicted of treason for broadcasting Japanese propaganda to US troops during World War II. Toguri, who was 60 at the time the 1976 petition was sent, had consistently maintained her innocence. In response to her petition, the JACL (Japanese American Citizens League) apologized to Toguri for not rallying to her defense at the time of her arrest.

NOVEMBER

◆ *The Panama Canal Convention* was signed in 1903. This treaty proclaimed that the canal would be under the administration of the United States.

❖ In 1805, the Female Charitable Society was organized in Wiscosset, Maine in the home of Mrs. Silas Lee. The society is often recognized as being the first women's club in the United States.

● During this month in 1991, Orlando Patterson won the *National Book Award* in the nonfiction category for his book *Freedom in the Making of Western Culture*. The book was the first volume in a series that was planned about freedom and slavery.

■ The Oglala Sioux announced in 1978 that they had become the first Native American Nation in the US to apply to the FCC for a license to operate a television station on a reservation. Oglala Sioux spokesperson Tim Giago, Jr., said that the tribal council was planning a news program in the Lakota language and a *Sesame-Street* type program entitled *As Long As the Grass Shall Grow*. A series about Native Americans in general called *Unkita Oyate* was also planned.

Key: ▲ Asian American ◆ Hispanic American ❖ European American ● African American ■ Native American

▲ Reverend Syngman Rhee, named after the first elected president of South Korea, was appointed successor to the president of the National Council of Churches in a meeting held in Pittsburgh, Pennsylvania, in 1991. Rhee, who was educated at the Yale University Theological Seminary, became the first Korean American to hold the position.

# 19
# NOVEMBER

◆ In 1493, during his second voyage to the New World, Christopher Columbus landed on the island of Puerto Rico. Columbus claimed the island for Spain, naming it San Juan Bautista. Later the name was changed to Puerto Rico and its capital took on the name of San Juan.

❖ President Abraham Lincoln delivered his famous Gettysburg Address in 1863. The occasion was the commemoration of a cemetery on the sight of the Battle of Gettysburg, Pennsylvania (July 1863). The featured speaker was Edward Everett, one of the best US orators of his day. Everett's lengthy speech lasted for two hours on this cold November day. When it was Lincoln's turn to speak, everyone later agreed, including Everett, that his brief (approximately 15 minutes) but eloquent message about the significance of Gettysburg within the context of the Civil War and the even larger context of the United States of America said much more in less time.

> "...that this nation, under God, shall have a new birth of freedom; and that government of the people, by the people, for the people, shall not perish from the earth."
>
> President Abraham Lincoln,
> *Gettysburg Address,*
> November 19, 1863

● Seventy-three-year-old former Klu Klux Klan member Robert E. Chambliss was convicted of first-degree murder on this day in 1977. Chambliss was charged with responsibility for the bombing of the Sixteenth Street Baptist Church in Birmingham, Alabama, resulting in the deaths of four African American girls in 1963.

■ In 1675, European American John Fenwick purchased a tract of land in New Jersey from Native Americans of the Delaware Nation. The land was located between the Delaware River, Game Creek and Cananhidkinck Creek.

# 20
# NOVEMBER

▲ During this month in 1913, the Ghador Revolutionary party was formed in San Francisco. The party was organized for political purposes, and it allowed representatives from various Asian Indian groups to form the Hindu Association of America. Many of the members were involved in the revolutionary movements for the independence of India.

◆ The anniversary of the revolution in Mexico is celebrated on this day. In 1910, under the leadership of Francisco I. Madero, the first phase of the revolution to overthrow the government of Porfirio Diaz began with small rebellions throughout Mexico.

❖ Lincoln Borglum announced the completion of the carvings of the busts of Presidents Washington, Jefferson, Lincoln and Theodore Roosevelt into Mount Rushmore in 1941. His father, Gutzon Borglum, who died on March 6, 1941, spent 14 years carving the president's heads into the mountain and, when he died, his son pledged to finish his father's work.

● *A Soldier's Play*, performed by the Negro Ensemble Company, opened at Theater Four in New York City in 1981. The play was written by Charles Fuller. Cast members for the production included Charles Brown and Adolph Caesar.

■ A group of 78 Native Americans took over and occupied Alcatraz Island in San Francisco Bay in 1969. Their demand was that the land on which the famous Alcatraz prison was located be made available for a Native American cultural center. They offered to buy the prison and the land, which have been vacant since 1963, for $24 in beads and cloth.

▲ In 1927, the case of *Gong Lum et al v Rice et al* was being heard in the Supreme Court of Mississippi. The case had been initiated by Gong Lum, the father of Martha Lum, a student who was barred from the Rosedale High School on the grounds that she was a person of the Mongol race and, therefore, not entitled to enter an all-white school. The case for Gong Lum maintained that as a US citizen Lum was eligible to be educated in any school. Furthermore, the school's actions violated the fourteenth amendment. The court ruled on November 21st, saying that the state had the right to segregate white children from children of other races. In doing so, the court upheld the "separate but equal" doctrine.

**21**

NOVEMBER

◆ The book *La Vida: A Puerto Rican Family in the Culture of Poverty--San Juan and New York* was published by Random House on this day in 1966. The book, which was written by Oscar Lewis, described the family life of three generations of a Puerto Rican family both in their homeland of San Juan, Puerto Rico, and in New York.

◈ In 1922, 87-year-old Rebecca Latimer Felton, a Democrat from Georgia, became the first woman to serve in the US Senate. Felton, whose senatorial term lasted only one day (November 21-November 22), received her place in the Senate by appointment.

● Walter Washington, previously chairman of the New York City Housing Authority and the "commissioner" of the newly reorganized government of the city of Washington, DC, was officially appointed as mayor of Washington, DC, by President Lyndon B. Johnson in 1967. Washington was then confirmed by the US Senate.

■ The largest Native American nation in the US, the Navaho, elected Peterson Zah to the new position of president in 1990. They hoped that the new position and Zah would help the Navaho resolve and move beyond many of their internal scandals and problems, such as factionalism.

**22**

NOVEMBER

▲ *The Treaty of Commerce and Navigation of 1894* between Japan and the United States was a pact that was concluded on this day in 1895. This treaty was one of the most comprehensive ever negotiated by the two nations. It provided for freedom of travel for Japanese citizens in the US, as well as trade, import and export duties and equality of shipping and port regulations.

◆ The works of Spanish painter Salvador Dali made their United States debut in a New York gallery in 1934. Dali, who established himself as a surrealistic painter when he created *Persistence of Memory,* was often described by US critics as creating works that were either "erotic" or "neurotic."

◈ President John F. Kennedy was shot and killed by a sniper's bullet as he rode in a motorcade in Dallas, Texas in 1963. He became the fourth president to be assassinated and the first in 62 years. Texas Governor John Connally was also wounded. Several hours later, Lee Harvey Oswald was arrested and charged with the crime.

● Elijah Muhammad joined the Nation of Islam in their Detroit temple in 1930. Muhammad became assistant minister to the founder of the sect, Wallace D. Ford. When Ford unexplainedly vanished in 1934, Elijah Muhammad took over as head of the movement with the title "Minister of Islam."

■ People born between November 22nd and December 21st have the elk as their totem, according to Sun Bear's Earth Astrology.

▲ Kinro-Kansha-No-Hi, Labor Thanksgiving Day, is celebrated by Japanese Americans.

◆ Oscar Lord, general manager of the Puerto Rican musical group Menudo, announced in 1990 that group members Sergio Gonzales and Ruben Gomez had been fired for their possession of marijuana, discovered by US Customs agents at Miami airport. Lord said the two were fired because the alleged possession of the drugs would tarnish Menudo's "wholesome image."

❖ The opera *Gale* was performed by the Chicago City Opera Company in 1935. Ethel Leginska (Legins) wrote the opera and conducted its first performance. She became the first woman to write an opera and conduct it in a major opera house. The opera was a one-act arrangement of a Cornish legend adapted from *The Haunting* (1922) by Catherine A.D. Scott.

● African American farmer and inventor Andrew Jackson Beard was awarded a patent for his "Jenny" coupler in 1899. The coupler allowed train cars to be joined together simply by bumping them against one another. The device cut back on serious injuries, such as the loss of limbs, that occurred frequently using previous coupling methods.

■ In 1977, 50 members of the United American Indians of New England began a fast that lasted from sundown on this day until sundown on the following day, which was Thanksgiving. The president of the group, Frank James, who was known as Wamsutts by his people, said of the fast that "Native Americans have nothing to be thankful for." The 1977 fast marked the eighth for the group, who gathered in Plymouth, Massachusetts, to conduct the ritual annually.

**N**OVEMBE**R**

▲ Earlier this month in 1962, Daniel Inouye was elected to serve in the US Senate as senator from the new state of Hawaii. He was also the first representative from Hawaii to be elected to the House of Representatives, thus becoming the first Japanese American to serve in Congress. A heavily decorated World War II hero who lost his arm in battle, Inouye has continued to serve his country by being continuously reelected as senator.

◆ During this month in 1990, President Bush announced that Robert Martinez, former governor of Florida, would serve as drug policy director for his administration.

❖ Following the murder of President John F. Kennedy two days earlier, alleged assassin Lee Harvey Oswald was shot and killed by Jack Ruby while being escorted from a Dallas jail. The event, captured by television cameras waiting to photograph Oswald, became the first nationally televised murder. Ruby was immediately apprehended following the incident.

● During this week in 1969, the play *Slaveship* opened in New York. The play documents the reactions of Africans who were kidnapped from their homeland and brought to America to be enslaved by European American colonists. The play was written by LeRoi Jones (later changed to Amiri Baraka) and staged by Gilbert Moses.

■ Logansport, Indiana, was named for the Shawnee chief Spemicalawba, who died on this day in 1812 from wounds he received during battle. As a boy, Spemicalawba was taken prisoner by General Logan of the United States. Logan raised the boy and gave him the name of James Logan. James Logan became a captain in the military and fought on the side of the US during the War of 1812.

*President John F. Kennedy*

▲ In 1882, 55 planters, agents and others met to form an organization called the *Planter's Labor and Supply Company*, which published the *Planter's Monthly*. The organization changed its name on this day in 1895 to the *Hawaiian Sugar Planters Association*. The main purposes of the association were to improve the sugar industry, to support an experimental lab and station, to maintain a sufficient supply of labor and to develop agriculture in general.

◆ Puerto Rico was granted autonomy from Spain on this day in 1897.

❖ On this day in 1963, Irish American President John Fitgerald Kennedy was buried at Arlington National Cemetery in Virginia following a mass at St. Matthew's Roman Catholic Cathedral. The burial became the first to be featured as a national televised event, as millions mourned the loss of their youngest president, who had been killed days earlier by a sniper's bullet. Kennedy's burial spot became one of the most visited gravesites in the Arlington National Cemetery and is marked by an "eternal flame."

● In 1955, the Interstate Commerce Commission (ICC) banned segregation in travel coaches, buses and waiting rooms of transportation service companies involved in interstate travel. This act preceded the initiation of the famed Montgomery, Alabama, bus boycott by two weeks.

■ In 1922, the entire Rio Grande Pueblo Nation joined together to resist the passage of the Benson Bill. The bill would have given rights to European American squatters on Pueblo lands. In response to the Pueblo protest, the general public supported the Native Americans, leading to the creation of the Pueblo Land Board. The job of the board was to establish a fair method for the resolution of land ownership when disputes arose.

▲ Korean American Olympic weightlifter Tommy Kono won the gold medal in the light-heavyweight category at the 1956 Summer Olympics in Melbourne, Australia. Kono broke two world records, one in the jerk lift at 385.75 pounds and one in the snatch lift at 292 pounds. He also broke the Olympic record for the press lift at 308.5 pounds. All of these lifts were for a world-record total of 986.25 pounds.

◆ President Carlos Salinas De Gortari of Mexico met with President Bush of the US in 1990 to discuss possible free trade between the two countries. The trade agreement allowed US companies to open facilities in Mexico, providing jobs for Mexican workers.

❖ In 1973, Rose Mary Woods, personal secretary of President Nixon, testified that she was responsible for the 18-minute gap on one of the tapes subpoenaed by the federal court investigating the Watergate break-in. The tape in question was one contained a conversation between President Nixon and H.R. Haldeman three days following the break-in at the Democratic National Headquarters in 1972.

● During this week in 1967, the Chase Manhattan Bank Foundation gave a grant to the United Negro College Fund providing an opportunity for African American colleges to hire six economists as professors or advisors. The economists included Bertrand Fox (Harvard), Henry C. Wallich (Yale), Paul McCracken and Yal Brozen (University of Chicago), Walter Hesler (University of Minnesota) and Raymond Sauliner (Columbia).

■ The first conference of Eskimo, Lapps and Native Americans from the Arctic areas of Alaska, Greenland, Norway, Canada and Sweden met for four days in Copenhagen, Denmark, in 1976. The meeting was to demand recognition of the separate identities of groups and a share in the decision-making regarding use of their land and sea resources.

▲ ● *Flower Drum Song* was released as a motion picture during this month in 1961. The film was based on the Rodgers and Hammerstein musical play about Chinese Americans living in San Francisco's Chinatown. Featured actors in the movie included Japanese Americans Miyoshi Umeki, James Shigeta and Reiko Sato as well as Chinese American actors Jack Soo and Nancy Kwan. Also in an important role was African American Juanita Hall as a Chinese American.

◆ Mexican muralist Diego Rivera held a show of his latest works in his Mexico City gallery. The show included 150 paintings and drawings of people and places in Russia. During his lifetime, Rivera had become known for his communist ideals. In this particular display, he was recognized as trying to emulate Soviet art.

❖ The musical *Fifty Million Frenchmen* by Cole Porter and Herbert Fields opened at the Lyric Theater in New York City in 1930. This show, described as a "musical comedy tour of Paris," went on to become Porter's first success.

● In a speaking engagement in New York City in 1906, Booker T. Washington gave his views of what was described as an improvement in the acceptance of African Americans. In the speech, Washington repeated his assertion that those of his race must work for advances in jobs and education instead of trying to win social equality with European Americans. Washington backed up his views by telling his audience that, in the South, European Americans had praised the progress made by African Americans, particularly those who were attending the Tuskegee Institute in Alabama.

■ The Bureau of Indian Affairs (BIA) announced in 1970 that the bureau would undergo extensive reorganization in an effort to bring decision-making authority closer to tribal officials. BIA commissioner Louis Bruce described the reorganization as a way to "assist Indian people to take control over their own destinies."

*"...to assist Indian people to take control over their own destinies."*

Stated purpose of reorganization of BIA, Louis Bruce, 1970

▲ In 1910, Sara Choe was the first of 951 picture brides to arrive in Hawaii. Choe's picture appeared in an album of picture brides prepared for newly arrived Korean Americans working in the sugarcane and pineapple fields of Hawaii.

◆ Proclamation of US military occupation occurred in the Dominican Republic in 1916. This was done to quell recent outbreaks of violence, and it stimulated great opposition from the Dominican Republic and resulted in the removal of US military presence.

❖ Truman Capote produced the year's social sensation when he threw a party at the Plaza Hotel in New York City. The party was held to celebrate the success of Capote's new "nonfiction novel," *In Cold Blood*, published in 1966.

● In 1961, Ernie Davis, a record-setting halfback for Syracuse University, became the first African American college football player to win the *Heisman Trophy*. This trophy is annually awarded to the "best" college football player in a given year.

■ On this day in 1785, the Cherokee entered into their first treaty with the United States at Hopewell, South Carolina. The treaty outlined specific boundaries of Cherokee territory and promised restraint of US citizens from further trespassing into the new Cherokee territory.

▲ Syngman Rhee arrived in Hawaii on this day in 1904. Upon his arrival, Rhee immediately began to organize the Korean immigrants who were living on the island for the Korean national liberation movement.

◆ Los Angeles millionaire and management consultant Benjamin Fernandez announced in 1978 that he was a candidate for the Republican presidential nomination in 1980. With his announcement, Fernandez claimed he was the "first Hispanic to seek a major party's presidential nomination." Fernandez, who was born to Mexican parents in Boxcar, Kansas, had worked his way up from picking crops as a small boy to a successful business career. In 1972, he worked as a fund raiser in the 1972 campaign of President Nixon.

❖ In 1926, Nelie Taloe Ross, the first woman elected governor of a state, celebrated her 100th birthday. Ross, a Democrat from Wyoming, summed up her career in politics as "a milestone in the battle for women's equality." Ross died in 1927.

● Granville T. Woods was granted a patent for his induction telegraph system in 1887. The system permitted communication between moving trains, making train travel safer.

■ Troops led by Colonel John M. Chivington massacred Cheyenne and Arapaho tribal members at Sand Creek in 1864. The massacre led to much public criticism. The tribal members had been ordered to camp at the Sand Creek site while en route from Kansas to Colorado for a conference. While camping, approximately 200 Cheyenne and Arapaho were killed in the attack, mostly women and children. Chivington was later censured by a Senate committee, but was not court-martialed.

NOVEMBER

▲ In 1933 the Filipino Labor Union was founded. The union established a number of branch offices throughout central California by the end of the year.

◆ The National Association of Puerto Rican Civil Rights presented an award to Mexican American César Chávez in 1970. Chávez, who normally does not accept awards, chose to accept this award because he saw the aims of the organization as being very similar to his own.

❖ Mark Twain (AKA Samuel Clemens) was born in 1835 in Florida, Missouri. He is considered by many to be the greatest humorist in United States literature and a giant among the authors of US fiction. Many of his books were reflections of his childhood or places he had been. Among the praise given to him is an observation that one of his greatest accomplishments was to develop a writing style so distinctly "American" and not an imitation of English writers. His satirical wit and sharp social criticism remain a unique mark on the pages of US literature.

● Gordon Parks, award-winning poet, photographer and movie producer, was born in 1912 in Fort Scott, Kansas. Parks quietly but with determination made his mark in each of the three categories mentioned above. He was a staff photographer for *Life* magazine (1949-1970) and won the *ASMP* award in 1961 as *Magazine Photographer of the Year*. His poetry and photographic ability came together in 1968 with the publishing of his book, *A Poet and His Camera*. He directed several movies, among them the film version of his autobiography *The Learning Tree*, *Shaft*, and *Leadbelly*. In 1972, he received the *Springarn Award* from the NAACP. In 1977, he and three other partners gained control of *Essence* magazine.

> **"Viva la huelgo"**
> **[Long live the strike]**
>
> César Chávez,
> United Farm Workers Slogan,
> 1960s

■ During this month in 1769, a school founded 20 years earlier by the Reverend Eleazar Wheelock for the purpose of educating Native Americans became Dartmouth College. At the new college's inception, 10 of the 28 students attending the school were Native Americans.

# MY PERSONAL LIST

Hispanic Americans have been at the forefront of many significant accomplishments in science and technology. One such pioneer is astronaut and scientist Franklin Chang-Diáz. Born in San Jose, Costa Rica, Chang-Diáz took an early interest in space exploration.

As a young adult, he wrote a letter to the German rocket scientist Werner von Braun. Surprisingly, the reply Franklin later received was not from Von Braun, but from the American space agency, NASA. NASA thanked Diáz for his interest in the space program and suggested ways for him to pursue his dream.

Franklin knew his future in space exploration lay in the US. After graduating from high school in 1968, he left Costa Rica for the US. He learned English in classes at Hartford High School in Hartford, Connecticut. He then received a scholarship to the University of Connecticut. Graduating in 1973 with a degree in mechanical engineering, Chang-Diáz next enrolled in the Massachusetts Institute of Technology and earned a Ph.D. in plasmaphysics. In 1980, Diáz joined the NASA space program as a member of the ground crew that worked with the first spacelab mission. Finally, in 1985, he became a member of the US space-shuttle crew. On January 12, 1986, Franklin Chang-Diáz became the first Hispanic American in space. While aboard the shuttle, he made history again when he spoke in Spanish to audiences in both the US and Latin America.

Franklin Chang-Diáz continues to be a pioneer in the field of space science, working on a rocket that could greatly increase the speed of spacecraft. As long as the US space program continues to grow, Chang-Diáz will be among its most innovative leaders.

Astronaut Franklin Chang-Diáz's response when the president of Costa Rica congratulated him on his first space mission:

**"Muchas Gracias, Senor Presidente. Este es un gran honor para mi. Y estamos muy contentos que pudimos establecer esta comunication entre los estados unido y los paises Latino Americanos ... Para mi es un honor poder hablar a todos los paises sur Americano ... Yo quiero darle gracia de nuevo por tu querida llamada. Me gustaria mucho ir y visitar a Costa Rica ... Muchisima Gracias!"**

" Thank you, Mr. President. This is a great honor for me. We are so happy that we were able to establish this communication between the United States and all Latin American countries ... For me this is a great honor--to be able to speak to all South American countries ... I want to thank you again for your very nice call. I would like very much to go and visit Costa Rica. Thank you so much!"

◀ *Franklin Chang-Diáz*

> *"Put in your history books the Indians' part in the World War. Tell how the Indian fought for a country of which he was not a citizen, for a flag to which he had no claim, and for a people who have treated him unjustly. We ask this, Chief, to keep sacred the memory of our people."*
> Grand Council Fire of American Indians, 1927

◆ In 1821, an "Independent State of Spanish Haiti" was declared. This new state was under the protection of Colombia and also included the territories of Venezuela, Panama and Ecuador. The new state of Spanish Haiti lasted only two months. In February, President Boyer invaded the Spanish colony with 12,000 soldiers, and the Spanish part of the island came under the control of the Republic of Haiti.

❖ On this day in 1917, Irish American priest Father Flanagan founded Boys Town in Nebraska.

● Rosa Parks, a Montgomery, Alabama, seamstress, was arrested by Montgomery police for refusing to move to the back of the bus and give up her seat to a white passenger. This incident led to the successful boycott of the Montgomery, Alabama, city bus system by African Americans in 1955.

■ The Grand Council Fire of American Indians presented a memorial to the mayor of Chicago in 1927. The memorial included some words of instruction to their white audience that began when the Native American group stated that they were the first true "Americans."

▲ The *Cairo Declaration* was issued on this day in 1943. The declaration stated that the US, China and Russia, "... mindful of the enslavement of the people of Korea, are determined that in due course Korea shall become free and independent."

DECEMBER

◆ During this month in 1976, Governor Jerry Brown of California appointed Vilma S. Martinez to serve on California's Board of Regents. Martinez, who also served as the Mexican American Legal Defense Fund's first female president, became the first Chicano to serve as a regent.

❖ Barney Clark, a Utah dentist, became the recipient of the first artificial heart ever implanted in a human being in 1982. The heart was the design of Dr. Robert Jarvik of the University of Utah Medical Center. The heart, known as the Jarvik-7, had two chambers, one that received blood from the body and another that pumped blood throughout the body. Barney Clark lived for 112 days after the heart was implanted. He died in March 1983.

● Joan S. Wallace was sworn in as assistant secretary of administration of the US Department of Agriculture in 1977. Wallace became the first woman and the first African American to hold this position.

■ In 1970, the US Senate voted 70 to 12 to approve a federal grant that would give the Taos Pueblo people title to 48,000 acres of land in New Mexico.

▲ From the 2nd through the 5th of this month in 1952, President-elect Eisenhower visited the combat zone in Korea. The trip was the first step in the implementation of Eisenhower's pledge to stop fighting in Korea. While in Korea, the president-elect met with Asian military commanders, Korean officials and Korean President Rhee.

**Key:** ◆ Hispanic Americans   ❖ European Americans   ● African Americans   ■ Native Americans   ▲ Asian Americans

◆ Mexican President Gustavo Diáz and President Lyndon B. Johson met on this day in 1966 to inspect the Amistad (Friendship) Dam that was being built across the Rio Grande. The $78-million structure was being paid for in equal amounts by both Mexico and the United States. During the meeting, the presidents issued a joint statement proclaiming that the dam was "an outstanding example of how two neighbor countries can resolve their common boundary problems with benefit to both."

**D**ECEMBE**R**

❖ European American composer George Gershwin appeared as a soloist at a concert in Carnegie Hall in New York City on this day in 1925. Gershwin played his *Concerto in F*. This was the first jazz concert for the piano in musical history.

● Karen Farmer, a real-estate salesperson from Detroit, became the first African American woman to be admitted as a member of the Daughters of the American Revolution (DAR) in 1977. This was a significant event because of the group's racist image. In 1939, the DAR had barred singer Marian Anderson from performing in Constitution Hall in Washington, D.C., because Anderson was an African American.

■ In 1639, the Bronx portion of New York was purchased from Native Americans. The purchase was made by Danish immigrant Jonas Bronck, a farmer, for whom the region is currently named.

▲ On this day in 1977, the US government announced that it would accept 10,000 Vietnamese refugees called "boat people" who had left Vietnam in small boats. During the previous summer, the US had approved the emergency admission of 15,000 Indochina refugees, many of whom came from Vietnam.

◆ Mexican American union official César Chávez was jailed in Salinas, California, in 1970 for contempt of court after he failed to call off a nationwide boycott of lettuce. The boycott was part of an attempt by the AFL-CIO to unionize Salinas Valley lettuce growers.

❖ Rosalyn S. Yalow, a senior medical investigator for the US Veterans Administration, became the first woman to receive the *Albert Lasker Basic Medical Research Award* in 1976. The award, worth $10,000, was given in recognition for her role in the discovery of the radioimmunoassay -- a method of measuring tiny concentrations of hundreds of substances in body tissues. Today, these assays are used to detect the hepatitis virus, among other things, in potential blood donors.

**D**ECEMBE**R**

● *The Amsterdam News*, the largest African American-owned newspaper in New York City and the largest weekly community newspaper in the United States, was started in 1909 in the New York City home of James H. Anderson.

■ During this month in 1963, the American Indian Arts Center opened in New York City, New York. The arts center was devoted to increasing public awareness of the high standards in workmanship and wealth of art produced by Eskimo and other Native American groups.

▲ During this week in 1968, Dr. Samuel I. Hayakawa was named acting president of San Francisco State College. Hayakawa's appointment followed racial unrest between African Americans and European Americans that led to the temporary closing of the school. Hayakawa, born to Japanese American parents in Canada, said of his appointment, "I stand in the middle. I am neither white nor black." His hope was that his own color would help him become "a channel to bring blacks and whites together."

> "Animals struggle with each other for food or for leadership, but they do not, like human beings, struggle with each other for things that stand for food or leadership ... such things as money, bonds, titles."
>
> Samuel I. Hayakawa,
> *Language in Thought and Action*,
> 1968

*Mae C. Jemison*

◆ Columbus arrived on the island of Quesqueya on his first voyage in 1492. He named the island *La Española*. It later became known as Hispaniola and today is called the Dominican Republic/Haiti.

❖ The Rand Corporation, a research and development organization, announced the appointment of the first two women to sit on their 21-member board of directors in 1972. The women were Sonia Mentschikoff and Dr. Eleanor Bernert Sheldon.

● In 1992, Mae C. Jemison was the first female astronaut of African American descent to go into space. Her first mission was a cooperative effort between the US and Japan which focused on experiments in space to gain more knowledge about the life sciences.

■ During this month in 1973, Native Americans of the Menominee Nation of Wisconsin formed the National Committee to Save the Menominee People and Forests. This organization was formed to get back Menominee forestland that had been taken away by the federal government. One of the key people in the battle to protect the Menominee rights was Ada Deer, cofounder of the militant group DRUMS and head of the Menominee Common Stock and Voting Trust.

▲ During this month in 1964, the Kennedy family called a press conference to announce that Chinese American architect Ieoh Ming Pei had been selected to design the new John F. Kennedy Memorial Library. The library was being built as a shrine to slain President Kennedy. In explaining her choice of Pei as the designer for the building, Jacqueline Kennedy said, "We wanted the memorial to my husband to be built by an American architect, and Pei--why he just loves things to be beautiful."

# 5
## DECEMBER

**Discovery by Columbus Day**
Haiti

# 6
## DECEMBER

◆ Governor of Puerto Rico Luis Munoz Marin received the *Presidential Medal of Freedom Award* in 1963.

❖ Shirley Hufstedler, a US Appeals Court judge and the highest-ranking woman jurist in the United States at the time, was sworn in as the US's first secretary of education in 1979. She was nominated for the position by President Jimmy Carter, who also created the new federal department.

● The Thirteenth Amendment to the Constitution was ratified in 1865, ending the institution of slavery in the United States by law. The true end of slavery came on April 19, 1865, when the Confederate troops of the South surrendered to the Union troops of the North.

■ Annie Dodge Wauneka, daughter of Navaho chief, Chee Dodge, was awarded the *Presidential Medal of Freedom Award*, the United States's highest civilian honor in a White House ceremony in 1963. Wauneka, who was the first Native American woman to receive the award, was also the first woman to sit on the Navaho Tribal Council. Wauneka was cited for her "long crusade for improved health programs" on the reservations. Her break with many of the traditional ways of her people resulted in much criticism, but her work in education and health programs that resulted in better living conditions for the Navaho improved the standard of living for her people.

▲ Patsy Mink, the first Japanese American woman to be elected to Congress, was born on this day in 1927. Mink, from the state of Hawaii, held a degree in law from the University of Chicago Law School. Mink began to serve in Congress in 1965 and held her seat there until 1976, when she ran for the Senate. Although she did not win a Senate seat, she continued her public service as Assistant Secretary of State for Oceans and Environmental Affairs.

**Key:** ◆ Hispanic Americans ❖ European Americans ● African Americans ■ Native Americans ▲ Asian Americans

◆ During this month in 1857, the Cart War, a Mexican border incident that attained international significance, was brought to an end. Mexican teamsters who controlled a very lucrative trade between San Antonio and the coast of Texas became the victims of violent attacks by European American businesspeople who were attempting to take over the route. The attacks on the Mexicans escalated to such a degree that Texas Rangers had to be called in.

◆ Republican Edith Norse Rogers of Massachusetts began her first term of Congress in 1925. Rogers, who holds the distinction of being the woman who served the greatest number of years in Congress, served a total of nineteen terms. Her final term ended with her death on September 10, 1960.

● The Reverend W. Sterling Cary, a New York minister, became the first African American to be elected president of the National Council of Churches in 1972. The National Council of Churches brings together people of different faiths. "Together they make a common witness to their faith and, with others, serve the churches and the world."

■ During this month in 1895, Lieutenant V.E. Stottler was placed in charge of the Apache group known as the Mescalero. Under Stottler's power, the Mescalero men were required to cut off their braids and wear European clothing instead of their traditional apparel. In order to ensure that the Mescalero followed his demands, Stottler refused to give tribe members food, employment or other necessities until they met his requests. Stottler also disbanded the Mescalero tribal court system, taking on the role of judge and jury himself. The actions of Stottler are considered to be one of the worst abuses of power in dealing with Native Americans.

▲ In 1975, President Ford made a stopover in the Philippines on his return trip from China. The purpose of Ford's visit was to meet with President Ferdinand Marcos to renew the terms of a US-Philippine air and naval-base agreement.

DECEMBER

DECEMBER

◆ During this week in 1846, the Battle of San Pasqual took place. This military skirmish between Californians and US forces resulted in about 19 deaths, including that of Colonel Stephen Kearney of the US forces. The battle, which took place near San Diego, occurred during the height of the Mexican American War.

◆ John Lennon, former lead guitarist of the famous music group called the Beatles, was shot to death in New York City outside his apartment building, the Dakota, in 1980. Although he never gave up his British citizenship, Lennon had lived in the United States for many years and contributed greatly to the musical development of this country. A prolific songwriter, Lennon wrote and sang many songs both as a member of the Beatles and as a solo artist. Some songs attributed to Lennon include: *Imagine, Eleanor Rigby* and *Woman*. The last of these songs appeared on Lennon's comeback album, which featured songs performed by both Lennon and his wife Yoko Ono.

● Althea Gibson received a *Springarn Award* from the NAACP in 1956. As the pioneer African American female tennis player, she was honored for her sportsmanship and for opening up a new field of endeavor to young African Americans.

■ The BIA (Bureau of Indian Affairs) signed a contract in 1966 with RCA (Radio Corporation of America) to establish the first "family-centered" residential training center at Philadelphia, Mississippi. The center is located adjacent to the Choctaw reservation. The training was initiated to promote employment among the Choctaw peoples.

▲ In 1906, an investigation conducted in San Francisco in 1906 determined that Japanese students numbered only 68 of the total school population of 28,736. Twenty-five of the Japanese students were US citizens by birth.

◆ During this week in 1898, the United States and Spain signed the *Treaty of Paris* to end the Spanish American War. Under this treaty, the US acquired the islands of Puerto Rico, Guam and the Philippines. The islands cost the US $20 million.

### DECEMBER

✦ Noah Webster established *The American Minerva,* New York's first daily newspaper, on this day in 1793. Webster pledged that his newpaper would be "...the friend of government, of freedom, of virtue, and every species of improvement."

● In 1872 P.B.S. Pinchback became the first, and, as of 1992, the only African American governor of the state of Louisiana. This event occurred during Radical Reconstruction (1865-1877). This period, a result of the North's victory over the South in the Civil War, permitted African Americans a chance at upward mobility in various fields, particularly in politics in the South.

■ During this year in 1960, *Apology to the Iroquois*, a book by Edmund Wilson, was published. This book dealt with the history of the Iroquois in the United States.

▲ On this day in 1943, the Senate passed Senate Joint Resolution 93, which granted the Philippines independence by presidential proclamation soon after the Japanese had been defeated and normal conditions had been restored on the islands.

### DECEMBER

◆ Gabriella Mistral, Chilean poet and educator, was awarded the *Nobel Prize for Literature* in 1945. Mistral gained American as well as international fame for her collected works, including *Desolacion* (*Desolation*--1922) and *Ternura* (*Tenderness*--1924). In addition to her career as a writer, Mistral served as a delegate to the United Nations.

✦ Sinclair Lewis was awarded the 1930 *Nobel Prize for Literature*. He was the first US author to win the prize in that category. His body of work exposed the weaknesses he saw in US social life, expressed in such books as *Main Street* (1920), *Babbitt* (1922) and *Elmer Gantry* (1927).

● Dr. Ralph Bunche, a United Nations mediator, personally accepted the 1950 *Nobel Peace Prize* award in Oslo, Norway, becoming the first African American to receive this award. The award recognized Bunche's efforts in negotiating an end to the fighting between Arabs and Jews in Israel, formerly known as Palestine, in 1948.

> *"A son, a son, a son! I wanted a son of yours and mine, in those distant days of burning bliss when my bones would tremble at your least murmur and my brow would glow with a radiant mist."*
>
> Gabriella Mistral,
> "Poem of the Son,"
> *Desolacion,*
> *1922*

▲ Two young Chinese American pharmacists, Chen-Ning Yang and Tsung-Dao Lee, were awarded the 1957 *Nobel Prize for Physics*. Yang, a physics professor at Princeton's Institute for Advanced Study, and Lee, a physics professor at Columbia University, discovered a law of nature that negated the previously existing one, the "Principle of the Conservation of Parity," which had been formulated about 30 years earlier.

◆ Rosa Delores Alvarino (later changed to Rita Moreno) was born in 1931 in Humacao, Puerto Rico. As Rita Moreno, the singer-dancer-actress enjoys a successful career in the United States. One of her most memorable roles was her *Academy Award*-winning performance in the popular film *West Side Story*.

◆ Diane Feinstein, a former city supervisor, became the first woman to serve as mayor of San Francisco, California in 1979. In 1992, she was one of two women from the state of California elected to the Senate.

● On December 11, 1939, boxer Henry Armstrong, who fought early in his career under the name "Melody Jackson," defeated Jimmy Garrison in a welterweight title bout. Armstrong won the fight by a knockout in the seventh round.

■ Recognition of the Heritage College's national pilot of the COMP (College Opportunities Mentorship Program) project was read into the *Congressional Record* on this day in 1989. Heritage College is a private, nondenominational school located in the Yakima Valley of Washington State. The school, which incorporated in July 1981, has a mostly Native American population. The COMP project, which was funded by the state of Washington's Higher Education Coordinating Board, is devoted to using minority students as mentors in their own communities to help increase awareness in college attendance among persons of multicultural backgrounds.

*Rita Moreno*

▲ A bilateral cotton-textile agreement was concluded between the governments of Korea and the United States on this day in 1967.

**D ECEMBE R**

◆ During this month in 1978, Mexican American professional golfer Nancy Lopez was formally named "Rookie of the Year" and "Player of the Year" by the Ladies Professional Golf Association (LPGA). Lopez became the first professional golfer, male or female, to win both titles in the same year.

◆ Oscar S. Strauss of New York City became the first person of Jewish heritage to be appointed to a presidential cabinet position in 1906. Mr. Strauss served as Secretary of Commerce and Labor under President Theodore Roosevelt.

● Joseph H. Rainey of Georgetown, South Carolina, was sworn in as a member of the US House of Representatives in 1870, becoming the first African American member of Congress. Rainey, a Republican, was sworn in to fill a vacancy created when the House declared the seat of Benjamin Franklin Whitmore vacant. Joseph H. Rainey served in the Congress for two years.

■ A lower court ruling requiring Native American students in Oklahoma to cut their hair to meet school regulations was upheld by the US Supreme Court during this week in 1973.

▲ During this week in 1963, Korean Park Chung Hee was sworn in as the chief executive in Korea's new civilian government.

*Katherine Dunham*

◆ In 1968, part of the city of El Paso, Texas, came to be owned by Mexico. The change in ownership resulted from a change in the course of the Rio Grande, which serves as the boundary between Texas and Mexico.

◆ Diana Kilmury was elected to one of five vice-presidential positions with the International Brotherhood of Teamsters in 1991. Since joining the Teamsters in 1974, Kilmury had served as a delegate to their 1981 convention and worked as a truck driver for the film industry in Vancouver, British Columbia. She was the first woman elected to a national office within the Teamster organization.

● During this month in 1983, Katherine Dunham, African American dancer, choreographer and anthropologist, received a *Kennedy Center Honor* -- the highest award an artist in the US can receive. Four years before receiving her *Kennedy Center Honor*, Dunham was presented with an *Albert Schweitzer Music Award* at Carnegie Hall in New York City.

■ Ross O. Swimmer, chief of the Cherokee Nation, relinquished his position as chief in 1985 to assume the post as assistant secretary of the Interior for Indian Affairs. Swimmer was sworn in at a ceremony in Washington, DC.

▲ On this day in 1943, President Franklin D. Roosevelt signed the bill to repeal the Chinese Exclusion Act which established quotas. The law enabled 105 Chinese aliens per year to become US citizens.

◆ During this week in 1991, Mexican American actor Martin Sheen (Ramon Estevez) opened in a revival of Arthur Miller's *The Crucible* at the Belasco Theater in New York. The play deals with the events that occurred during the infamous Salem (Massachusetts) witch trials of 1692.

◆ In 1971, Detective Frank Serpico, an Italian American member of the New York City Police Department, testified to the Knapp Commission about corruption in the New York City Police Department. According to Serpico, there were many police officers in the department who were guilty of taking payoffs. The testimony of Detective Serpico led to the indictments of several corrupt police officers.

● During this week in 1943, the National Institute of Arts and Letters (NIAL), along with authors Carl van Doren and Upton Sinclair, elected African American sociologist and historian W.E.B. DuBois to membership. DuBois was the first African American elected to membership in the NIAL.

■ Wilma P. Mankiller was installed as the principal chief of the Cherokee Nation in 1985. Prior to her installation, she was deputy chief. Mankiller was the first Native American woman to become chief of a major nation. She managed 1,000 Cherokee national employees of a 75,000-member nation with an annual budget of $47 million.

▲ In 1916, the Senate passed the Burnett Bill, a restrictive immigration bill. The bill contained a provision that would restrict the immigration of Asians by administering a literacy test. The bill was sent to President Wilson who vetoed it, citing the provision as his reason for doing so. Congress overrode the veto, and it became an official immigration act on February 5, 1917.

◆ On this day in 1961, President and Mrs. Kennedy stopped in Puerto Rico while en route to Venezuela and Colombia for a state visit to inspect the Alliance of Progress projects in those countries. The Kennedys were greeted at the San Juan Airport by Puerto Rico Governor Luis Munoz Marin. After a brief stay on the island, the president praised the progress of the economic program that had been put in place, saying that the program had "given us the inspiration to feel that we can carry on a great cooperative effort throughout the hemisphere."

● African American jazz innovator and trumpeter, Miles Davis, was awarded the *Sonning Prize* for musical excellence in Copenhagen, Denmark, in 1984. As part of the award, Davis was given a cash endowment of $9,000.

● African American farmer and inventor, Andrew Jackson Beard, invented a plow on this day in 1887. Beard sold the plow and patent for $5,200. An earlier plow that had been invented by Beard was patented in 1881.

■ In 1890, Chief Sitting Bull, the leader of the Sioux Nation, was killed by Red Tomahawk during an arrest. Red Tomahawk was a member of a Native American police agency connected with the US Army.

▲ On this day in 1978, the People's Republic of China and the United States announced that full diplomatic relations between the two countries would resume on January 1, 1979.

**D**ECEMBE**R**

*"Let us help ourselves...let us pull ourselves up by our bootstraps."*

Luis Munoz Marin,
Governor of Puerto Rico
1940s

◆ A militant Mexican American group called *Catolicos Por La Raza* was founded in Los Angeles, California during this month in 1969. The name of the group translates in English to Catholics for the Race.

◆ In Ohio, Florence E. Allen became the first woman to sit as a justice on a state supreme court (1922).

**D**ECEMBE**R**  ● Longtime civil rights activist and former member of the SCLC (Southern Christian Leadership Conference) during the 1960s, Andrew Young was appointed United States ambassador to the United Nations in 1976 by President Jimmy Carter. Young became the first African American to hold this important position.

■ During this week in 1962, Native Americans of the Sioux Nation joined farmers living in Mound City, South Dakota, in a protest against the Department of Agriculture. The Native Americans were encouraged to join the protest by Standing Rock tribal chairman, Alijoe Agaard. The protest was being held in response to the Agriculture Stabilization and Conservation Service's announcement that it was moving its offices from the Mound City location to Herreid, South Dakota. The farmers were protesting the move, believing that movement of the office would take jobs away from the small town.

▲ The US Supreme Court handed down its ruling in *Endo v United States* in 1944. In its decision, the court ruled that the retention of Japanese American citizens was a violation of Constitutional rights and, therefore, was not authorized by law.

◆ Romana A. Banuelos was sworn in as the 34th treasurer of the United States in 1971. Appointed by President Richard Nixon, Banuelos became the first Hispanic American to hold this government position. The job of the treasurer is to oversee the US Savings Bond Division, the US Mint, and the Bureau of Engraving and Printing. Ramona Banuelos later left government service and operated her own business, Ramona's Mexican Food Products of Gardena, California.

**DECEMBER**

❖ On this date in 1903, brothers Orville and Wilbur Wright made history when they achieved the first successful flight made in a self-propelled heavier-than-air craft near Kitty Hawk, North Carolina. In 1907, the brothers built an airplane for the US government able to carry two men.

● Paul Robeson and William I. Patterson led a delegation of African Americans to the United Nations in 1951. The group presented a petition that charged the US government with having a policy of genocide against persons of color who are citizens of the United States.

■ The Ford Foundation announced that a $654,000 grant would be given to Native Americans to assist them in a variety of ways. From the grant, $310,000 was to go to the National Congress of American Indians Fund, $100,000 was to go to the Alaska Federation, $150,000 to the Center for the Arts, $38,000 to the Citizens Crusade Against Poverty and $56,000 to the University of Alaska. The money was targeted for assistance in promoting and expanding Native American cultural affairs and for help in educational and economic developments.

▲ In 1944, President Franklin Delano Roosevelt, on the advice of Secretary of War Stimson, made the announcement that he was rescinding the Exclusion Act which led to the infamous Executive Order 9066 ordering Japanese American citizens and Japanese aliens to be interned. The following day, the War Relocation Authority (WRA) made its termination policy public. According to the WRA, all centers under WRA jurisdiction were to be emptied within six months to a year.

❖ The movie *El Cid* was released during this week in 1961. The movie was presented as a historical film about the medieval Spanish hero.

❖ In 1979, Robert Bergland, Secretary of Agriculture, announced that his department would stop funding labor-saving research, because it was generally felt that farm mechanization was having an adverse effect on the lives of the migrant laborers.

**DECEMBER**

● In 1865, the Thirteenth Amendment to the Constitution was ratified. The amendment abolished slavery.

■ The movie, *Tell Them Willie Boy Is Here,* made its premiere in 1969 at theaters in New York. The movie, which starred actors Robert Blake, Robert Redford and Katherine Ross, is the account of a Native American boy who is on the run with a girl whose father he has killed in self-defense. The movie was released by Universal Pictures.

▲ Edward Bing Kan, interpreter for the US Immigration and Naturalization Service (INS), filed his application for citizenship on this day in 1843. On January 18, 1844 in Chicago, Illinois, Kan became the first person of Chinese descent to become a naturalized citizen following the repeal of the Chinese Exclusion Act.

◆ Texas became the 28th state to join the union in 1845 after a vote was held in which Texans supported annexation to the United States. Prior to becoming part of the US, Texas had belonged to Mexico. However, the United States seized much of this land during the Mexican American War.

◆ The first installment of *The American Crisis* by Thomas Paine appeared in *The Pennsylvania Journal* on this day in 1776. This marked the beginning of a series of essays designed to bolster the morale of American patriots during the Revolutionary War.

**D**ECEMBE**R**

● Doubleday/Doran Publishing Company announced the establishment of the *George Washington Carver Memorial Award,* worth $2,500, in 1943. The award was to be given annually to the author of any book that dealt with "American Negroes in a manner that seems worthy of special recognition."

■ In 1675, King Philip, chief of the Wampanoag Nation, went to war with English soldiers. King Philip feared the destruction of his people and their land. Both sides suffered many losses of men, women and children. Native troops were defeated, but King Philip escaped for a time. He eventually was killed at a swamp near present-day Bristol, Rhode Island, in 1676.

▲ One of the earliest efforts by General John B. DeWitt of the US to have Japanese aliens placed in internment camps while the US was involved in World War II was initiated on this day in 1941. In this early communication, DeWitt urged the internment of aliens of all countries with whom the US was at war, including Japan, Germany and Italy.

◆ Opposition to the Vietnam War grew in the Hispanic community as significant numbers of Hispanic soldiers and sailors, particularly those from the Southwest, were losing their lives in Vietnam. Rosalio Munoz, a former student-body president at UCLA, who refused induction into the military, organized the first Chicano anti-Vietnam rally in the United States in 1969. The rally was held in Los Angeles, California. It was estimated that 2,000 people were in attendance.

**D**ECEMBE**R**

◆ Samuel Slater, a British expert in textile machinery, started the first successful mill in the United States at Pawtucket, Rhode Island in 1793. Slater has been called the "Father of American Manufacturers." He is considered one of the most influential figures in the introduction of the "Machine Age" in the United States.

● Michael Bennett's musical, *Dream Girls,* featuring an all-African American cast, opened on Broadway in 1982. The musical, which had a successful multiyear run on Broadway, was loosely tied to the rise and fall of the Motown 60s musical trio, the Supremes.

■ In 1835, many members of the Cherokee Nation who lived in Georgia were driven from their land by European American settlers. The Cherokee land was taken because gold was discovered on it.

▲ In 1932, Congress passed the Hare-Hawes-Cutting Act. The act excluded Filipinos from emigrating to the United States and also ruled Filipinos as ineligible for US citizenship.

♦ In 1991, Linda Chávez published her first book, *Out of the Barrio,* in 1991. The book addresses concerns of Hispanics and, in particular, the issue of assimilation. In 1992, Chávez was preparing to write her second book on multiculturalism.

### DECEMBER

♦ A group of "Pilgrims" from the ship *Mayflower* landed at Plymouth, Massachusetts, in 1620. Called Pilgrims because of their search for religious freedom, this group of diverse people left their native England for the shores of North America. England already had various settlements up and down the Atlantic coast, but this one would be a permanent foundation for the founding of the US.

● The boycott of the Montgomery, Alabama, bus system had been in effect for more than a year in 1956. On this date, for the first time since the boycott began (December 5, 1955), African Americans could again ride the buses as racial segregation within the transportation system came to an end.

■ At about 10:00 A.M., 38 imprisoned Sartee warriors were hanged in the town of Manketo in 1862. The execution, which was sanctioned by President Lincoln earlier in the month, has been described by some as "America's greatest mass execution."

▲ More than 50,000 Chinese students gathered in the People's Square in 1989 to make their wish for democratic reforms, including the freedom of the press, known to officials of China. The government denounced the demonstration as an illegal act and killed many of the demonstrators.

### 22

### DECEMBER

♦ During this week in 1969, a demonstration took place in front of the new St. Basil's Cathedral in Los Angeles. The demonstrators were part of a group called *Catolicos Por La Raza* (Catholics for the Race) and they were protesting extravagant church expenses in a time of great social need. The group were demanding better distribution of funds for the poor.

♦ The Continental Naval Fleet was actively organized on this day in 1775 and placed under the command of Ezek Hopkins, a former New England sea captain. The fleet consisted of two frigates, two brigs and three schooners.

● Lucy Ann Stanton-Sessions of Cleveland, Ohio, became the first African American woman college graduate in the US during this month in 1850. Ms. Stanton-Sessions received a Bachelor of Literature degree from Oberlin College in Oberlin, Ohio.

■ In 1835, Sam Houston, John Forbes and John Cameron were appointed by the Grand Council of Provisional Government of Texas as Indian commissioners. Governor Henry Smith ratified the appointments on December 28th.

▲ A joint Japanese-US automobile-manufacturing venture between General Motors Corporation, the largest automobile manufacturer in the United States, and Toyota of Japan was approved by the Federal Trade Commission (FTC) in 1977. The venture was to include the building of a plant in Freemont, California, at which 200,000 to 250,000 automobiles would be produced annually.

◆ In 1962, 1,113 Cuban rebels who had been captured in the invasion attempt of 1961 were returned to the US in exchange for food and medicine valued at $53 million.

◆ In 1894, Henry Ford completed construction of his first successful gasoline engine. His first motorcar was assembled in 1896. Powered by a two-cylinder, four-cycle gasoline motor, it made a successful run.

**23**
**D**ECEMBE**R**

● Madame C.J. Walker, the first African American millionairess, was born in 1867 in Delta, Louisiana. Madame Walker, a beautician by trade, acquired her fortune through the making of hair and skin products for African Americans. She employed many African Americans in her business and, by 1910, the company had sales of $1,000 a day -- a great deal of money for those times.

■ On this day in 1890, Big Foot of the Miniconjou Sioux and other tribal members abandoned their village near the Cheyenne River and traveled toward Pine Ridge, South Dakota. The move averted the arrest of Big Foot on orders of General Miles.

▲ The Celestial John Theater in 1852 was the first Chinese theater to open in the United States. The theater was located on Telegraph Hill in San Francisco, California. The theater seated 1,400, had no levels or seat boxes and used no scenery.

**24**

**D**ECEMBE**R**

◆ The Spanish Governor Juan de Onate announced on this day in 1599 that the subjugation of New Mexico was complete. The struggle to conquer this territory was long and bitter. Onate met fierce resistance from the Native Americans in the war. The measures he took were often harsh. When one Native American village resisted, he ordered that a foot be cut off every man more than 25 years of age and that every man in the pueblo offer him 25 years of service.

◆ President-elect George Bush announced that he had chosen Elizabeth Hanford Dole to serve as secretary of labor in his administration in 1988. Dole had previously held a cabinet post as secretary of transportation in the Reagan administration. Following the nomination of Carla Hills as special trade representative, Dole became the second woman chosen to sit on President Bush's cabinet.

● Jupiter Hammon became the first published African American poet in 1760 when his poem, *An Evening Thought, Salvation by Christ, with Penitential Cries,* was published. At the time of its publication, Hammon was enslaved. He was owned by a Mr. Lloyd of Long Island, New York. Hammon's work reflected his deep religious beliefs. When not writing, Hammon enjoyed preaching. A better-known work of his was *An Address to the Negroes of the State of New York*, a prose piece that was delivered to the African Society of New York City in September 1786. The following year, the speech was published.

■ The snow goose is the totem for people born between December 22nd and January 19th according to Sun Bear's *Earth Astrology*. The sun goose is also the totem of the Earth Renewal Moon. It is highly respected by the Chippewa.

▲ During this week in 1864, a law was passed in Hawaii with instructions from King Kamehameha V establishing the Bureau of Immigration. This provided strict governmental control over the flow of contract laborers entering Hawaii.

◆ Following the discovery of Española (Haiti) earlier in the month, Columbus's ship the *Santa Maria* was destroyed while off the coast of the island in 1492. In preparation for the trip back to Spain (January 4, 1493), Columbus decided to leave behind 38 men in Española. The men, who became the first Spanish settlers of the colony, were left with enough food and ammunition for one year.

### DECEMBER

◆ A 1956 Gallup Poll released during this month reported that for the tenth time in 11 years, Eleanor Roosevelt, the widow of former President Franklin Delano Roosevelt, headed the list of most-admired women in the United States.

● African American Jack Johnson became "heavyweight champion of the world" in Sydney, Australia, in 1908 after defeating Australian boxer Tommy Burns in the 14th round of the fight. Johnson remained champion until 1915 when he was forced to "throw" a fight to keep from going to jail. Johnson "lost" the fight against boxer Jess Willard in Cuba in the 26th round.

■ In 1854, more than 100 Jicarilla and Ute destroyed a settlement located on the Arkansas River. Fifteen European Americans were killed in the attack. In addition, the women and children were taken prisoner and the livestock was set free. The battle was one of many between the Native Americans and European Americans living in the plains region at the time.

▲ During this month in 1949, Ts'ai Ch'ang, one of the earliest women involved in the CCP (Central Committee party), chaired the committee of 165 delegates from 14 Asian countries at the Asian Women's Conference held in Peking. This was the first of a series of international meetings showing the newly noted importance given to the liberated women of the new China.

### DECEMBER

◆ The Davis Cup was regained by the United States during this week in 1958 when Hispanic American Alejandro "Alex" Olmeda defeated Australian tennis champ Ashley Cooper in the singles competition.

◆ During World War II, the Greek War Relief Association in the US reported that it had sent more than $9 million in supplies and money to Greece. This money had been donated by Greek Americans as well as other European Americans from all over the US.

● On this day, the celebration of Kwanzaa begins for many African Americans. Kwanzaa is a celebration of culture and cooking. The celebration last until New Year's Day. This celebration was created by Maulana (Ron) Karenga in 1966.

■ In 1967, Mrs. Ramona Zephier, a member of the Cheyenne River Sioux Nation, was among the ten finalists in the *Mrs. America* contest held in San Diego, California. She viewed her experience as a way of ending Native American stereotypes.

▲ During this week in 1943, Wilbur Carl Sze was commissioned as a second lieutenant, becoming the first US Marine Corps officer of Chinese descent. Although born in Washington, DC, Sze had returned to China at age five. He returned to the United States when he was 16.

> **"I don't presume to speak for the Indian people, but maybe this will show Indians that they can do anything if they really want to do it."**
>
> Ramona Zephier,
> Referring to her experience
> as a *Mrs. America* finalist,
> 1967

◆ The Law of Burgos was passed in Spain in 1512, giving New World natives protection against abuse. However, this law also authorized the use of Africans as slaves in place of these native people.

◆ In 1987, Gayle Sierens became the first woman to deliver the play-by-play commentary for a televised NFL game. Sierens announced the regionally shown game between the Seattle Seahawks and the Kansas City Chiefs. The game was telecast by NBC.

## 27
### DECEMBER

● Dr. Charles Drew, a pioneer in the isolation and storage of blood plasma, established the first blood bank of its kind in New York City in 1941. His efforts helped many United States military personnel during World War II to stay alive through the use of transfusions. Drew also worked as a surgical consultant to the US Army. Tragically, in 1950, Dr. Drew himself died of blood loss from a car accident because the hospital treating him had no plasma.

■ During the winter of 1814, Marie Dorion, a Native American of the Iowa Nation, was serving as a guide for European Americans on an expedition in the north central states. At some point in the expedition, members of the exploring party were massacred, but Marie Dorion managed to escape with her babies. For 55 days, she and her children survived the harsh winter in a makeshift tepee. They were rescued in the spring by members of the Walla Walla tribe. Two years before this disastrous event, Dorion had also served as a guide for the William Price Hunt group that explored the St. Louis-Astoria region.

▲ The United States, the Soviet Union and Britain in 1945 agreed to establish a joint US-USSR commission in Korea. The intention of the commission was to help Korea reestablish itself as an independent state.

◆ On this day in 1961, the New York Film Critics Association announced that the film version of the musical *West Side Story* had been chosen as the best motion picture of 1961. The musical, whose composer was Leonard Bernstein, told a "Romeo and Juliet" type story between an European American boy and a Puerto Rican American girl. *West Side Story* became the first musical to win this award.

◆ On this day in 1832, Vice President John C. Calhoun, who was at odds with President Andrew Jackson, resigned from his office. Calhoun became the first vice president in US history to resign.

## 28
### DECEMBER

● Poet Paul Laurence Dunbar published *Oak and Ivy* during this month in 1893. Dunbar, who began writing poems when he was a young boy, was one of the first African American poets to become famous in the US.

■ For the week beginning December 28, 1990, and ending January 1, 1991, the Exhibitor Relations Company reported that the movie *Dances with Wolves* was the fourth-place box-office hit. The movie told the story of a US soldier's relationship with Native Americans in the 1800s.

▲ The War Brides Act was enacted on this day in 1945. This act permitted Chinese men who had served in the US armed forces to bring their wives and minor children to the United States.

◆ During this week in 1777, Juan de Miralles, a citizen of Cuba, left his country for the purpose of establishing a diplomatic liaison between the government of Spain and the Continental Congress of Philadelphia.

❖ *Time* magazine named General George C. Marshall, Army Chief of Staff, as its "Man of the Year" in 1943 for transforming the United States into the world's most effective military power. Marshall would later formulate an economic plan to help Europe after World War II. The plan was called the Marshall Plan.

### DECEMBER

● Whitney M. Young, Jr., executive director of the African American organization National Urban League (NUL), was appointed to a 3-year term as "Class C" director of the US Federal Reserve Board New York Bank in 1970. Young's appointment was announced by the Federal Reserve Bank of New York.

■ The infamous massacre at Wounded Knee took place in 1890. The massacre resulted in the killing by US troops of Sioux Chief Big Foot and hundreds of his followers. In 1990, ceremonies marking the 100th anniversary of the massacre were held at the Wounded Knee Reservation. The ceremony was attended by about 400 people who sat down beside a mass grave.

▲ During this week in 1965, Zubin Mehta, a native of India, made his debut as a conductor at the Metropolitan Opera House in 1965. Mehta conducted a highly acclaimed performance of *Aida*. In 1992, he held the position of conductor and director of the New York Philharmonic.

### DECEMBER

◆ Sons of the Cuban leader Fulgencio Batista arrived in New York in 1958 to warn that Cuba was about to come under the control of Fidel Castro. Castro later became the premier of Cuba.

❖ In 1940, one of President Roosevelt's famous "Fireside Chats" was broadcast during this week. He clearly expressed to the public that the US would give full aid to Britain, no matter what threats were received from other countries.

● A 1992 report issued by the Tuskegee Institute stated that 1952 was the first year in 71 years in which no lynchings took place in the United States.

*President Franklin D. Roosevelt*

■ Fairchild Semi-Conductor Corporation, the largest employer of Native American workers at the time, announced in 1968 that it planned to add an additional 500 workers to its Shiprock, New Mexico, production crew. At the time of the announcement, the company was temporarily housed in a building it was leasing from the Navaho people.

▲ Ferdinand E. Marcos was inaugurated as president of the Philippines on this day in 1965. Marcos, who won on the Philippine National party ticket, became the sixth president of the country.

◆ Roberto Clemente, all-star Puerto Rican American baseball player, died in a plane crash off the coast of Nicaragua in 1973. Clemente, a lifetime .300-hitter and a member of the Pittsburgh Pirates, was on his way to Nicaragua with relief supplies to help victims of a recent earthquake. Later the same year, Clemente was posthumously elected to baseball's *Hall of Fame*.

◆ A dispute over royalty payments to an unemployment fund led to the start of a strike by members of the American Federation of Musicians in 1947. The strike, called by Federation president James C. Petrillo, forbade the musicians who were union members to participate in the recording of phonograph records. The reason for this prohibition was that recordings often replaced live musicians, thus depriving them of work.

● In 1775, General George Washington ordered recruiting officers to accept into the army free Africans who were living in the colonies. The order was in response to the proclamation of Lord Dunmore on November 7, 1775, that offered freedom to slaves who would join the British forces in their fight against the American soldiers.

■ In 1845, the US House of Representatives requested an investigation of Choctaw claims in an attempt to redress Choctaw grievances.

▲ Japanese Americans celebrate their New Year's eve as *Omisoka*, or the Grand Last Day.

DECEMBER

# MY PERSONAL LIST

From the decks of overcrowded ships, millions of immigrants from eastern and southern Europe excitedly glimpsed the symbol of the "New World's" promise in New York Harbor--the Statue of Liberty. For immigrants in the late 1800s and early 1900s, however, the shining promise of the US clashed harshly with reality as soon as they reached Ellis Island, where the Bureau of Immigration opened its facilities in January 1892.

The new wave of European immigrants were Russian and Polish Jews, Italians, Hungarians, Roman Catholics from a variety of countries, Greeks, Slavic peoples and others. These immigrants were put through seemingly endless legal and medical tests. These tests were supposed to measure their intelligence and detect any diseases they might have brought into the US. After all examinations were complete, some immigrants were sent back home, and others were allowed to leave Ellis Island for mainland US.

In 1914, immigration slowed down and, by 1920, became almost nonexistent because of quota laws that were passed. Between 1920 and 1954, Ellis Island became a detention center for those to be deported, a hospital facility for wounded soldiers and sailors, and a Coast Guard station. The island was declared "excess federal property" in 1954, and was boarded up and closed.

A commission to restore Ellis Island and the Statue of Liberty formed in 1982. The statue was restored and rededicated on its centennial, 1986. The Ellis Island Registry was restored and turned into a museum of immigration in 1990. If relatives of yours emigrated to the US through Ellis Island, records of their stay may well be on display there today.

---

On the pedestal of the Statue of Liberty appear these words by Emma Lazarus:

" ...A mighty woman with a torch, whose flame is the imprisoned lighting, and her name Mother of Exiles ... cries she with silent lips. Give me your tried, your poor, your huddled masses yearning to breathe free....I lift my lamp beside the golden door!"

---

◀ *The Statue of Liberty*

*Ben Nighthorse Campbell*

◆ Jacqueline Means became the first woman in the US to be ordained as a Protestant Episcopal priest in 1977. She was ordained in Indianapolis, Indiana.

● The Emancipation Proclamation, signed by President Lincoln in December of 1862, took effect on this day in 1863. This act set free all enslaved Africans in the South on principle, if not in fact. The act also allowed free African Americans and escaped slaves already living in the North to join forces with the Union Army against the Confederacy during the Civil War.

▲ On this day in 1979, President Carter finished establishing normal diplomatic relations with The People's Republic of China, a process started by President Richard Nixon. It was the first time since 1949 that the two countries had exchanged ambassadors and diplomats and engaged in trade with each other.

# *1*
# JANUARY

◆ In 1959, Cuban dictator Fulgencio Batista resigned and went into exile in the US following several attempts to overthrow his government. Fidel Castro became the new leader slightly more than one month after the collapse of the Batista regime. Many Cubans fled their homeland to seek freedom in the US.

■ Ben Nighthorse Campbell fulfilled his duties as co-grand marshall of the 1992 Tournament of Roses Parade in Pasadena, California. In 1992, Campbell, a Democrat from Colorado, was the only Native American serving in the US Congress and in the 1992 election, he was elected as senator from Colorado, becoming first Native American senator.

# *2*
# JANUARY

◆ Construction of the Brooklyn Bridge began on this day in 1870. The bridge would span the East River to connect Manhattan and Brooklyn, and its construction employed the labors of many European Americans.

● Olympic gold medalist Wilma Rudolph was awarded the Amateur Athletic Union's (AAU) *Sullivan Memorial Trophy* as the year's outstanding amateur athlete in 1961. Rudolph won gold medals in both the 100- and 200-meter dash in the 1960 Olympic Games.

▲ About this day in 1979, large groups of Vietnamese refugees began to arrive in Manila, Philippines. The refugees, called "boat people," left their homeland in any type of seacraft possible and crossed the South China Sea to get to the Philippines. Eventually, many settled in the United States.

◆ In 1949, Luis Munoz Marin was inaugurated as Puerto Rico's first elected governor. Previous governors of Puerto Rico had been appointed by the United States. As one of the most powerful and influential figures in the history of Puerto Rican politics, Marin was a champion for Puerto Rico's poor. He also fought for Puerto Rico's independence from the United States during the 1930s. *Operation Bootstrap*, a self-help program developed by Marin during World War II, got Puerto Ricans involved in improving health and education opportunities in agriculture and industry.

■ In 1730, a group of Native Americans of the Yazoo tribe attacked and defeated the US Army garrison on Native American land that had been designated as Fort St. Peter, Mississippi.

❖ Helen Gahagan Douglas became the first female actor to hold a Congressional seat on this day in 1945. Douglas served in Congress from January 3, 1945, until January 3, 1951.

● In 1984, the Reverend Jesse Jackson successfully negotiated the release of Lieutenant Robert Goodman, a US Navy pilot who had been shot down over Damascus, Syria, by Syrian artillery forces fighting in Lebanon. Goodman was captured by the Syrians in 1983. Jackson went to Syria and negotiated with its government to obtain Goodman's release.

▲ While in the midst of an agricultural expansion, the Royal Hawaiian Agricultural Society agreed in 1852 that field labor was needed for the sugar plantations. To meet this need, 200 Chinese men called "coolies" were imported from Amoy under a policy similar to indentured servitude. Each "coolie" was bound to work the fields in Hawaii for a $3.00-per-month salary plus food, clothing and housing for five years.

◆ In 1969, Julia Rivera de Vincenti became the first woman to hold a cabinet post in Puerto Rico. De Vincenti was appointed to the position of secretary of labor of the Commonwealth of Puerto Rico. Three years later, Vincenti gave up the post to become the first female member of the US Mission to the United Nations.

■ During this month in 1971, Dee Brown's *Bury My Heart at Wounded Knee* was published. The book chronicled the plight of Native Americans as Europeans began to colonize the United States, up to and including the massacre at the Wounded Knee reservation.

# 4
## JANUARY

❖ During this month in 1849, Amelia Jenks Bloomer began to publish *Lily*. The publication was the first woman's journal actually published by a woman. In addition to being a publisher, Bloomer was active in the women's rights movement of the 1860s. Bloomer is known today for beginning the clothing fad of the Turkish style pants that bear her name.

● Dr. Melvin H. Evans became the first elected governor of the US Virgin Islands in 1971. All previous governors had been appointed by the president of the United States.

▲ Patsy Mink, a Democrat from Hawaii, became in 1965 the first Japanese American woman to serve in the Congress. Mink served a total of 12 years in Congress. After Jimmy Carter was elected to the presidency, Mink was appointed to the position of assistant secretary of state for Oceans and International Environmental Affairs (1977). After 13 months, Mink resigned from her appointed position and went on to become president of the Americans for Democratic Action.

◆ In 1493, Christopher Columbus set sail for his return trip to Spain from the "New World." In addition to his crew, Columbus took with him six Native American interpreters (whom he dubbed "Indians"). The interpreters were Arawak village people from South America.

> "Like the beautiful flower from which it derives its name, we shall strive to make the *Lily* [a newspaper] the emblem of 'sweetness and purity' and may heaven smile on our attempt to advocate the great cause of temperance reform!"
>
> Amelia Jenks Bloomer,
> *Lily*,
> January 1, 1849

◆ Nellie Ross became the first woman to be governor of a state when she was inaugurated as governor of Wyoming in 1925. Ross took over for her husband, William, following his death in October 1924. She ran for his office and was elected in November. Ross later became the first woman director of the US Mint (1933-1953).

● Portia Mittleman in 1989 accepted a position as staff director of the Senate Special Committee on Aging. Mittleman thus became the first African American woman to serve as a staff director of a full Senate committee.

▲ Sometime during the past week in 1942, the United States Army fought its first significant battle of World War II, using an army largely made up of Filipino soldiers.

◆ The Voting Rights Act was enacted during 1965. Under the Voting Rights Act, literacy tests given in English were banned as prerequisites for voter registration. As a result of this legislation, Puerto Ricans who were non-English speaking were permitted to register as voters if they could prove that they had completed at least six years of school.

■ Peter MacDonald was inaugurated in 1971 as tribal chairman of the 129,000-member Navaho Nation. MacDonald, who was an ex-Marine, was the first tribal leader to have a college education. He won the election for the position in November of 1970 when he defeated incumbent chairman Raymond Nakai.

**5**

**J A N U A R Y**

**George Washington Carver Day**

**6**

**J A N U A R Y**

◆ In 1970, Richard Nixon headed the annual Gallup Poll list of "Men Most Admired by Americans." The American Institute of Public Opinion reported that others included in the top ten were Billy Graham, Spiro T. Agnew, Lyndon B. Johnson, Edward M. Kennedy, Harry S Truman, Hubert Humphrey and Pope Paul.

● In 1773, Africans living in the Massachusetts colony sent a petition to the governor. The petition requested equal rights for Africans as well as an end to enslavement of Africans living in the colony. A second petition that contained more signatures and made the same request was sent to the governor two weeks later.

▲ In 1977, Maxine Hong Kingston won the National Book Critics Circle Award in the nonfiction category for her book *The Woman Warrior*. The book was an attempt by Kingston to bring together her past, represented by her parents who were born in China, and her present, represented in the book as herself, an Asian born in the US who felt neither completely Chinese nor "American." In her book, Kingston focuses mainly on her relationship with her mother.

◆ On this day in 1912, New Mexico, a territory earlier dominated by Spain, was admitted to the Union as the 47th state of the US.

■ In response to protests by Native Americans and feminists, a distributor of home video games announced that it would not market the adult video game called *Custer's Revenge* (1983). The video, which had been purchased months earlier by *Game Source*, had a naked male character who was to capture and rape a naked Native American woman before he himself was killed by arrows.

"I learned to make my mind large, as the universe is large, so that there is room for paradoxes."

Maxine Hong Kingston
*The Woman Warrior*

**Key:** ◆ European American ● African American ▲ Asian American ◆ Hispanic American ■ Native American

◆ After moving from Philadelphia, Pennsylvania, in 1776, the Continental Congress convened in Washington, DC. In January of 1777, the Congress commissioned Mary Katherine Goddard of Baltimore, Maryland, to act as printer of the first official version of the Declaration of Independence which had been approved by the delegates on July 4, 1776. In addition to her work as a printer, Goddard also published Baltimore's only newspaper and was postmaster for the city from 1775 to 1789, an appointment she received from Benjamin Franklin.

# 7
## J A N U A R Y

● On this date in 1943, Marian Anderson sang to a full house in Constitution Hall in Washington, DC. Prior to this year, the Daughters of the American Revolution (DAR), who ran the hall, had a discriminatory policy that prevented African Americans from performing there. The DAR first prevented Anderson from singing at Constitution Hall in 1939, so she sang instead to a crowd of 75,000 at the Lincoln Memorial. Public pressure following this appearance resulted in the DAR changing this segregationist policy.

▲ Missionaries working on the Asian Pacific islands of Hawaii began to publish the first known textbooks written in Hawaiian in 1822.

◆ Many Hispanics from New Orleans helped General Andrew Jackson win the Battle of New Orleans in 1815. This was the final battle of the War of 1812, which was fought between the United States and Britain.

*Marian Anderson*

■ Russel Means, cofounder of the militant Native American group AIM (American Indian Movement), announced his retirement from that group in 1988. During his announcement, Means claimed that AIM had been so successful in reaching its goals that the organization had "worked itself out of a job."

# 8
## J A N U A R Y

◆ Ella Tambussi Grasso of Connecticut in 1975 became the first elected woman state governor who was not married to a man who had previously held that position. Prior to serving as governor, Grasso held several positions in government. These positions included membership in the Connecticut General Assembly, the state legislature and the House of Representatives.

● Toni Morrison was among the winners of the *National Book Critics Circle Award* of 1978 for her 1977 book, *Song of Solomon*. Morrison was the first African American woman author to win this award.

▲ Sometime in 1979, the government of The People's Republic of China adopted what is called the Pinyin system of spelling. By this system, many of the Western spellings for Chinese names and places were changed. For example, using the Pinyin spelling method, the name of Chinese revolutionary leader *Mao Tse-tung* is spelled as *Mao Zedong*. Today, the US government recognizes and uses the Pinyin spelling in its dealings with China.

◆ Julian Nava was chosen by President Jimmy Carter as US ambassador to Mexico in 1980. Nava was the first Mexican American chosen for this post. Prior to his assignment as ambassador, Nava was an assistant to the president of California State University at Northridge. He was also the first Hispanic to serve as president of the Los Angeles County School Board.

■ Sometime in 1660, the first New England church for Native Americans was founded by John Eliot, who is recognized as the first missionary to the Native Americans in New England. The church was founded in the town of Natick, Massachusetts. Six years later, Eliot published *An Essay to Bring the Indian Language into Rules, for the Help of Such as Desire to Learn the Same, for the Furtherance of the Gospel Among Them*. The publication was a grammar text written in the language of the Massachuset Nation.

❖ Women's suffrage leader Carrie Chapman Catt was born in Ripon, Wisconsin, in 1859. Catt was instrumental in the 1920 passage of the nineteenth Amendment to the Constitution, which gave women the right to vote. She was president of the national American Suffrage Association at the time. In 1920, she founded what is today called the *League of Women Voters* to provide women with information on using their new and hard-earned right. Her suffrage work took her to Canada and Europe. She was also an antiwar activist and formed the *National Committee on the Cause and Cure of the War* in 1925.

**J A N U A R Y**

● On this day in 1866, Fisk University, a college dedicated to the education of African Americans, was founded in Nashville, Tennessee.

▲ A San Francisco judge ruled in 1885 that, under the fourteenth Amendment, a 10-year-old Chinese girl named Mamie Tape had the constitutional right to attend public school in the US.

◆ In 1964, rioting erupted when United States students living in the Panama Canal Zone ignored an agreement that the US and Panamanian flags should fly side-by-side. On the following day, Panama broke relations with the United States and denounced the Canal Zone treaties. Two weeks later, President Johnson announced that the United States would engage in a "full and frank" review of all controversial issues related to the Canal Zone.

■ Native Americans belonging to the Cheyenne Nation escaped from their imprisonment by the US at Fort Robinson under the direction of Dull Knife in 1879.

❖ Thomas Paine, writer and revolutionary, published his pamphlet *Common Sense* in 1776. Paine's pamphlet stated the desires of the American colonists at the time of the American Revolution: complete independence from England and a strong, established federal union. *Common Sense* quickly became the most widely circulated document in the history of America at the time.

● During this month in 1972, African American member of Congress Shirley Chisholm of New York announced her plans to run for the presidency of the United States. Chisolm was the first woman to seek the nomination for this office.

**J A N U A R Y**

▲ During this month in 1910, a processing center for newly arrived Chinese immigrants opened in San Francisco, California. This center was built to replace the Angel Island Detention Center which had served as the immigration center for the West Coast. Inhumane conditions at this first center prompted Chinese leaders' letters of protest to both US and Chinese authorities and boycotts of US imports in China. In response to the protests, construction on the new site was begun.

> *"Society in every state is a blessing, but Government, even in its best state, is but a necessary evil; in its worst state, an intolerable one."*
>
> Thomas Paine,
> *Common Sense* (1776)

◆ Juan de Onato of the Spanish army led an attack on the Keres of Acoma in New Mexico in 1599. The Spanish army attacked the Native Americans after tribal members refused to surrender their pueblo to the Spanish.

■ Vice President Walter Mondale met with leaders of several large southwestern Native American tribes in Albuquerque, New Mexico, in 1978 to discuss their concerns about treaty-rights issues. One of the main concerns of the Native Americans was the protection of natural resources on reservation lands. In particular, the group was concerned about the attempts of several US oil companies to gain access to oil on reservation soil.

　**Key:** ❖ European American　● African American　▲ Asian American　◆ Hispanic American　■ Native American

❖ Marianne Moore was awarded the *Bollinger Prize* for poetry in 1951 for her volume of *Collected Poems*. Her subject matter tends to be of things in nature, such as exotic animals.

● Charles W. Anderson was elected to the legislature of the state of Kentucky in 1936. He became the first African American in the history of the state to hold that position.

**J A N U A R Y**

▲ In the January 11, 1960, issue of *Newsweek* magazine, movie cameraman James Wong Howe was recognized for his achievements. The article stated, "Among movie cameramen, none ranks higher than Jimmy Howe, a Chinese American veteran of forty-two years."

❖ A group of nations consisting of Mexico, Panama, Colombia and Venezuela met for the second time during this week in 1983 and formed the Contadora Group. The meeting took place on the island of Contadora (located off the coast of Panama), from which the group took its name. The purpose of the meeting was to "promote *detente* and put an end to situations of conflict in Central America." The resolutions resulting from this and other such meetings were fully supported by the US government.

■ The state of Alabama, named for the Native American group known as the Alibamon (of the Creek confederacy), was admitted to the union in 1861. The state was readmitted to the union following the Civil War on June 25, 1868.

**J A N U A R Y**

❖ During this month in 1993, President Bill Clinton appointed several women to key positions in his new administration. Among these nominations were Madeleine K. Albright as US Ambassador to the United Nations, Carol Browner as Director of the Environmental Protection Agency, Alice Rivlin as Deputy Budget Director, Laura D'Andrea Tyson as chairperson of the Council of Economic Advisers and Carol Rasco as Assistant to the President for Domestic Policy.

● The US Supreme Court handed down a ruling that gave African Americans the right to study law at state institutions. The ruling, given in 1948, was based on the court case, *Sipuel v University of Oklahoma*. In this case, Ada Lois (Fisher) Sipuel, an African American, was refused admission into the law school of the University of Oklahoma. With legal help from the NAACP, she sued the university. A lower Oklahoma court ruled against the suit, citing the 1938 *Gaines* decision, and the state supreme court agreed with this decision. However, the US Supreme Court reversed the Oklahoma court's decision and Sipuel was admitted to the university.

▲ Franklin Chang-Diáz became the first astronaut of Asian and Hispanic descent to travel in space on this day in 1986. Chang-Diáz, of Chinese and Costa-Rican heritage, studied mechanical engineering at the University of Connecticut and earned a doctorate in plasmaphysics from the Massachusetts Institute of Technology (1977). Chang-Diáz served as one of seven astronauts aboard the space shuttle *Columbia*, which took off from Cape Canaveral in Florida on January 12, 1986, and landed at Edwards Air Force Base in California on the 18th.

◆ In 1954, the Puerto Rico House of Representatives passed a resolution approving the island's status as a United States commonwealth.

■ On this day in 1864, a patrol under the command of Kit Carson encountered a band of Navaho near the west end of the Canyon de Chelly. Eleven Navaho were killed by Carson's men. This was just one of many attacks on the Navaho led by Carson and one of many examples of the constant conflicts between Native Americans and European settlers in the 1860s.

♦ In 1976, European American Sarah Caldwell became the first woman to conduct at the Metropolitan Opera in New York. The performance conducted by Caldwell was Verdi's opera, *La Traviata*.

● President Lyndon B. Johnson announced the appointment of Dr. Robert Weaver to the position of secretary of Housing and Urban Development in 1966. Weaver became the first African American member of a president's cabinet. Weaver was confirmed to the position by the Senate on the 16th of the month.

# 13

## JANUARY

▲ About 100 Koreans arrived in Hawaii aboard the *SS Gaelic* in 1903. The Koreans were inspected while aboard the ship. Later, they were divided into small groups and sent to work as laborers on plantations.

♦ Newly elected Puerto Rican Governor Hernandez Colon appointed six women to his cabinet in 1973. Four of the women were appointed as the directors of the Civil Defense Office, Personnel Office, Office of Economic Opportunities and the Right to Employment Administration. The other two appointments were secretary of education and special aide to the governor in charge of long-term policy.

■ The Chilocco Indian School was established and opened during this month in 1884. The school, located in northern Oklahoma, was organized mainly as an industrial school. Financial support for the school was provided by the federal government.

# 14

## JANUARY

"We of the second generation also know the anguish and the agony of war....But we have no complaints....We who have tasted freedom know that we must earn freedom by fighting for it."

Carmen Padilla, 1944

♦ After 28 years of political service, Evelyn Gandy became the first woman to hold the position of lieutenant governor of Mississippi on this date in 1976. With her election to this position, Gandy became only the third woman in US history to hold the second-highest political office of a state.

● In 1957, Jackie Robinson, the first African American to play major league professional baseball, announced his retirement from the sport. Robinson had recently been traded to the New York Giants.

▲ In 1944, Carmen Padilla gave a speech entitled *Of Second Generation Filipinos* in Fresno, California. She encouraged Filipinos to teach their children about their native land, people and culture.

♦ On this day in 1778, the Royal Cedula was forced to divide the royal lands in Puerto Rico. As a result, citizens were permitted to own land that had been previously owned by Spain.

■ Louise Erdrich, a Turtle Mountain Chippewa, won the *National Book Critics Circle Award* in 1985 for her 1984 book *Love Medicine*. The book, set in and around a North Dakota reservation from 1934 to 1984, explored how love is put to the test through various trials within the context of Native American reservation life. Two families, the Kashpaws and the Lamartines, are the main characters in the story.

**Key:** ♦ European American  ● African American  ▲ Asian American  ♦ Hispanic American  ■ Native American

◆ At the age of 30, Jessica Tuchnan began her job as a key advisor to President Jimmy Carter in 1977. With this appointment, Tuchnan became the top staff person within the National Security Council's Global Issues unit.

● The Reverend Dr. Martin Luther King, Jr., was born on this date in 1929. As a civil rights leader in the '50s and '60s, Dr. King was a leader in the struggle to eliminate laws that discriminated against African Americans in the southern United States. In 1955, King led a boycott against the segregation policies of the Montgomery, Alabama, city bus system. King was the main speaker at the March on Washington rally in 1963, won the *Nobel Peace Prize* in 1964 and led the famous march from Selma to Montgomery, Alabama, in 1965. King was also an early critic of the Vietnam War. On April 4, 1968, King died from an assassin's bullet in Memphis, Tennessee. His birthday became a national holiday in 1983.

▲ On this day in 1872, the Iwakura Mission led by Prince Iwakura was dispatched to the United States by the emperor of Japan. The mission arrived in San Francisco before proceeding to Washington, DC, in order to negotiate a new treaty between the two nations. Fifty-three Japanese students remained to study in the US.

◆ An inter-American conference convened on this day in 1942 in Rio de Janeiro. The conference was summoned in order to unite the American republics against aggression by foreign powers.

■ Virginia Klin Kole was elected president of the Mescalero Apache Tribal Council of New Mexico in 1959. Kole, who served a term of one year, became the first woman to head the Mescalero.

*"I have a dream that one day on the red hills of Georgia the sons of former slaves and the sons of former slaveowners will be able to sit down together at the table of brotherhood."*

Rev. Martin Luther King, Jr.
Speech at Civil Rights March on Washington
(August 28, 1963)

◆ Actress Lillian Russell was issued a patent in 1912 for a dresser trunk she designed to make it easier to move her elaborate costumes and cosmetics from one place to another. Lillian Russell was a superstar in the musical theater during the Gay Nineties of the 1800s. In 1922, Russell took on a role in the government when she accepted an appointment from President Harding as special investigator on immigration problems.

● The first African American sheriff in the South since Reconstruction, Lucius D. Amerson, took office in 1968. Amerson became sheriff of Macon County, Alabama. Three deputies, two of whom were African American, were sworn in at the same time.

▲ A meeting of miners in Shasta County, California, held during this week in 1856, decided that a resolution was needed to prevent Chinese "coolies" from working as laborers in the mines.

◆ The first San Juan Biennial was held in Puerto Rico on this day in 1970. The exhibition included 700 works from 180 Latin American artists, including the prominent Mexican artist Clemente Orozco. During the biennial, 16 artists signed a proclamation stating, "With our participation in this biennial, we give homage to the liberation struggle for the peoples of Latin America."

■ On this day in 1891, the American Indian Wars came to an end as the Dakota Sioux surrendered to Colonel Nelson Miles at Wounded Knee, South Dakota. Nineteen days earlier, US Army troops had fired on the encampment, killing 62 Native American women and children.

*Patricia Roberts Harris*

◆ For the first time in ten years, a prisoner was executed in the United States in 1977. Gary Gilmore, sentenced to death for the murders of two Brigham Young University students, was executed by firing squad at the Utah State Prison.

● Patricia Roberts Harris was nominated for a Cabinet position as secretary of Housing and Urban Development by President Jimmy Carter during this month in 1977. Harris was confirmed by the Senate, becoming the first African American woman to hold a Cabinet position.

▲ A special ceremony was held on this day in 1982 to dedicate the renovated Korean Friendship Bell Pavillion in Los Angeles, CA. The Korean Friendship Bell Pavillion is located in Angel Gate Park. During the ceremony, a Certificate of Property Transfer was presented to Los Angeles Mayor Tom Bradley.

◆ During this week in 1973, legislators of Puerto Rico's Popular Democratic party urged Premier Fidel Castro of Cuba to free the estimated 60,000 political prisoners, including 58 members of the news media, who were being held in his country.

# 17
# JANUARY

■ Rebekah Harkness received the *Shield Award* of the American Indian and Eskimo Cultural Foundation in 1967. Harkness was honored for her "outstanding contributions to the advancement and encouragement of American Indian arts and crafts." The presentation was made by Solomon McCombs, an artist of the Creek Nation and the president of the foundation, at the Harkness Gallery of the Dance in New York City.

# 18
# JANUARY

◆ Constance Berry Newman was nominated by President Bush in 1989 to head the Office of Personnel Management. Newman had worked for the federal government since 1961 when she began a job as a clerk typist for the Department of the Interior. She later worked her way up to various management positions, including director of VISTA (Volunteers in Service to America) and assistant secretary of HUD (Housing and Urban Development).

● In 1989, African American performers Otis Redding and Stevie Wonder were inducted into the Rock and Roll Hall of Fame in a New York City celebration. Redding's induction occurred posthumously. In the same ceremony, The Temptations, an African American musical group of the '60s, was also inducted into the Hall of Fame.

▲ Edward Bing Ken of Chicago, Illinois, an interpreter for the US Immigration and Naturalization Service (INS), became the first person of Chinese descent to become a naturalized citizen in 1944. Ken was permitted to become a citizen as a result of the repeal of the Chinese Exclusion Act. President Franklin D. Roosevelt signed the bill on December 17, 1943. Prior to the signing of the bill, no Chinese had been allowed to emigrate to the United States without restrictions, and Chinese already living in the US could not become citizens. The act permitted an annual quota of 105 Chinese immigrants to enter the US.

◆ On this day in 1960, Texas Governor Price Daniel proclaimed that February 27th would be celebrated as Navarro Day. The day was set aside to honor the accomplishments of Mexican American Jose Antonio Navarro who was involved in the creation of the Texas Constitution.

■ During this month in 1687, the explorer La Salle visited the Akasquy, a Native American tribe that is now extinct. The tribe was characterized by clothing made from bison hair with bird-feather adornments. The tribe lived in Texas near the Brazos River.

❖ In 1889, the state of Georgia made January 19, Robert E. Lee's birthday, a legal holiday. Lee, a general of the Confederate Army during the Civil War, is a hero of the South. Lee's birthday was later made a legal holiday in the states of Kentucky, Louisiana, Mississippi, North Carolina, Tennessee, Texas and Virginia.

**J A N U A R Y**

● Sheriff James G. Clark of Selma, Alabama, arrested 65 African Americans who refused to enter the Selma County Courthouse through an alley door (1965). The next day, the sheriff and his deputies arrested 150 more African Americans who were trying to register to vote. The sheriff was later reprimanded by the court for his actions and those arrested were set free.

▲ In 1948, the US Supreme Court ruled that Fred Oyama, a Japanese American born in the US, was the rightful owner of land in California that had been purchased by his father, who was born in Japan. The ruling went against California's Alien Land Law which would have given the state title to the land.

❖ Oscar Gonzales Suarez, elected president of the Puerto Rican Bar Association, was sworn in on this day in 1968 at the New York State Supreme Court building.

■ Native Americans and civil rights activists across the nation began a call for the resignation of Interior Secretary James Watts in 1983 following remarks he made about the living conditions of Native Americans on reservations. During a television interview, Watts told the nation, "If you want an example of the failures of socialism, don't go to Russia, come to America and see the American Indian reservations." As a result of criticism brought on by Watts's comments, his resignation was requested by Congress on January 27.

> *"If you want an example of the failures of socialism, don't go to Russia, come to America and see the American Indian reservations."*
> Interior Secretary James Watts, 1983

**J A N U A R Y**

❖ On this day in 1941, Franklin D. Roosevelt was inaugurated for a record-breaking third term as president of the United States. No president before him had ever served more than two four-year terms. FDR would later break this record by being elected to a fourth term.

● During the 1992 *Image Awards*, sponsored by the NAACP, the following African Americans were honored for their contributions to the entertainment industry and the African American community: Natalie Cole (*Best Female Recording Artist, Best Jazz Album* and *Best Music Video*) for a technological compilation of the song "Unforgettable" by both Natalie Cole and her father Nat King Cole who had recorded the song many years before his death; Arsenio Hall (*Key of Life Award*) for his efforts to help the homeless and eliminate drug-abuse problems; Janet Jackson (*Chairman's Humanitarian Award*) for her work in encouraging completion of high school and higher education. among US youth.

▲ The drafting of the constitution for the Fifth Republic of Korea officially began on this day in 1980. A draft of the constitution was prepared under the guidance of 30 experts. The constitution in its final form was finally voted on by the people in October of 1980 and received a 91.6 percent endorsement.

◆ During 1972, Antonia Pantoja was named to serve as director of the recently established Puerto Rican Research and Resource Center in Washington, DC. The center was created to serve as a general resource to the experiences of Puerto Rican Americans living on the island or on the mainland.

■ According to Sun Bear's Earth Astrology, the otter is the totem for people born between January 20 and February 18. Sun Bear was a Chippewa medicine man and medicine chief for the Bear Tribe Medicine Society of Washington. He also served as publisher of the magazine *Wildfire* and author of *At Home in the Wilderness, The Bear Tribe's Self-Reliance Book* and *Buffalo Hearts*. In addition, Sun Bear taught Native American philosophy at the University of California, Davis.

◆ In 1890, Elizabeth Cochrane, (journalistic pen name Nellie Bly), arrived in San Francisco, California, and was greeted by a large crowd after traveling almost completely around the world by herself. Bly began her solo trip on November 14, 1889, from Jersey City, New Jersey, when she set sail for England. After traveling through Europe and China, she reached San Francisco to begin the last leg of her journey, the trip across the United States. Cochrane completed the trip when she reached Jersey City by train on January 25. The complete journey took 72 days, 6 hours and 11 minutes.

**21**

**J ANUAR Y**

● Author and journalist Carl T. Rowan was appointed director of the United States Information Agency (USIA) in 1964 by President Lyndon B. Johnson. Rowan became the first African American to head this agency, which is the official disseminator for information about the United States to the rest of the world. Rowan resigned from the USIA in July of 1965.

▲ In 1974 the United States Supreme Court ruled on the case of *Lau et al. v Nichols et al.* and declared that a bilingual education must be provided for non-English-speaking students of Asian and other origins.

◆ During this month in 1943, the "Sleepy Lagoon" case was being tried in California. The case involved the beating to death of a young Mexican named Jose Diaz. On the basis of a gang fight that had occurred near a popular swimming hole known as Sleepy Lagoon on the previous night, 23 Mexican Americans and one European American gang member of the 38th Street gang were arrested and later indicted by a Grand Jury on charges ranging from murder to criminal conspiracy . The trial was concluded during January of 1943, and resulted in guilty verdicts for 17 of the gang members on a variety of charges. The trial, it was generally felt, was handled with anti-Mexican feelings. In 1944, the case was dismissed for lack of evidence, and the prosecutors and judge in the trial were heavily criticized for their conduct.

■ During this week in 1968, under the direction of the tribal chairperson Raymond Nakai, the Navaho celebrated the 100th anniversary of the establishment of the Navaho Indian Reservation.

**22**

**J ANUAR Y**

◆ As a result of Polish American agitation, President Woodrow Wilson delivered a speech to the Senate in 1917 that called for support of "a united, independent and autonomous Poland" when World War I reached its conclusion.

● On this day in 1962, Jackie Robinson became the first African American major league baseball player to be inducted into baseball's *Hall of Fame*. Robinson gained fame when he broke the "color barrier" in baseball by becoming the first African American to play professional baseball in the major leagues during the 20th century.

◆ In response to Father Miguel Hidalgo y Castillo's cry for Mexican independence from Spain on September 16, 1810, a short-lived revolt by Mexicans took place on this day in 1811. Castillo sympathizers, under the leadership of former army captain Juan Batista de Las Casas, were active in the revolt.

■ In 1968, President Lyndon B. Johnson spoke to the Navaho by telephone during ceremonies celebrating the 100th anniversary of the signing of the treaty that set up their reservation in 1868.

**Key:** ◆ European American ● African American ▲ Asian American ◆ Hispanic American ■ Native American

◆ Working with 13 other founders, feminist Gloria Steinem released the first issue of *Ms.* magazine in 1972. In only 9 days, the magazine sold out all 300,000 copies of its first issue.

◗ On this day in 1976, Paul Robeson, world famous actor, singer, athlete and lawyer, died. Robeson was the first African American to graduate from Rutgers University, Phi Beta Kappa, the first African American college football player to be named an All American and one of the greatest singers of folk and spiritual music.

**2 3**

**J A N U A R Y**

▲ Delbert E. Wong was appointed to the Los Angeles municipal bench by Governor Edmund G. Brown of California in 1959. Wong was the first Chinese American to become a judge.

◆ In 1868, Dr. Ramon Emeterio Betances called for a Provisional Constitution of the Puerto Rican Revolution, leading patriots in Lares to declare a republic on this day. The revolt of these patriots was quickly squelched, however, leaving Puerto Rico under Spanish rule.

■ Charles Curtis of Kansas became the first Native American to serve as a US senator in 1907. Curtis served two full terms in the Senate. He resigned after his second term to assume the vice presidency under Herbert Hoover.

**2 4**

**J A N U A R Y**

◆ During this week in 1916, President Woodrow Wilson appointed Louis D. Brandeis to the Supreme Court. Brandeis was confirmed by the Senate on June 1. Upon his confirmation, Brandeis became the first American of the Jewish faith to hold a seat as a Supreme Court justice.

● In an unusual ruling for its time (1966), the Mississippi Supreme Court reversed the grand-larceny conviction of an African American man, M.L. Hopkins, on the grounds that no African Americans had been considered to serve on his jury. Mississippi was one of the most segregated states of the South during the 1960s, and African Americans on trial for crimes were frequently judged by all-white juries.

▲ Japanese Premier Kishi was greeted by 10,000 supporters in Tokyo when he returned from a trip to the United States during which he and President Eisenhower had signed a new US-Japan defense treaty (1960).

◆ Nine Mexican American leaders made what was considered an unusual official appearance in Mexico City in 1978 to meet with Mexican President Jose Portillo. The purpose of the meeting was to seek support from the Mexican government to oppose a bill proposed by President Jimmy Carter to strictly limit illegal Mexican migration into the US. For many poverty-stricken Mexicans, legal immigration was not affordable, and the Carter bill would have made it almost impossible for them to gain entry. The nine Mexican American leaders seeking support and closer ties to their home country were: Eduardo Morga, Jose Angel Gutierrez, Franciso Schaffer-Corona, Antonio Gil Morales, Jose Hernandez, Eduardo Terrones, Reies Lopez Tijerina, Manuel Lopez and Carlos Falcon.

■ Shirley Plume, an Oglala Sioux, became the first Native American to be appointed superintendent of a Bureau of Indian Affairs agency in 1974. Plume had been designated as acting superintendent of the Standing Rock Agency in Fort Yates, North Dakota, in August of 1973.

◆ Julia Ward Howe, author of the "Battle Hymn of the Republic," became the first woman elected to the National Institute of Arts and Letters in 1907. The organization was founded in order to pay national tribute to great United States writers working in a variety of genres.

# 25
## J A N U A R Y

● African American abolitionist Sojourner Truth delivered a speech at the first Black Women's Rights Convention in Akron, Ohio, on this day in 1851. In her speech, Truth spoke about the problems of being both enslaved and an enslaved woman. This speech later became known as the *Ain't I a Woman* speech.

▲ James Marshall's discovery of gold on the American River in the Sierra Nevadas during this week in 1848 began the gold rush. In response to the gold rush, people from all over the United States and other countries flocked to the region. Many of these people were from China and had been hired to mine gold for the profit of others.

◆ The battleship *USS Maine* arrived at Havana, Cuba, on what was described as a "friendly visit" in 1898. The real purpose of the *Maine* was to protect the life and property of US citizens there. A short time after its arrival, the *Maine* mysteriously exploded while anchored at Havana harbor. The destruction of the *USS Maine* ultimately served as the precipitating factor in the Spanish American War.

■ At the invitation of the Sobaipuri of the San Xavier del Bac region (near what is today Tumaccocori National Monument in Arizona), a Jesuit missionary named Father Eusebio Francisco Kino came to the region during this month in 1692. Kino, who had developed a good reputation for his work of establishing missions for Native Americans in southern California, met with Sobaipuri leaders. He also said a mass and baptized some of the infants during his visit.

# 26
## J A N U A R Y

◆ The first German American daily newspaper, the *New Yorker Staats-Zeitung*, went into publication today in 1850. The newspaper, published in New York City, had for 16 years been published as a weekly.

● Actor and singer, Paul Robeson announced in 1947 that he would postpone his career for two years to begin a campaign against racial discrimination in the US.

▲ The Korea-America Cultural Exchange Committee was in its second day of meetings in Washington, DC (1982). This was the first session held by the committee. Their goal was to discuss ways to facilitate cultural exchanges between the United States and Korea.

◆ In 1928, President Coolidge ordered an additional 1,000 marines to be sent to Nicaragua to combat guerilla leader, General Sandino. Sandino was known as the "Pancho Villa of Nicaragua" and was thought of as a bandit by the United States.

■ In 1821, President James Monroe presented the *Treaty of Indian Springs* to the US Congress for ratification. The treaty called for the cession of 5 million acres of Creek land between the Chattahoochee and Flint rivers. The treaty also called for the reserved use of a village named Buzzard Roost by the Creek Nation. In return, the US agreed to pay the Creek Nation $10,000 cash and an additional $40,000 "as soon as practicable after the ratification of the convention; $5,000 annually for two years thereafter; $16,000 annually for five years thereafter; and $10,000 annually for six years thereafter." The money was to be paid to the Creek in either goods or currency, as decided by the Creek.

**Key:** ◆ European American ● African American ▲ Asian American ◆ Hispanic American ■ Native American

❖ Gunnar Myrdal's book *An American Dilemma: The Negro Problem and Modern Democracy* was published in 1944. Myrdal's book offered an in-depth analysis of the problems of race relations in the United States, particularly those of African Americans and European Americans. Myrdal, who was born in Sweden, wrote the book after he moved to the United States.

● Mississippi-born opera singer Leontyne Price made her debut in *Il Trovatore* at the Metropolitan Opera in 1961. Price, a soprano, received her training at the prestigious Juilliard School of Music in New York City.

▲ In 1973, Nguyen Thi Binh signed the *Paris Treaty* on behalf of the North Vietnamese Liberation Front. The treaty brought about an end to the Vietnam War. Madame Binh, who was born in Saigon, South Vietnam, was the head of Foreign Affairs in North Vietnam at the time the treaty was signed.

◆ During the year of 1962, Puerto Rican American Herman Badillo Rivera was named as commissioner of the newly formed Office of Relocation in New York. The office was created to assist in the relocation of Puerto Ricans to New York City. Badillo continued his work in government and later became borough president of the Bronx (1965).

■ On this day in 1913, Native American athlete Jim Thorpe of Carlisle, Pennsylvania, was stripped of the amateur honors that had won him fame in the 1912 Olympics. Thorpe confessed that he had played professional baseball prior to the Olympic Games and, therefore, did not qualify as an amateur athlete. Thorpe declared that, due to his professional athlete status, he would give back the *Pentathalon Trophy* which had been presented to him by the king of Sweden and the *Decathalon Trophy* that had been presented to him by the czar. The awards were then to be given to the athletes who had finished second to Thorpe.

❖ President Nixon announced that the war in Vietnam would end on January 28 and that, within 60 days, the United States's remaining 23,000 troops would be brought home (1973). More than 58,000 US troops were killed during the Vietnam War.

● Harvey Gantt became the first African American to enroll in any educational institution with white students in the state of South Carolina in 1963 when he became a student at Clemson College. In 1992, Gantt was elected mayor of Charlotte, North Carolina.

*Pope John Paul II*

▲ Secretary of State Rusk visited Korean President Park Chung Hee in 1964. Rusk went to Korea to assure President Hee that the United States would continue to provide military aid to Korea.

◆ On this day in 1979, Pope John Paul II paid a visit to Mexico. The pope was greeted by large crowds and a ceremonial welcome at Notre Dame de Guadalupe, Guadalajara and Oaxaca. The visit was a brief stop before a scheduled conference with other religious leaders.

■ During 1913, the US government issued the "buffalo-head" nickel designed by James Earl Fraser. In addition to the buffalo head, the nickel featured a composite portrait of 13 Native American chiefs. Among those included on the coin were Chief Big Tree of the Iroquois, Chief Two Moons of the Cheyenne, and Chief Iron Tail of the Sioux.

❖ During this week in 1947, Dr. Lee DeForest was awarded the *Edison Medal* for his "pioneering achievement in radio." Dr. DeForest invented the electron tube in 1906.

● California member of Congress Yvonne B. Burke was unanimously elected to lead the Congressional Black Caucus in 1976. Burke was the first woman to lead the organization. The Caucus was formed to lobby within government branches for legislation to benefit the African American community. In 1966, Yvonne Burke was the first African American woman elected to the California State Assembly. She was first elected to the US Congress in 1972.

# JANUARY

▲ In 1947, the United States announced that it would abandon its peace mediation between the Chinese communists and the Chinese nationalists. At the time of the mediation, the two factions were involved in a civil war. In addition to pulling out of the negotiations, the US called for the return of most of its 12,000 troops from China. The troops had been sent to fight on the side of the nationalists.

❖ Hispanic American Linda Chávez, director of the White House Office of Public Liaison, announced her bid to succeed Senator Charles Mathias, Jr., when his seat became vacant at the end of the 1986 congressional session.

■ Under the direction of Brigadier General Patrick E. Connor, volunteers from Nevada and California defeated Shoshones in a battle that took place in 1863 on Bear River near the Utah-Idaho state line. The battle was partly caused by Native American attacks on European Americans who had stolen their land and destroyed much of the game in the region as well as the grazing areas of the animals on which the Shoshones depended for food.

# JANUARY

❖ Franklin D. Roosevelt, the 32nd president of the United States, was born in 1882. The only president elected to four terms, his New Deal programs aided many people suffering through the economic collapse of the Great Depression (1930-1941). Some of Roosevelt's programs included the Social Security Act, the Federal Bank Deposit Insurance Corporation (FDIC), the Federal Housing Authority and the National Labor Relations Act. Roosevelt led the US during most of its four-year involvement in World War II (1941-1945). His leadership during that period was exemplified by his "fireside chats" in which he spoke to people of the US via radio in a relaxed manner, reassuring citizens about US progress in the war. He was the first president to appear on both radio and television.

● Franklin A. Thomas was named president of the Ford Foundation in 1979. Thomas, a lawyer, became the first African American to head a major philanthropic organization in the United States. From 1967 to 1977, Thomas was president and chief executive officer of the Bedford-Stuyvesant Restoration Corporation. With his guidance, the corporation helped to establish neighborhood businesses, renovate buildings and provide jobs within the Bedford-Stuyvesant community.

▲ President Ngo Dinh Diem of South Vietnam was removed during a coup in 1963. His removal came about due to his administration's growing more and more corrupt. He lost the US support previously given to him by President Eisenhower.

❖ A *US News and World Report* study published on January 30, 1978, showed how the ethnic makeup of the Congress of 1978 had changed from that of the Congress of 1953. The Hispanic makeup of the House had increased by three members in 1978 as compared to 1953. For the same years, however, only one Senate seat was held by an Hispanic American (1953) and no seats were held by Hispanic Americans in 1978.

■ About this day in 1861, Navaho leader Delgadita persuaded more than 650 Navaho to surrender at Fort Wingate because of harsh weather conditions and lack of food and clothing, the result of long-term fighting between US soldiers and Navaho warriors. The disputes were over land taken from the Navaho by the US.

**Key:** ❖ European American ● African American ▲ Asian American ◆ Hispanic American ■ Native American

◆ Captain Charles Blair made aviation history on this day in 1951 when he flew his converted *Mustang* fighter plane from New York to London in only 7 hours and 48 minutes. With this time, Blair broke the record established by Pan American Airways the previous November.

● On this day in 1941, Richard Wright received the *Joel Springarn Medal* from the National Association for the Advancement of Colored People (NAACP) for the "highest achievement in any honorable field of endeavor." Wright was both a poet and a novelist. He is best known for his novels, *Black Boy* and *Native Son*.

▲ During this week in 1912, North American Business, Inc., was established by Korean American Ahn Chang-ho. The company was the first business of its kind to be owned by a person of Asian ancestry. North American Business, Inc., makes investments in business and agriculture.

◆ In 1974, the governments of Mexico and the United States agreed that an estimated 120,000 illegal Mexican immigrants living near the border region of the two countries would be legalized as residents of the United States. In addition, the new Mexican Americans would receive contracts guaranteeing that their salaries would be at least minimum wage in the United States.

■ On January 31, 1870, the War Department announced that its White Mountain homeland would become the reservation for all Apache then living in Arizona and New Mexico.

# MY PERSONAL LIST

February was designated as Black History Month largely through the efforts of Carter G. Woodson to raise the national consciousness of the history of African Americans. Born in West Virginia in 1875, he worked his way up from the coal mines to earn a Ph.D. from Harvard University in 1912. Called the "Father of Black History," Dr. Woodson wanted to disprove the notion that African Americans had no history of their own. He was among a small group of scholars who promoted the study of African American history. Dr. Woodson's organization, the Association for the Study of Negro Life and History, was the living proof of his commitment to his craft.

Woodson's efforts laid the foundation for the civil rights movement of the 1960s. Two dominant African American leaders in the movement were the Reverend Dr. Martin Luther King, Jr., and Malcolm X. Dr. King was a Baptist minister who advocated *nonviolent resistance*, or disobeying unfair segration laws in peaceful ways to publicize and change the law. Malcolm X was a black Muslim minister who preached *black separatism*, the concept that African Americans should live apart from whites. The black Muslims did not believe in nonviolence. They felt that African Americans should fight back and defend themselves when attacked.

Dr. Carter G. Woodson, Dr. Martin Luther King, Jr., and Malcolm X are three leaders who captured the hearts, minds and consciences of many people in the United States. Their legacy of self-actualization lives on today.

> "Education is our passport to the future, for tomorrow belongs to the people who prepare for it today."
>
> *Malcolm X*

◀ *Martin Luther King, Jr., (left) and Malcolm X (right).*

● African American students in Charlotte, North Carolina, sat at the lunch counter of a Woolworth's on this day in 1960 to protest the denying of counter service to African Americans unless they stood. Lunch counters of eight local businesses closed in fear. The protest event was repeated the next day in Greensboro, North Carolina, by four African American college students who sat down peacefully at a lunch counter and refused to leave when they were denied service. These were two of the earliest attempts to integrate public facilities in the South.

▲ The provisional government of Hawaii was recognized by US Minister to Hawaii John L. Stevens in 1893. Stevens ordered the raising of the US flag and declared the island a protectorate of the United States. This occurred after a revolution had ousted Queen Lilioukalani from power.

◆ Sometime in February 1895, the Marti and Cuban Revolutionary party called for a war of independence on the island of Cuba. The war was intended to free Cuba from Spanish rule.

■ The Dawes Act went into effect during this month in 1887. The act, also called the General Allotment Act, gave land to individual Native Americans in an attempt to discourage them from living in tribes. The act was also intended to assimilate Native Americans into mainstream US society via individual ownership of land.

❖ During this week in 1880, Land League President and leader of the Irish Home Rule movement Charles Stewart Parnell toured the US in an effort to gain support from the Irish American community for agrarian reform in Ireland. As part of his visit to the United States, Parnell addressed Congress on the second of this month to publicize Irish issues.

# FEBRUARY

# FEBRUARY

● Twenty-six-year-old Autherine J. Lucy became the first African American student admitted to the University of Alabama (1956) following orders issued to the school by a federal court. The admission of Lucy to the university led to rioting by segregationists.

▲ On this day in 1981, Republic of Korea's President Chun Doo Hwan met with US President Ronald Reagan at the White House. The purpose of the meeting was to reaffirm the friendship and positive diplomatic relations between the two countries. Chun was the first foreign head of state to meet with President Reagan.

◆ The US and Mexico signed the *Treaty of Guadalupe Hidalgo* in 1848, bringing the war between the two countries, which started in 1845, to an end.

■ In a speech given during this month in 1973 at Western New England College in Springfield, Massachusetts, LaDonna Harris, wife of Oklahoma Democratic Senator Fred Harris and a citizen of the Comanche Nation, said that "We must teach Indians they can succeed and live happy lives as Indians." The Native American activist also called upon US institutions not to regard Native Americans as "apples." *Apples,* according to Harris, are "Indians who are red on the outside and white on the inside."

❖ *The Language of Fashion,* the first dictionary compiled by a woman in the US, was published in New York City in 1940. The dictionary, which was edited by European American Mary Brooks Picken, was devoted entirely to the topic of wearing apparel.

> "The strength of Indian peoples, both individually and collectively, is in the tribe. We have something we can identify with, a collective strength."
>
> LaDonna Harris, 1992

---

● In 1962, African American Barbara Jordan became a candidate on the Democratic ticket for a seat in the Texas House of Representatives. Jordan was the first African American woman to run for that office. Jordan lost the primary that year and in the next election year as well. In her third try for the seat, Jordan won both the primary and the general election.

▲ In 1973, this day was the first day of the Chinese New Year. It was designated the Year of the Ox. President Richard Nixon and Vice President Spiro Agnew sent messages of congratulations to many Chinese Americans.

**F EBRUAR Y**

◆ Gloria Molina was elected to the Los Angeles City Council in 1987. Molina was the first Hispanic American to be elected to the council. Hoping that others would follow her precedent, Molina endorsed another Hispanic American, Lucille Roybal Allard, to fill the seat she vacated in the California State Assembly.

■ ◆ ◇ Mexican Native American singer Richie Valens (Richard Stephen Valenzuela) died at age 17 in an airplane crash on this day in 1959 while en route to Fargo, North Dakota. The plane crash occurred following a concert performance in Iowa at which Valens performed his rock 'n' roll rendition of the Mexican folk song *La Bamba*. Shortly after his death, the single on which Valens recorded the songs *Donna* and *La Bamba* reached the number-two spot on the national rock music charts. European American musical performers J. D. Richardson ("the Big Bopper") and Buddy Holly also died in the crash.

● On this day in 1822, free African Americans settled and established the new West African nation of Liberia. This began in 1815 when Paul Cuffe, a free African American, took 38 other free African Americans on a voyage to West Africa at his expense. The transportation of the Africans was in response to demands by European Americans that free African Americans were a disruptive influence and should be deported to Africa.

**F EBRUAR Y**

▲ The first Chinese New Year celebration in the United States occurred during this month in 1851.

◆ Juanita Castro, sister of Cuban Premier Fidel Castro, took the oath of allegiance and became a United States citizen in 1982. Castro, who took the oath in the Dade County Auditorium in Miami, Florida, had helped her brother rise to power by toppling the Batista government in 1959. Juanita and her brother then parted company the following year. Juanita, who lived in the United States for 17 years before becoming a citizen, owned a small pharmacy.

■ In 1991, President Bush proposed a 14.8 percent increase in the Smithsonian Institution's budget. The new budget included $16.3 million for a new National Museum of the American Indian.

◇ In 1955, 18-year-old swimmer Lynne Cox became the first woman to swim across the Cook Strait which is located between the north and south islands of New Zealand. Her marathon 14-mile swim was completed in 12 hours and 15 minutes.

> "Every Cuban living has a desire to go back home. If everything changes there and we have freedom, I would go back. My heart is there but my life is here."
>
> Juanita Castro, 1982

● Two significant events involving African Americans that had taken place on this date include:
    1884--a US patent was granted to W. Johnson for an egg beater.
    1956--L. R. Lautier became the first African American to be admitted as a member
        of the National Press Club.

▲ President Wilson vetoed a bill passed by Congress on December 14, 1916, but Congress overrode his veto and the bill became law on this day in 1917. The law, known as the *Asiatic Barred Zone Act*, excluded immigration from South and Southeast Asia. Asian Indian immigration was also prohibited by law.

◆ Promulgation of the Constitution Day is celebrated in Mexico. In 1917, the Mexican Congress drafted a new constitution, which is still the basis of the Mexican government.

■ During a Frank McGee television newscast in 1967, the term "red power" was used to describe a Native American movement for independence. This is believed to be the first time the term was used publicly. The movement for independence came as a result of a National Congress of American Indians conference.

❖ In 1989, Judith Richards Hope became the first woman elected to the Harvard Corporation. Hope was elected to serve on the board which acts as the chief governing body of Harvard University.

**5**

FEBRUARY

**6**

FEBRUARY

● *Native Son*, a novel by African American author Richard Wright, was published during this month in 1940. The novel became one of the best-sellers of the year and is still a classic.

▲ On February 6, 1982, United States Economic Council President Henry Taylor visited Korea. Taylor was received by Korean President Chun Doo Hwan. On this same day in 1949, the new United Nations Commission on Korea assumed its duties in Seoul.

◆ In 1975, the Voting Rights Act of 1965 was amended to make the ban on literacy testing permanent and to require any state with greater than a 5 percent minority voter population to provide ballots in the native language of specific ethnic groups. The groups included in the amendment were persons of Spanish heritage, Native Americans, Asian Americans and Alaskan natives. Six years later, in 1982, this new provision of the Voting Rights Act of 1965 was amended again to remain in effect until 1992.

■ In 1788, Massachusetts, named for the Native American tribe that lived near Milton River, was admitted to the union as a state.

❖ Patent #187,695 was issued to Ms. S. Brooks of Helena, Arkansas, in 1877. Brooks received the patent for a method that allowed people to "produce lubricated molds in plaster." The cooking method allowed for a way to make decorative ornamental designs with butter.

> *"We live here and they live there. We black and they white. They got things we ain't. They do things and we can't. It's just like living in jail."*
>
> Richard Wright,
> *Native Son,*
> *1940*

- Lowndes County, Alabama, was found guilty of "gross systematic exclusion of members of the Negro race from jury duty" by a federal court in 1966. With its finding, the court ordered Lowndes County officials to produce a new jury list and to desegregate its school system within two years. The court also required schools in the county to introduce remedial programs to ensure that African Americans received the same educational quality offered to white children.

▲ Chinese American Gerald Tsai, Jr., made economic history this month in 1966 when he persuaded investors to buy 42-million shares of the newly created Manhattan Fund. Investors bought into the fund based mostly on Tsai's reputation for being an economic whiz. Tsai, who founded the fund, also served as its president.

**F E B R U A R Y**

◆ In 1979, Lieutenant Colonel William Landgraf of the US Army announced that a ban which had prohibited Hispanic American soldiers from communicating with each other in Spanish had been rescinded. Landgraf added, however, that he would continue to discourage the speaking of Spanish among soldiers who were on duty. In response to Langraf's announcement, Army Secretary Clifford Alexander said that the army "does not and will not restrict the use of any languages used by soldiers to communicate with each other."

■ In 1974, Russell Means of the American Indian Movement was reelected as president of the Oglala Sioux tribe at the Pine Ridge, South Dakota, reservation. At the same time, Joseph American Horse was defeated by incumbent David Long on the vice-presidential ballot.

❖ During this week in 1912, the play *He and She* by Rachel Crothers opened in New York. The play dealt with the struggle of women to balance home and career at the same time. The subject matter of the play was unusual for its time because women had not yet entered the workforce at large. This was only one play in which Crothers explored women's roles in society.

- The Orangeburg Massacre took place on this day in 1968. The massacre occurred when police officers opened fire on a crowd of African American students who were holding a racial protest at South Carolina State College in Orangeburg, South Carolina. Three students were killed and twenty-seven were wounded in the massacre.

**F E B R U A R Y**

▲ The government of Hawaii paid for the passage of Japanese workers and their families who arrived in Honolulu on this day in 1885. A total of 943 Japanese, two-thirds of whom were men, were brought to Honolulu to serve as agricultural laborers. The men, who would be paid $9.00 per month, were bound to work in Honolulu for a period of three years.

◆ In 1519, Hernan Cortes left Cuba to sail for the Mexican coast. Cortes was originally sent to explore Mexico by King Ferdinand of Spain.

■ The Office of Economic Opportunity awarded a $65,000 grant to Native Americans of the Seminole tribe in Florida in 1967. The grant was awarded for the development of a 9-month Head Start program for 75 Seminole children.

❖ James Blair of Virginia was provided with a grant to found the College of William and Mary. The charter for the college, which is the oldest college in the United States, was signed on this day in 1693. Blair was given the grant to "furnish Virginia with a seminary of ministers, to educate the youth in piety, letters and good manners and to propagate Christianity among the Indians."

*Orangeburg Massacre*

● On this day in 1961, the US Senate confirmed the nomination of Robert C. Weaver as administrator of the Housing and Home Finance Agency, which later became the Office of Housing and Urban Development (HUD). At the time of his appointment, Weaver had the highest federal post ever held by an African American.

▲ On this day in 1907, delegates from the San Francisco Board of Education met with President Theodore Roosevelt at the White House to defend its policies of segregating children of Chinese, Japanese and Korean descent in separate "Oriental schools." The meeting resulted in several Japanese American students being able to attend the public schools in exchange for a more restricted emigration policy for Japanese wishing to come to the US.

◆ In 1822, President Boyer of Haiti invaded the Independent State of Spanish Haiti (the Dominican Republic) with 12,000 soldiers. The Spanish part of the island was overtaken by Boyer's troops and once again came under the control of the Republic of Haiti.

■ Harvard University's Peabody Museum announced in 1979 that, due to financial difficulties, it was going to sell its collection of 106 oil paintings of Native Americans of North America. The paintings were created by artist Henry Inman. Scholars who wanted to study the paintings protested the sale because they feared the collection would be sold to private owners.

❖ Andrew Bradford of Philadelphia published the first magazine in America during this month in 1741. The magazine was a monthly periodical which Bradford called *The American Monthly Magazine*, or "A Monthly View of the Political State of the British Colonies." The magazine was published in Philadelphia, Pennsylvania. Later in the month, Benjamin Franklin began to publish *The General Magazine*.

F E B R U A R Y

F E B R U A R Y

● Ronald Brown from New York was elected chairman of the Democratic National Committee in 1989, becoming the first African American to head a major US political party.

▲ The Hungop Chusik Hoeska (Business Promotion Corporation), a small business company operated by Ahn Sok-jung, was established on this day in 1910. This was one of the first Korean businesses established in the continental United States.

◆ Late this month in 1844, Trinitaria "separatist movement" leaders and their followers met in Santo Domingo at the Gate of La Misericordia. Here they fired a shot into the air to symbolize their independence from the Haitian government. This was the first of two declarations of independence by the Dominican Republic. The second announced their independence from Spain.

■ Chief Redbird of the Cherokee Nation expressed his disappointment in President Jimmy Carter in 1978. Redbird had sent the president a handmade feathered headdress. The headdress was soon returned to Redbird with the explanation that President Carter had a policy of not accepting gifts from the public. The chief had sent a headdress to every president since Woodrow Wilson. At the time the headdress was returned, Chief Redbird was in a nursing home recuperating from cancer surgery.

❖ Elizabeth Watson, who had been nominated for the position of chief of police of Houston, Texas, by Mayor Kathryn Whitmire one month earlier, was officially confirmed to the position on this day in 1990. Watson became the first female police chief of a major city in the history of the United States.

● In 1990, Nelson Mandela was released from prison in South Africa. Mandela had served a 27-year sentence as a political prisoner. He was a member of the African National Congress (ANC)--an organization dedicated to the removal of South Africa's laws of racial segregation.

▲ On this day in 1968, United States Presidential Envoy Cyrus Vance went to Seoul, Korea, to consult with Republic of Korea officials about Korean security. The concern of the United States was the result of an attack on a US ship and an assassination attempt on the Korean president by North Korean military forces the previous month.

*Luis Munoz Marin*

◆ As governor of Puerto Rico from 1948 to 1964, Luis Munoz Marin pledged his support to the formation of an anti-Communist alliance aimed at Cuban Premier Fidel Castro. The alliance was formed in Miami, Florida, by Cuban Revolutionary Council President Jose Miro Cardona. Miro served as chairman of the group, which had the support of many Latin American leaders.

■ Twenty-four Native Americans held a rally on Alcatraz Island in San Francisco Bay before beginning a 3,000-mile walk to Washington, DC. The march was a protest against legislation that would nullify Native American treaties. The leaders also wanted to complain about efforts to limit their hunting and fishing rights. As the marchers proceeded across the country, several hundred Native Americans joined in, finally arriving in Washington, DC, on July 15, 1978.

◆ US inventor Thomas Alva Edison was born on this date in 1847. Edison patented more than 1,000 inventions. Among his most important inventions were the incandescent lightbulb, the phonograph, the mimeograph, the vote recorder, and the electric pen. He also was one of the first people to produce movie pictures.

---

## 12 FEBRUARY

● On this day in 1909, the NAACP was founded in New York City. It is the oldest civil rights organization in the US and has fought against discrimination against African Americans in all aspects of life by bringing lawsuits and organizing rallies and protest marches.

▲ A joint resolution was passed by the Colorado legislature during this week in 1870 to welcome Chinese immigrants. The attitude that led to the resolution, however, did not last long.

◆ Militant Mexican American nationalist Reies Lopez Tijerina began a movement to regain land in New Mexico for Chicano workers in 1962. His organization, the Alianze Federal de los Pueblos Libres (Federal Alliance of Free City States), existed to push for the return of millions of acres of land that Spain granted to Mexico before the 1848 war. The US territorial government honored the land grants that were "communally" owned by Mexican Americans until the 1900s when, through legal maneuvering and taxation, European Americans took the land.

■ The trial of AIM leaders Dennis Banks and Russell Means opened in St. Paul, Minnesota, in 1974. Banks, a Chippewa, and Means, a Sioux, were on trial for charges stemming from the 1973 occupation of the Wounded Knee village on the Pine Ridge reservation in South Dakota. In opening statements, Means said that Wounded Knee was taken over "to dramatize the need for reform." Dennis Banks said that Wounded Knee was "an event that is destined to change the course of Indian history."

◆ President Lincoln's birthday was once celebrated as a national holiday on this date. The celebration was later combined with George Washington's birthday into the federal holiday called President's Day. Abraham Lincoln, 16th president of the United States, was born in 1809.

*Queen Lilioukalani*

● Joseph L. Searles III became the first African American member of the New York Stock Exchange on this day in 1970.

▲ The *Hawaiian Native Claims Settlement Act* was presented by a Congressional subcommittee on Indian Affairs on this day in 1975. Hearings were held on each of the six Hawaiian islands in an attempt to reimburse native Hawaiians for their loss of identity and property as a result of US intervention in the overthrow of the Queen Lilioukalani monarchy in 1893.

◆ A *New York Times* article published on this day in 1970 stated that the Puerto Rican revolutionary and proindependence group, *MIRA*, had acknowledged responsibility for 19 terrorist acts that had taken place over the past one and one-half months. Seven of these acts occurred in New York City.

■ Sometime in 1847, the citizens of Norwich, Connecticut, erected a monument to the memory of Uncas, chief of the Mohegan [Mohican]. Uncas became widely known in the fictional tale, *The Last of the Mohicans*, by James Fenimore Cooper. Regionally, Uncas was known for his assistance to European American settlers in their dealings with members of the Pequot and Narragansett tribes.

❖ Dorothy Hammill emerged from the 1976 Winter Olympics in Innsbruck, Austria, as a star after winning a gold medal on this day. Hammill won her gold medal in figure skating.

## St. Valentine's Day

● In 1867, the US Post Office released a 25-cent stamp honoring Frederick Douglass, "the Great Emancipator," liberator and abolitionist, who was born on this day in 1817. The stamp, part of a series of 25, was the only one to honor an African American. As founder of the African American newspaper, *North Star*, Douglass used this platform to help bring about an end to the enslavement of Africans in the US. An eloquent speaker and a talented writer, Douglass advised President Lincoln and was appointed minister to Haiti in 1889.

▲ On this day in 1953, Senator Pat McCarran received a letter from Suziburo Kujiraoka of Tokyo, Japan. The letter thanked the senator for making it possible for Kujiraoka to emigrate to the US. Kujiraoka was the first Japanese citizen to receive a visa to the US under the McCarran-Walter Act.

◆ Robert Garcia, who ran on both the Democratic and Liberal party tickets, won the senatorial seat that had been held by Herman Badillo in the 21st Congressional District in 1978. Badillo had stepped down to become deputy mayor of New York City in Mayor Ed Koch's administration.

■ On or around this date in 1950, Jim Thorpe was declared the greatest US athlete and football player of the half-century. Thorpe, of Native American descent, won gold medals in the decathlon and pentathlon in the 1912 Olympics. He was an All-American college football player and a successful major league baseball player.

❖ Earlier this month in 1984, the space shuttle *Challenger* was launched into space from the Kennedy Space Center, Florida. On this mission, the Manned Maneuvering Unit and Manipulator Foot Restraint were checked out in two space walks. Astronauts McCandless and Stewart performed the two space walks.

● Heavyweight boxing champion Muhammad Ali lost his title to Leon Spinks in Las Vegas, Nevada (1978). The decision in the fight was considered controversial because of a liquid in a brown bottle that was administered to Spinks during the fight. Six months later, the fighters had a rematch in which Ali won back the title.

▲ Chang-Lin Tien was named to the position of chancellor at the University of California at Berkeley in 1990. Tien, an engineer and administrator at the university, was the first Asian American to head a major research university.

## FEBRUARY

◆ The presidents of Colombia, Bolivia, Peru and the United States met in Cartagena, Colombia, on this day in 1990. There, the dignitaries signed the *Cartagena Declaration*, pledging their governments to more strenuous efforts in fighting the illegal trafficking of cocaine into the United States and to other parts of the world.

■ In 1966, Native Americans in the state of Washington staged a "fish-in" to protest state laws that forbade net fishing.

❖ In 1950, Mildred "Babe" Didrikson Zaharias was voted the greatest woman athlete of the past 50 years in an Associated Press poll of sportswriters. Born in Port Arthur, Texas, Babe excelled in many sports, such as baseball, golf and track and field. In the 1932 Olympics, she set world records in the 80-meter hurdles, the javelin and the high jump. After taking up golf in the early 1930s, Babe began her domination of this sport. She won the *US Women's Amateur Tournament*. In 1948, 1950 and 1954, she won the *US Women's Open*. Babe was also one of the founding members of the Ladies Professional Golf Association (LPGA).

● *Soul On Ice*, a book about the rage of African Americans because of society's injustices in the US, was published in 1968. The book was written by Eldridge Cleaver.

▲ *The Chung Sai Yat Po* (*The Chinese Western Daily Newspaper*) released its first issue on this day in 1900 in San Francisco, California. The four-page newspaper was founded by Ng Poon Chew. Chew served as the president and managing editor of the paper until his death in 1931.

## FEBRUARY

◆ On this day in 1959, Fidel Castro was sworn in as the new premier of Cuba. Castro's rise to power followed the takeover of the Batista regime using guerilla-warfare tactics.

■ More than 50 Native American leaders of reservations met during this week in Billings, Montana, in 1971 and agreed to form a national tribal council association. The purpose of the council was to devise unified policies for all Native Americans. The group felt that the council was needed because BIA Commissioner Louis Bruce was listening to demands that came mostly from Native Americans living in urban areas and from militant Native American groups.

❖ In 1804, a band of pirates from Tripoli captured the US Naval frigate *Philadelphia* in Tripoli harbor off the northeastern coast of Africa. On this day, Stephen Decatur of the US Navy led a daring nighttime raid in the harbor, setting fire to the *Philadelphia* while it sat in Tripoli Harbor in captivity.

> *"It [Arizona] is my land, my home, my father's land, to which I now ask to be allowed to return. I want to spend my last days there and be buried among those mountains."*
>
> Chief Geronimo
> to President Ulysses S. Grant

● Inventor A.C. Richardson, who held a patent for a hame fastener (a horse and wagon device), was awarded a patent for a churn on this day in 1891. Richardson, who continued to create devices, was later granted patents for a casket-lowering device (1894) and an insect killer (1899).

▲ On this day in 1942, US Attorney General Francis Biddle sent a memorandum to President Roosevelt in an effort to stop the evacuation and relocation of persons of Japanese ancestry. Biddle was opposed to the plan because he believed that all needed precautionary measures had already been taken to ensure the safety of the US. He also believed that such actions were in violation of the constitutional rights of Japanese Americans. Biddle later became a champion of civil liberties.

◆ Sometime in 1953, an office called The Coordination of Spanish Catholic Action was established by the Archdiocese of New York. The office was established to study the needs of Puerto Ricans who had emigrated to New York City. The office also coordinated efforts among the city's Catholic parishes to provide religious services for the new immigrants.

■ Apache Chief Geronimo, who was in his eighties, died while he was a prisoner of war at Fort Sill in 1909. Pneumonia was the reported cause of Geronimo's death.

❖ Esther Morris was appointed as the first female magistrate (judge) in America in 1870. Officially, Morris was appointed justice of the peace for the community of South Pass, Wyoming. While in office, Morris tried 70 cases.

● The National Urban League named *Time* publisher Henry Luce its chairperson for its drive to raise funds for "Negro" economic self-help projects during this week in 1947.

▲ An agreement on the restriction of Japanese immigration was reached through a note sent to the US ambassador to Japan. The note acknowledged President Theodore Roosevelt's mandate of March 1907. In 1908, due to anti-Japanese sentiment at the time, the Japanese government agreed not to issue any more passports to Japanese laborers who wanted to emigrate to the United States.

◆ Daniel Fernandez was posthumously awarded the *Congressional Medal of Honor* in 1966, becoming the first Mexican American to win such an award. Fernandez, serving in the US Army during the Vietnam War, was cited for "conspicuous gallantry and intrepidity at the risk of his life above and beyond the call of duty." Fernandez was fighting through enemy fire to rescue a wounded soldier when an enemy hand grenade was thrown near his wounded ally. Concluding that there was no time for the others to protect themselves, Fernandez threw himself on the grenade as it exploded.

■ Federal agents called a meeting with Native Americans at Fort Lyon to sign a treaty in 1861 that provided a small reservation in southeastern Colorado. The treaty was made with Cheyenne Chiefs Black Kettle and White Antelope and Arapaho Chief Little Raven. Chief Little Raven was the first signer of the *Treaty of Fort Wise* in Colorado.

❖ A group of Dutch American Quakers living in an area of Pennsylvania called Germantown made the first formal protest against slavery in the Western Hemisphere in 1688.

● The first *Pan African Congress* convened for three days of meetings in 1919 at the Grand Hotel in Paris, France. The conference was organized by African American W.E.B. DuBois.

▲ US troops landed in Iwo Jima, Japan, on this date in 1945. The US forces fought the Japanese until the Japanese were defeated in battle on March 16.

◆ On this day in 1821, Spain gave up control of what is today Florida by signing a treaty with government officials in Washington, DC. Andrew Jackson was appointed the new governor of the region. Official transfer of authority was handed over to Jackson during ceremonies held at the Plaza Ferdinand VII in Pensacola, Florida.

■ After being captured by members of his own tribe for a reward, Chief Leschi of the Nisqualli and Yakima was condemned and hanged on this day in 1857. One year earlier, Leschi had led a war party composed of more than 1,000 warriors in an attack on Seattle, Washington. The war party was driven off by bombardment from a ship in the harbor.

❖ In 1941, General O'Ryan formed the Committee for American Irish Defense. O'Ryan and other Irish Americans published an open letter to President Roosevelt to urge support of air and naval bases in Ireland.

## FEBRUARY

"Your can count on the Irish, Mr. President...to preserve the freedom of the seas and to keep inviolate our Icelandic outpost..."

Committee for American Irish Defense, 1941

## FEBRUARY

● During this month in 1968, Henry Lewis was named director of the New Jersey Symphony orchestra. He was the first African American to head a US symphony orchestra.

▲ The United Citizens League was formed by 1,500 US-born Japanese citizens living in Los Angeles, California, in 1942. The organization was created to oppose the evacuation of "loyal aliens" and Japanese American citizens.

◆ During this week in 1990, the Sandanista government of Nicaragua, which had been in power since 1979, was voted out of office by a 14-party coalition. The coalition was led by Violeta Barrios Chamorro, Nicaragua's first female president.

■ The first known scalpings of Native Americans by white settlers occurred in 1725. The scalpings, which were encouraged by a bounty offered by the city of Boston, took place in New Hampshire. A hunting party in search of Native Americans came across ten sleeping Native Americans and scalped each of these people. They then took the scalps to Boston, where they were paid 100 pounds for each scalp.

❖ Colonel John Glenn of the US Marine Corps became the first US astronaut to orbit Earth on this day in 1962. As one of the original *Mercury* astronauts, Colonel Glenn became the third US citizen to be sent into space.

**21**

**FEBRUARY**

● While speaking in New York City, Malcolm X (birth name: Malcolm Little; Muslim name: El Haji Malik El Shabazz) was shot and killed in 1965. Malcolm X served as the spokesperson for the African American Muslim movement, leading the struggle for human rights in the United States and around the world. He also traveled around the world to organize Africans around Muslim principles.

▲ During this month in 1942, *Executive Order 9006* resulted in the imprisonment of thousands of Japanese Americans in internment camps. This order issued by President Roosevelt was, in part, a response to the attack on Pearl Harbor in 1941 marking entry of the US into World War II.

■ In 1828, the first edition of *The Cherokee Phoenix*, a weekly newspaper that was printed both in English and Cherokee, was published in New Echota, Georgia, by Elias Boudinot, a full-blooded Cherokee. Boudinot was educated in Cornwall, Connecticut, in a foreign mission school formed by a philanthropist whose name Boudinot adopted.

❖ In 1947, European American Edward Land, president of the Polaroid Corporation, demonstrated a new camera that produced a developed negative and a positive print one minute after the photograph was taken.

**22**

**FEBRUARY**

● Actor Richard B. Harrison is featured in the role of "De Lawd" in the opening performance of *Green Pastures*. The play opened on Broadway in this month in 1930.

▲ During this month in 1972, President Richard Nixon visited the People's Republic of China. This was the first step toward normalizing relations between the two countries since the Chinese Communist party took control of the Chinese mainland in 1949. The normalization process was completed by President Carter during his administration.

❖ During this month in 1968, Cesar Chavez, president of the United Farm Workers Union, began a fast as a symbolic act of rededication to the principles of nonviolence.

■ *The Treaty of Dancing Rabbit Creek* was ratified by Congress during this week in 1831. This treaty, made between the federal government and the Choctaw Nation, gave all Choctaw-owned land east of the Mississippi River to the United States. The treaty also provided for the removal of all Choctaw living east of the Mississippi River to the Indian Territory set up under the *Indian Removal Act*. The Choctaw became the first Native American group to be removed to the West under this act.

❖ The birthday of George Washington (born in 1732), the first President of the United States, was at one time celebrated on this day. During the Revolutionary War, he was a general in charge of the Continental Army. His most decisive victory was the Battle of Trenton. In his home state of Virginia, Washington was a farmer and a horseman. Washington owned African slaves and ordered them freed upon the death of his widow, Martha. His birthday is now celebrated as part of President's Day.

● During this week in 1932, the African American singing group, the Mills Brothers, made their third appearance at Manhattan's Palace Theatre in New York. The group quickly gained notoriety for their unique *a capella* ability to simulate the sounds of musical instruments with their voices. The group consisted of four brothers--Herbert, Harry, Don and John.

▲ In 1905, the *San Francisco Chronicle* attacked Japanese immigrants in the United States through the use of inflammatory headlines that proclaimed the dangers that would result from the excessive immigration of these peoples.

**23**
**FEBRUARY**

◆ Mexican President Antonio Lopez de Santa Anna led an army of conquest into Texas in 1836 to slow down the number of European Americans entering Texas, then a part of Mexico. Mexico had first given European Americans permission to settle in Texas, but Mexico felt it had lost control of the territory as thousands of immigrants in the region began to make their own laws in conflict with those of Mexico. About one month later, almost 200 European Americans made a final stand against several thousand Mexican soldiers at the Alamo.

■ On or about this day in 1973, a group of Oglala Sioux barricaded themselves in the Pine Ridge Indian Reservation in Wounded Knee, South Dakota, to protest the murders of Native Americans by European Americans in the Dakotas and the alleged corruption in the administration of the Oglala Sioux tribal council president Richard Wilson.

❖ In 1956, Branch Rickey, former major league baseball executive, received the *National Conference of Christian and Jews Human Relations Award* for helping to break the color barrier in baseball by signing Jackie Robinson to play for the Brooklyn Dodgers. Mr. Rickey was the general manager of the team at the time.

**FEBRUARY**
**Mexican Flag Day**

● In February of 1908, bishops of the African Methodist Episcopal Church issued a joint statement condemning the "monstrous injustices" that occurred at a race riot in Brownsville, Texas, and the "lily white" racial policies of the Republican administration that they felt led to a pervasive climate of racial injustice in the country.

▲ Japanese artist Yoko Ono accepted the *Best Album Grammy Award* for 1981 on behalf of her late husband, John Lennon, for *Double Fantasy*. The album was released shortly before his murder in New York City and was performed by both John Lennon and Yoko Ono.

◆ The Plan of Iguala was signed in 1821 and was the final step of a process allowing Mexico to declare its independence from Spain..

■ The ongoing intense conflict between European Americans and Native Americans has taken many forms over the years. To many, the death of Anna Mae Aquash was the symbol of that intense conflict. Aquash, a Micmac from Nova Scotia, was a member of the American Indian Movement (AIM) and had smuggled food to those who barricaded themselves in the Pine Ridge Reservation in South Dakota in 1973. On this day in 1976, she was found shot to death on the reservation. Many in the movement suspected the death was caused by the FBI.

❖ During this month in 1873, James W. Gerard, a lawyer and member of the Society for the Prevention of Pauperism, delivered a report on juvenile delinquency in New York. His report criticized the arraignment process which placed young offenders in the same facilities as older, more hardened, criminals. This report led to the creation of the first separate institution for juvenile offenders in the US, the New York House of Refuge, on January 1, 1925.

*Yoko Ono*

*Sheila Young*

● On this day in 1870, Hiram Revels of Mississippi became the first African American to be elected US senator. Under the Radical Reconstruction provisions of the federal and state governments (1865-1876), African Americans were given the opportunity for the first time to run for elective office.

▲ In 1942, the US government activated the Varsity Victor Volunteers, a military unit made up of young Nisei (US-born Japanese) men who were formerly with the University of Hawaii ROTC. This unit performed construction and defense duties as a part of the 34th Combat Engineers Regiment.

◆ The First Spanish-language worship service at the Metropolitan Community Methodist Church in Harlem, New York City, was held in 1962. Adults and children came together in a small room for the service, led by lay preacher Jose Rosado. The service was an attempt to bring together the Hispanic and African American communities of the neighborhood in what Rev. William M. James described as a "common Christian fellowship."

■ Scarlet Night of the Crow Nation disappeared in 1867 while he was in Washington, DC, as part of a delegation of Native American leaders meeting with the government. An advertisement offering a $100 reward was run in the *Washington Chronicle*. Scarlet Night's body was found in Alexandria, Virginia, two weeks after his disappearance.

❖ Detroit's Sheila Young won the 500-meter speed-skating event in Stromburg, Sweden, in 1973. The 23-year-old athlete also became the first US woman from the US in more than 50 years to win the world cycling event. She was the first athlete to win world championships in both speed skating and track cycling.

● Joe Reed and Arthur Shores became delegates for the state of Alabama at the Democratic National Convention in 1968. The men, who ran unopposed for the delegate positions, were the first two African American delegates from Alabama at a major political party convention.

▲ Tetsuo Toyama was in the first group of Japanese aliens to be naturalized under the provisions of the McCarran Walter Act on this day in 1953. Toyama was publisher of the *Jitsugyono Hawaii Journal*. One year after receiving citizenship, he founded *The Citizen*, a bilingual newspaper that encouraged elderly Japanese to seek citizenship.

**26**

**F E B R U A R Y**

◆ The Real Great Society, Inc. was awarded a grant from the Federal Office of Economic Opportunity in the amount of $258,447 in 1968. The organization, which was started by former Puerto Rican gang members Carlos (Chino) Garcia and Angelo Gonzales, was given the grant in recognition of its *University of the Streets* program which offered a variety of traditional and nontraditional classes. The organization, which is designed to be a self-help group for Puerto Ricans, has produced at least two self-supporting businesses.

■ During this week, Napeshneeduta, a full-blooded Sioux, became the first Native American of the Dakotas to be baptized and accepted into the Christian church. When baptized, Napeshneeduta's name was changed to Joseph Napeshee. Napeshee was turned away by his people because he changed his name and faith. He later fought against the people he had once led.

❖ Robert Penn Warren was named the first official poet laureate of the US in 1986 by Daniel Boorstin, librarian of Congress. Warren, a writer of poetry, short stories and novels, won the *Pulitzer Prize for Fiction* in 1974 for his novel *All the King's Men*. His collection of poems, *Promises: Poems 1954-1956*, won the 1958 *Pulitzer Prize in Poetry*.

● At the 1986 *Grammy Award* ceremonies, held during this week, the all-star cast singing *USA for Africa* won *Grammy* awards for best record of 1985 and best pop group for their recording of *We Are the World*, the proceeds of which were to be sent to help the impoverished people of Africa. The recording was the concept of producer Quincy Jones and recording artist Michael Jackson. Whitney Houston was also recognized as the year's best female pop vocalist for her recording of *Saving All My Love for You*.

## FEBRUARY 27

▲ On this day in 1942, Canadian officials pursued a Japanese-removal plan that demanded total removal of all aliens in the mountain valleys of the Canandian interior. The property of those interned was sold to help pay the cost of their internments. Those who were interned remained in camps until March of 1949.

◆ On January 18, 1960, Texas Governor Price Daniel proclaimed February 27th *José Navarro Day*. José Antonio Navarro, a Mexican American, was born on February 27, 1795. Navarro was one of the signers of the Texas Declaration of Independence in 1836 and served on the committee that wrote the Texas Constitution in the same year.

■ In 1976, Canadian Eskimo leaders presented a proposal to Premier Pierre Trudeau. In the 61-page document, the Eskimo claimed that approximately one-fifth of the Canadian territory belonged to them and requested that they be given a 3 percent royalty on any natural resources located on the land they claimed.

❖ Irish American Senator John L. McClellan, a Democrat from Arkansas, received the *George Washington Award* during this week in 1970 from the Freedom Foundation for his "integrity and courage" in combating communism.

> "We are the world, we are the child. We are the ones who make a better day, so let's start giving. There's a choice we're making. We're saving our own lives. It's true we make a better day, just you and me."
>
> USA for Africa
> Chorus from
> *We Are the World*,
> 1985

## FEBRUARY 28

● African American poet Phillis Wheatley accepted the invitation of General George Washington to his Cambridge, Massachusetts, headquarters to thank her for a poem she had written in his honor in 1776. Wheatley was born in West Africa around 1753. She came to the US in 1761 and was purchased as a slave by Susannah Wheatley, the wife of a Boston tailor. Phillis was taught to read and write by Susannah Wheatley's daughter, Mary. Some of Wheatley's published poems include *A Poem by Phillis, A Negro Girl on the Death of Reverend George Whitfield*, *Poems on Various Subjects: Regions and Morals* and *Liberty and Peace*.

▲ In February 1878, the China Fire Company was formed by a group of 50 Chinese men in Hawaii.

■ Ten days after federal agents signed a treaty with Arapaho and Cheyenne chiefs (1861) that would provide a small reservation in southeastern Colorado for their peoples, Congress provided a territorial governor for the same region.

❖ The United States Steel Corporation, one of the most successful businesses in US history, was incorporated during this week in 1901. The two people responsible for the formation of the company were J.P. Morgan and Elbert Gary.

● Hattie McDaniel became the first African American to win an *Academy Award* for a performance in a motion picture. McDaniel won the Oscar in 1939 in the Best Supporting Actress category for her role in *Gone with the Wind*. In the movie, McDaniel played the role of a house servant in the Southern plantation home of Scarlett O'Hara.

FEBRUARY

▲ Chang Yin Huan, Chinese minister to Washington, negotiated an important treaty with Secretary of State Thomas Francis Bayard in 1888. Among other things, the treaty prohibited the emigration of Chinese labor to the US for a period of 20 years and provided full monetary compensation for damages inflicted against Chinese lives and property in the Rock Springs Massacre of 1885.

◆ The Panama Canal Commission was appointed by President Theodore Roosevelt in 1904. The seven-person commission was charged with overseeing the construction of the waterway in Panama.

■ During this month in 1908, Louis Tewanima, a Hopi from Arizona, competed in the Olympic Games in London, England. Tewanima finished ninth in the 26-mile distance race and brought home medals in the 5,000- and 10,000-meter races. He repeated these medal-winning performances in the 1912 games in which fellow Native American Jim Thorpe gained notoriety. Tewanima later became the first athlete to be placed in the Arizona Sports Hall of Fame.

❖ The 1992 Senate elections opened the door for four female Democrats to take their historic place among US senators in 1993. By February, their second month in office, the impact of the female senators was being felt. The three European Americans elected were Dianne Feinstein, Barbara Boxer and Patty Murray. Carol Mosely Braun, the fourth female elected, is the first African American woman to be elected to the Senate.

# MY PERSONAL LIST

# MY PERSONAL LIST

Two Chinese Americans are among the many women who have changed the face of television broadcast news over the past 20 years, at both the national and local levels. Connie Chung and Kaity Tong are now nationally recognized.

Connie Chung was the first Chinese American woman to become a successful national television news anchor. She has worked at CBS twice, most recently in 1992, and also has worked at NBC. Chung has anchored morning and Saturday evening national newscasts and served as a political analysis correspondent during the 1988 presidential elections. Awards she has received include the *Peabody Award* in 1980, and an *Emmy* in 1987.

Kaity Tong has enjoyed her broadcast journalism success in the US's largest local television area, the New York-New Jersey-Connecticut tri-state region. She has been co-anchor of the *Eleven O'Clock News* on New York City's ABC and, in 1992, was co-anchor on the *Emmy* award-winning ten-o'clock nightly newscast on New York City's WPIX.

Connie Chung and Kaity Tong have overcome many obstacles to reach the career success they now enjoy. They have opened doors for other Chinese Americans and women to achieve their goals in broadcast journalism.

---

Some advice from Kaity Tong in 1992:

"First and foremost, never give up, and believe in yourself! Whatever you want to do, you can, with patience, persistence, and, (let's face it), a little bit of luck. In general, I recommend that you get a good liberal arts education, then try to start in a smaller market. To break into broadcasting, learn your craft and refine your skills as a big fish in a small pond. Reporters in smaller markets cover many more kinds of news than their big city counterparts. You can always move into a bigger market once you've honed your skills. Whatever you decide to do--report, produce, direct, write, whatever--always aim to be the best that you can be. Good luck--and I hope to see you on the air someday soon."

◀ *Kaity Tong*

▲ Dr. An Wang and eleven other naturalized US citizens were recipients of the first *Medal of Liberty*. Dr. Wang was the founder and the chairman of the board of the computer company, Wang Laboratories, Inc. The medal, which was formally presented by the Statue of Liberty-Ellis Island Foundation during the Liberty celebration in July 1986, recognized the achievements of immigrants to America.

◆ Puerto Rican nationalists shot five members of Congress in the US House of Representatives as a protest in 1954. The Puerto Ricans sought independence for their country.

■ The first issue of the *Shawnee Sun* was printed on this day in 1835. The *Shawnee Sun* was the first semimonthly Native American newspaper and the first newspaper to be written in the Shawnee language.

❖ Beginning to develop his "New Frontier," Irish American US President John F. Kennedy signed an executive order to launch the Peace Corps on this day in 1961. An organization designed to help peoples living in underdeveloped countries, the Peace Corps program trained US volunteers to help "liberate independent nations from the bonds of hunger, ignorance and poverty." Peace Corps workers were sent to different nations to teach skills dealing with agriculture and health.

● Governor Nelson Rockefeller of New York appointed Wyatt Tee Walker as special assistant on Urban Affairs in 1966. Walker was a top executive with a publishing company in Yonkers, New York. He had also previously worked as a chief of staff for Martin Luther King, Jr.

# MARCH

**Constitution Day**
Panama

▲ The final episode of the hit TV series *M\*A\*S\*H* aired on this day in 1983. The long-running television satire chronicled the lives of a US medical team serving during the Korean War. One of the show's main themes was the need for peace, not only in Korea but in the world at large. The final show commanded the largest television audience for any program up to that date.

◆ The Jones Act was passed on this day in Washington, DC, in 1917. The act granted United States citizenship to people in Puerto Rico.

# MARCH

■ A Washington, DC, fund-raising gala was held at the Kennedy Center Opera House in 1982 for the benefit of Native Americans. The "Night of the First Americans" event drew more than 100 tribal leaders, including Peter MacDonald of the Navaho and Ted Hogan of the Crow. A total of 2,000 tickets at prices from $15 to $1,000 were sold for the event. Proceeds, which were to support the nonprofit consortium of the Council of Energy Resource Tribes (which trains Native Americans as engineers and fiscal managers), were estimated to be $200,000. The audience was entertained by performances of the Ponca Dancers and the Red Earth Players, among others.

❖ Robert Bly won the *National Book Award* in March of 1968 for his book of poems titled *The Light Around the Body*. This book of poems "reflects personal and political struggles" particularly in its antiwar expressions. Robert Bly was a founder of American Writers Against the Vietnam War.

● Congress passed the Reconstruction Act in 1867. This act allowed African American men to participate in political conventions, write new state constitutions and hold political office. As a result of this act, African Americans later gained 20 congressional and 2 senatorial seats.

"American historic longing for pure light, constant victory, has been destroyed by the Vietnam War and from now on, we will have to live with grief and defeat."

Robert Bly,
National Awards Dinner
1968

▲ In response to the Japanese attack on Pearl Harbor in December 1941, the United States government required that Japanese Americans be placed in internment camps. On this day in 1942, an estimated 100,000 Japanese Americans who were living in the West were marched into internment camps in California. The entire area to be evacuated included a 2,000-mile stretch of land along the Western seaboard.

**M A R C H**

◆ During this week in 1971, the American Museum of Natural History in New York City opened an exhibit on Puerto Rican contemporary life.

■ In 1881, Congress appropriated $1,000 to pay Captain Richard Pratt to act as the director of a Native American school located in Carlisle, Pennsylvania. The school, which opened in 1889, was initially supported with private funds.

❖ In 1879, Mrs. Belva Anne Lockwood of Washington, DC, became the first female lawyer admitted to practice before the US Supreme Court.

● During this week, Congress passed the Civil Rights Act of 1875. This act guaranteed African Americans equal rights in amusement centers and hotels, at public conveyances and on juries.

**M A R C H**

▲ During this month in 1962, Wing Luke was elected to a seat on the city council of Seattle, Washington. Luke became the first Chinese American to win a political seat in a northwestern state.

◆ During March of 1861, the Dominican Republic was annexed to Spain, ending a 17-year period of self-rule for Dominicans.

■ Native American Charles Curtis of Kansas began his second term as a US senator in 1915. His first term lasted from 1907 to 1913. Curtis remained in the Senate until 1929 when he resigned the position to assume the role of vice president under President Herbert Hoover.

❖ Jeannette Rankin began her term in 1917 as the first woman elected to the House of Representatives. She served as an at-large member of Congress from the state of Montana. Her term ended in 1919. She was elected to another single term in 1940. During her first term, she voted against the entry of the US into World War I. During her second term, she became the only member of Congress to vote against US entry into World War II.

● Two members of the Black Panther party, Fred Hampton and Mark Clark, were killed by police gunfire during a predawn raid on Clark's apartment in Chicago, Illinois, in 1969. The party was considered "subversive" by the federal government and by the FBI in particular. The Chicago police were at first accused of murder in the deaths of Hampton and Clark, but a coroner's jury acquitted the police of murder, saying that the shootings were justified because Hampton and Clark allegedly fired first. The Black Panthers were the subject of many investigations, infiltration and raids by law-enforcement officials.

▲ A two-day conference of Chinese American organizations, including 34 branches of the Chinese Consolidated Benevolent Association, began in 1957 in Washington, DC, to encourage the cooperation of Chinese Americans in the support of US policy toward China.

◆ During this month in 1977, Puerto Rican American Carmen Rosa Maymi gave up her position as the seventh director of the Women's Bureau. While serving in the director's spot, Maymi was the highest ranking Hispanic American in the federal government.

**5**

**M** A R C **H**

■ The US Supreme Court handed down its ruling in the *Cherokee Nation v Georgia* in 1831, stating that the Cherokee Nation did not qualify as a foreign state and, therefore, had to abide by the laws of the state. The case occurred in response to Andrew Jackson's removal act which took Cherokee land and forced them to move.

❖ During the Boston Massacre of 1770 (see below), Patrick Carr, a native of Ireland, was slain.

● Crispus Attucks was killed in the infamous Boston Massacre in 1770. Attucks, a runaway "slave," was part of a group of men who, along with most of the colonists in Boston, resented the presence of British soldiers in their city. These men decided to confront the British soldiers, who then fired into the group, killing Attucks first. Crispus Attucks was the son of an African man and a Native American woman. His name, *Crispus*, means "small deer" in his mother's Natick language.

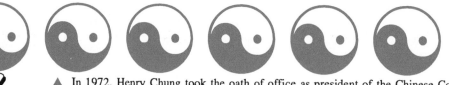

**6**

**M** A R C **H**

▲ In 1972, Henry Chung took the oath of office as president of the Chinese Consolidated Benevolent Association, making him the "figurehead" mayor of New York's Chinatown. The association, made up of the 59 community groups, chooses a new president every 2 years.

◆ After 12 days of fighting in 1836, the Alamo fell to the Mexican army under the leadership of General Santa Anna. The Mexican army massacred all the Texas defenders of the fort. Thereafter, the battle cry of the Texans' war for independence became "Remember the Alamo!"

■ President Johnson sent a message to Congress in 1968 requesting that Native Americans be given "an opportunity to remain in their homelands, if they choose, without surrendering their dignity; an opportunity to move to the towns and cities of America, if they choose, equipped with the skills to live in equality and dignity."

❖ European American Kathryn Sellers was reappointed to a second term as judge of the juvenile court of the District of Columbia in Washington, DC, in 1925. Judge Sellers held her position in the juvenile courts until 1934.

*Dred Scott*

● In 1857, a decision by the US Supreme Court seemingly guaranteed the continued existence of the institution of slavery. In the case of *Dred Scott v Sanford*, an African slave named Dred Scott sued to gain his freedom after his master's death. Scott's lawsuit was based on the fact that, having lived in the proslavery state of Missouri, Sanford took Scott to Illinois and Wisconsin, states where slavery was illegal. After his master's death, antislavery lawyers helped Scott file his lawsuit. The suit basically said that Scott was a free man. However, the US Supreme Court ruled against Scott with Chief Justice Roger B. Taney saying that Africans, whether enslaved or free, "had no rights which the white man was bound to respect."

▲ Dr. Choh Hao Li, a research associate and lecturer at the University of California, Berkeley, collaborated with the director of the Institute of Experimental Biology, Dr. Herbert M. Evans, to isolate the growth hormone in its pure form in 1944. Dr. Li, a graduate of China's Nanking University, came to the US in 1935. He claimed that the hormone has been tested on rats with some success and held hope that it could have a positive effect on the growth of human dwarfs. Dr. Li was also credited with purifying and isolating three other hormones produced by the pituitary gland.

**M A R C H**

◆ On this day in 1911, the US sent 20,000 troops to the Mexican border to protect US interests. A rebellion against Porfirio Diáz was spreading rapidly. Many rebel leaders were in the area of Chihuahua, across the Rio Grande from Texas and New Mexico. Diáz had even imprisoned Madero, a leader of the reform movement. The rebellion began when Madero fled to Texas and declared himself provisional president, urging the Mexican people to revolt.

■ During this week in 1991, the new Museum of the American Indian of the Smithsonian Institution announced that it had adopted a policy to return certain artifacts to Native Americans, including ceremonial and religious objects and objects that had been obtained illegally by the museum. The return policy of the museum was brought on in part by protests from a variety of Native American groups.

◆ Mary Foley Bitterman took office as the director of the Voice of America in 1980. Bitterman, who succeeded R. Peter Strauss, was the first woman to hold the position.

● The Messiah Baptist Church was founded in Brooklyn, New York, in 1965 by Reverend Elijah Pope. The dedication service of the church was presided over by Sandy F. Ray of the Cornerstone Baptist Church of Brooklyn.

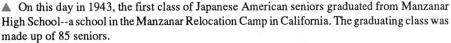

**8**

**M A R C H**

**International Woman's Day.**

▲ On this day in 1943, the first class of Japanese American seniors graduated from Manzanar High School--a school in the Manzanar Relocation Camp in California. The graduating class was made up of 85 seniors.

◆ President Franklin Delano Roosevelt appointed a committee in 1943 to reform the government of Puerto Rico. The committee was made up of Secretary Harold Ickes, Father Raymond A. McGowan, Senator Luis Munoz Marin, Abe Forbes, Martin Travieso and Jose Ramirez-Santibanez.

■ On this day in 1782, Glikhikan, a Delaware warrior, was killed and scalped by European Americans at Gnadenhuetten, near present-day Ohio. Glikhikan tried to win back members of his tribe who had been "Christianized" by whites. In 1769, he challenged to a debate the Moravian missionaries who had converted his peoples, but lost when he, too, was converted.

◆ The Hall of Fame of Great Americans was established in this month in 1900 by Henry Mitchell MacCracken at New York University. MacCracken was a former chancellor of the university.

● Phyllis Mae Daley, a registered nurse from New York City, became the first African American nurse to serve in the Navy Reserve Nurse Corp. Daley was sworn in as an ensign on this date in 1945.

## 9 MARCH

▲ The staff of the first Japanese embassy to a foreign power, led by Niimi Masoka, reached San Francisco on this day in 1860. The staff reached its final destination, Washington, DC, on April 25th but remained there for a period of only six weeks.

◆ Following the resignation of EPA (Environmental Protection Agency) administrator Anne McGill Burford in 1983, President Reagan named John Hernandez, the EPA's deputy administrator, as acting administrator of the agency. The appointment of Hernandez to the head EPA position was to remain in effect until a permanent nominee to the post could be selected by the president.

■ Actor-activist Jane Fonda and 13 Native Americans were arrested in this week in 1970 in Fort Lewis, near Seattle, Washington. The Native Americans were attempting to take over an area army post and turn it into a Native American cultural center.

❖ During this week in 1942, Dr. Frederick Arthur Willius and Librarian Thomas Edward Keys of the Mayo Clinic published the findings of their study of the health of George Washington, first president of the United States. According to their studies, George Washington suffered from a wide variety of illnesses during his lifetime. Among these illnesses were smallpox, dysentary, diptheria, pneumonia, malaria and rheumatism. Washington also suffered from some less-serious afflictions. Among these were a carbuncle, headaches, bad eyesight, the flu and tooth decay.

● African American inventor W. H. Jackson was granted patent #593,665 for a railway switch in 1877. Jackson received a second patent for another railway switch one week later.

## 10 MARCH

▲ Gerald Tsai, Jr., who came to be known as one of the top money managers on Wall Street, emigrated to the US from China on this day in 1928.

◆ General Fulgencio Batista seized power in Cuba on this day in 1952 when a coup under his direction ousted the government of President Carlos Prio Socarras. The coup was similar to that which had brought Socarras into power in 1933.

■ McGraw-Hill, Inc., in 1972 agreed to pay the estate of former Superintendent of the Pine Ridge reservation James H. McGregor after discovering that a book published by the company was not the original document it had been claimed to be. The agreement was based on the discovery that the 1971 McGraw-Hill title, *The Memoirs of Red Fox*, by William Red Fox, had been based largely on the 1940 book *The Wounded Knee Massacre: From the Viewpoint of the Sioux*, which had been published by another company.

❖ Alexander Graham Bell secured his place in history on this day in 1876. Bell transmitted the first clear telephone message to his assistant, Thomas A. Watson. Bell's words to Watson were, "Come here, Watson. I want you."

● During this month in 1961, Dollie Lowther Robinson became the first African American to be named assistant director of the Women's Bureau. Robinson held a degree in law from New York University Law School.

---

▲ In 1915 the Korean newspaper *The New Korea* was printed on an Intertype machine. The machine was invented by Korean Yi Dae-wi.

◆ During the 1972 school year, Herman La Fontaine was appointed to serve as director of the recently created New York City Board of Bilingual Education. The office, which functions under the auspices of the Bilingual Commission of the New York State Board of Education, was created to address the needs of the non-English-speaking children, most of whom were Puerto Rican, attending New York's public schools.

**M A R C H**

■ Robert Burnette and Henry Crow Dog of the Rosebud Sioux Nation of Mission, South Dakota, announced the formation of the Indian Civil Rights Council. The announcement was made in Washington, DC, in 1967. Burnette declared that the council would use the tactics of the "Negro" civil rights movement, including demonstrations.

◆ Around this day in 1961, Elizabeth Gurley Flynn became the first woman to chair the National Committee of the American Communist Party. She remained at the top of that organization until her death, in Moscow, in 1964. In addition to her activities with the Communist party, Flynn was a founding member of the American Civil Liberties Union (ACLU) in 1920, a columnist for *The Daily Worker* and in 1955 author of *I Speak My Own Piece: Autobiography of the Rebel Girl*.

> **"The American Indians have no constitutional or civil rights."**
>
> Robert Burnette and Crow Dog, 1967

● The play *A Raisin in the Sun* opened to a favorable review on Broadway in New York City in 1959. The play by Lorraine Hansberry described the challenges confronting an African American family from the inner city who, having lived in the slums, tried to improve their lives by leaving the city for a suburban area in the US.

 ▲ Chiang Kai-shek succeeded Sun Yat-sen as the leader of the Kuomintang, or People's party, on this day in 1925. Sun Yat-sen, known as the "Father of the Republic," died on this same day of cancer, presenting the need for a new leader. Chiang, who was trained in military affairs in Japan, had previously served as an aide to Sun Yat-sen.

**M A R C H** ◆ The University of Puerto Rico was established on this day in 1903. The university was established by an act of the Puerto Rican legislature. Enrollment at the prestigious school was about 36,000 students in 1992.

■ The Bureau of Indian Affairs (BIA) was organized during this month by the Confederate government in 1861. General Albert Pike of Arkansas was appointed head of the BIA

◆ President Franklin Delano Roosevelt, who had taken office only eight days before in 1933, introduced a new feature to US life when he broadcast the first of his "fireside chats." Speaking on the radio from the White House, the president explained informally to the nation how the reopening of the country's banks would be accomplished.

● Sidney Poitier received the *American Film Institute's Life Achievement Award* in a Hollywood ceremony in 1992. Poitier became the first African American entertainer to receive the honor. The honor is considered to be one of the highest in the film industry.

▲ The Board of Education of San Francisco, California, rescinded its order that students of Korean, Japanese and Chinese descent be segregated in Oriental schools after receiving criticism from the White House in 1907. However, the board also made three resolutions to allow segregation of Asians if (1) after examination of the student's educational qualifications, the principal of the school deemed segregation to be necessary; (2) Asian students had language deficiencies in English; (3) Asian students did not meet school age qualifications. The resolution stated that Asian students not meeting these requirements could be segregated in special classes or schools.

**13**

**M A R C H**

◆ Dr. Luis Alvarez of the University of California was named the recipient of the 1961 *Albert Einstein Award* for his contributions to physical theory and the development of the ground-control-approach blind-landing system for airplanes during the 1940s. Seven years later, Dr. Alvarez was awarded the *Nobel Prize in Physics* (*see December 10th*).

■ Following a conference in Omaha, Nebraska, in 1972, Native Americans from urban areas came together to form the National American Indian Council. The group pledged to help Native Americans living in cities and on reservations. A 20-member volunteer group was chosen to build the structure of the council and its objectives. John Folster, a Sioux from Oakland, California, headed this group. The establishment of a health-care council with income and educational improvements were some of the council's long-term goals.

❖ During this week in 1945, Governor Thomas E. Dewey of New York signed a bill setting up a commission for the elimination of discrimination in employment. This was the first such commission in the United States.

● Jean Baptiste DuSable, a French-speaking African pioneer, erected the first structure around 1773 on the site that would later become the city of Chicago. Because DuSable was a trapper and trader, the structure he built was probably a trading post. In 1992, the city of Chicago had a high school and a museum named in honor of DuSable. The school is predominantly African American.

**14**

**M A R C H**

▲ ◆ ● At the fifth annual Tidewater Conference of Republicans in Easton, Maryland, in 1982, Republican party members agreed to draft separate resolutions with the same wording for economic programs dealing with Asian Americans, Hispanic Americans and African Americans. The "separate but equal" resolutions for each group resulted from the perceived slighting of Asian American and Hispanic American needs in comparison to African Americans.

■ About this day in 1697, Mrs. Hannah Dustin, her week-old baby and the nurse who cared for the child were taken prisoner by a party of Abnaki. In the same raid, an additional group of whites, most of whom were women and children, also were kidnapped. About two weeks later, Dustin became a heroine when she escaped with several others who had been captured. The event marks one of the earlier conflicts between European Americans and Native Americans.

❖ In 1891, the lynching of 14 Sicilian immigrants who had been indicted for the murder of an Irish police chief in New Orleans caused an international crisis. The incident served to restrain immigration.

● In honor of the annual celebration of Negro Newspaper Week in 1953, the National Newspaper Publishers Association, an African American newspaper organization, announced the winners of the annual *John B. Russwurm Awards*. Ralph Ellison was among the winners for his book *The Invisible Man* which "shed new light on the American problem of racism." The *Russwurm Awards* honor outstanding achievements to "democratic principles" and give tribute to "upholding those highest traditions considered as the ideals of the American way of life."

▲ During this month in 1971, a quarterly publication entitled *Amerasia Journal* was started by the Asian American Students Association at Yale University. The *Amerasia Journal* was the only publication dedicated exclusively to Asian American history, as well as to contemporary issues and problems facing Asian Americans and their communities.

**M A R C H**

◆ Columbus returned to Spain on this day in 1493. After more than seven months, he arrived in Palos, Spain, along with his crew, natives (whom Columbus dubbed "Indians") from the lands he had visited, gold and other treasures. Upon his return, King Ferdinand and Queen Isabella gave Columbus many honors, including the titles of admiral of the ocean, viceroy and governor of the newly discovered territories.

■ A lawsuit filed by Native Americans of the Penobscot tribe in Maine was settled in 1980 when the tribe agreed to accept monies in the sum of $81.5 million. The tribe claimed that land had been taken from them in violation of the *Indian Non-Intercourse Act* of 1790.

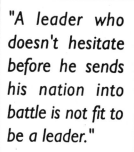

"A leader who doesn't hesitate before he sends his nation into battle is not fit to be a leader."

Golda Meir, 1967

◆ During this week in 1969, US-born Golda Meir was sworn in as the fourth prime minister and first female prime minister of Israel. Twenty-one years earlier, Meir had been one of the signers of Israel's Declaration of Independence. She was the only signatory to have emigrated to Israel from the United States. In the 1930s, Meir was active in the World Zionist Congress and campaigned in both Europe and the United States for the formation of the state of Israel.

● In 1933, the NAACP made its first attempt to stop segregation and discrimination in education via the legal system. On behalf of an African American student named Hocult, the NAACP filed a suit against the University of North Carolina.

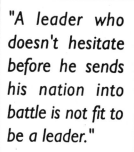

▲ US Marines defeated Japanese soldiers at Iwo Jima on this day in 1945. This battle became one of the most well known in World War II. A famous statue of US soldiers raising the US flag on the island commemorates this victory.

◆ In Hialeah Gardens, Florida, Gilda Oliveros was sworn in as mayor (1989). At the time of her swearing-in ceremony, Oliveros was the first Cuban American female to be elected mayor of a city in the United States.

**M A R C H**

◆ A bill introduced in the New York State legislature in 1976 by State Assemblyman Joseph Lisa sought to authorize the state to return ceremonial wampum (money) belts that ranged in age from 80 to 400 years to the Six Nations of the Iroquois Confederation.

● A repeat of a one-day protest earlier in the year (February 3, 1964) was held on this day in 1964. In the one-day protest, about 450,000 New York City school students absented themselves from school to show their support against *de facto* segregation in the schools.

▲ Architect Ieoh Ming Pei received the *Brunner Award for Architecture* from the National Institute of Arts and Letters in 1961. The award was given to Pei because of his design of concrete apartment towers built in Washington Square East in Philadelphia, Pennsylvania.

M A R C H

◆ The League of United Latin American Citizens declared its concern over the Simpson-Mazzoli Immigration Bill that was introduced in the Senate on this day in 1982. One of the provisions of the bill called for the imposition of $1,000 and $2,000 fines on employers who hired illegal aliens. The organization opposed the bill for fear that employers would cease to hire "Hispanic-looking" people in case they were illegal aliens.

**St. Patrick's Day
Ireland**

■ On this day in 1876, Colonel Joseph Reynolds attacked a Native American village in the Powder River Valley. The surprised Native Americans of Cheyenne and Oglala descent counter-attacked, forcing the US soldiers to withdraw.

❖ In celebration of the traditions of their homeland, Irish Americans nationwide celebrate St. Patrick's Day. The traditional celebration includes parades and the wearing of green by Irish Americans throughout the country. In New York City, the annual celebration is marked with a parade down Fifth Avenue. In 1989, a 229-year tradition was broken when Dorothy Hayden Cudahy became the first woman to serve as Grand Marshal of the parade.

● In 1865, the Navy's Medal of Honor was awarded to Aaron Anderson for his brave actions aboard the *USS Wyandank* during the Civil War.

▲ Japanese architect Kenzo Tange was awarded the $100,000 *Pritzker Architecture Prize* at a ceremony held at the Museum of Modern Art in New York City in 1987. Tange, the ninth person to receive the award, designed buildings in Europe, the Middle East and Japan.

M A R C H

◆ During this week in 1966, Teodoro Moscoso, a leading Puerto Rican economist and former ambassador to the US, was appointed as special consultant on Puerto Rican community affairs and economic development in New York City. The appointment was made by Mayor John Lindsay. Moscoso was to use his abilities to look into better job, housing and educational opportunities for the city's 730,000 Puerto Rican citizens. Moscoso accepted the position without pay.

■ A Native American uprising took place on this day in Jamestown, Virginia, in 1644. The uprising, led by the Powhatan Opechancanough, was suppressed. Eventually, a treaty was made between the Native Americans and the white immigrants. The treaty called for Native Americans to give up more land to the Jamestown territory and for peace between the two groups. The peace called for in the treaty lasted until 1675.

❖ The first Young Men's Hebrew Association (YMHA) in the United States was founded in New York City in 1874. The first president of this organization was Lewis May.

● William Henry Hastie received the *Springarn Award* of the National Association for the Advancement of Colored People (NAACP) as the outstanding American Negro in 1942. Hastie, a former federal judge and dean of Howard University Law School, accused the Army Air Force of "reactionary policies against Negroes." In 1946, President Harry Truman appointed Hastie governor of the US Virgin Islands.

▲ On this day in 1942, Public Law No. 503 passed both houses of Congress by unanimous voice vote making it a federal offense to violate all restrictions made by the military within a military area. The purpose of this law was to give credence and legal clout to Executive Order 9066 which called for the removal of Japanese aliens and US-born Japanese to internment camps.

◆ In its 25th year in 1953, the American Academy of Motion Picture Arts and Sciences presented Mexican American actor Anthony Quinn with an Oscar in the Best Supporting Actor category. Quinn won the Oscar for his performance in the film *Viva Zapata* portraying the wild and dissolute brother of Mexican rebel, Emiliano Zapata.

**St. Joseph's Day**
Columbia, Costa Rica,
Spain, Italy

■ During this week in 1966, Robert L. Bennett of the Seneca Nation was named commissioner of the Bureau of Indian Affairs (BIA). Bennett became only the second person of Native American descent to hold the post since 1870.

❖ During this week in 1949, architect Frank Lloyd Wright won the American Institute of Architects (AIA) *Gold Medal Award.* One structure Wright is well known for is the Guggenheim Museum in New York City.

● The New Negro Theater was founded in Los Angeles, California, in 1939 by Langston Hughes. *Don't You Want to be Free* by Langston Hughes was the first play produced at the theater.

M A R C H

▲ The spiritual leader of Buddhist Tibetans, the Dalai Lama, was reported missing on this day in 1959. Rumors suggested that the Dalai Lama might have been arrested by the Chinese forces occupying Tibet at the time. Most people, however, believed that the Dalai Lama had escaped to India to seek political asylum.

◆ Spanish-born singer and Metropolitan Opera star Lucrezia Bori made her final appearance in *La Rondine* at the Metropolitan Opera in New York City during this week in 1928.

■ During this week in 1889, President Benjamin Harrison opened the former Native American Territory of Oklahoma to "settlement" by European Americans, further reducing Native American land.

❖ Jane "Jennie June" Cunningham Croly served as the recording secretary for the General Federation of Women's Clubs which was organized at Madison Square Garden in New York City on this day in 1890. Croly previously served as vice president of Sorosis, the first women's professional club, which she founded in 1868.

● Jan E. Matzelinger, a native of Dutch Guiana, received a patent for his shoe-lasting machine in 1883. As an apprentice cobbler in Philadelphia, Pennsylvania and Lynn, Massachusetts, Matzelinger worked creatively with shoes. His machine reduced the cost of manufacturing shoes by 50 percent. After receiving his patent, he sold his machine to the United Shoe Machinery Company of Boston.

*The Dalai Lama*

▲ The Korean Resident Association was created in Hawaii on this day in 1921. Nineteen years later on the same day, Asian Americans representing the Japanese American Citizens League (JACL) met with army officials and US Intelligence Services to pledge their loyalty and cooperation to the United States.

◆ Mexican Americans celebrate the birthday of Benito Juarez. Juarez served in the Mexican House of Representatives, as president of the Supreme Court of Justice, and later as president of Mexico (1858). He was born in 1806.

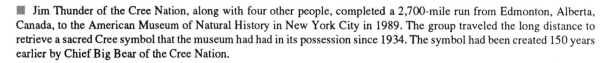

**21**

**M** A R c **H**

■ Jim Thunder of the Cree Nation, along with four other people, completed a 2,700-mile run from Edmonton, Alberta, Canada, to the American Museum of Natural History in New York City in 1989. The group traveled the long distance to retrieve a sacred Cree symbol that the museum had had in its possession since 1934. The symbol had been created 150 years earlier by Chief Big Bear of the Cree Nation.

✤ Svetlana Alliluyeva, the daughter of former Soviet leader Joseph Stalin, defected from the USSR and arrived in New York City in 1967. She defected to the US to "seek self-expression denied ... in Russia."

● African American inventors Latimer and Tregonin received a patent for a globe support for electric lamps in 1882. This was one of two patents received by the inventor team. Latimer is also the sole inventor and holder of three other patents.

**22**

**M** A R c **H**

▲ During this week in 1934, President Franklin Delano Roosevelt signed the Tydings-McDuffie Act. The act prohibited the emigration of Filipinos to the United States. It also promised political independence to the Philippine Islands ten years after the passage of the bill.

◆ Violence erupted during a Puerto Rican nationalist parade held in this week in 1937. The event, which came to be called the *Ponce Massacre*, resulted in 100 people being injured and 19 deaths.

■ In 1621, Massasoit, the chief of the Wampanoags, who lived in the Massachusetts and Rhode Island region, concluded a treaty with the Pilgrims. This treaty was the first in which land was given freely by Native Americans to European immigrants. On this same date one year later, the first reported massacre of white settlers by Native Americans occurred in Jamestown, Virginia. The massacre reportedly resulted in the deaths of 347 people, one-third of the entire colony.

✤ *The New York Times* reported the wedding of Czechoslavakian Olympic discus thrower Olga Fikotova and United States gold medalist Harold Connolly in 1957. Fikotova later became a US citizen and went on to qualify as a member of the US Olympic team. She continued to compete for the US in the next three Olympics.

● A civil rights delegation, led by African American labor leader A. Philip Randolph, visited President Truman in 1948. Randolph, founder and president of the largest African American labor union of that time, the Brotherhood of Sleeping Car Porters, went to discuss US defense policy as it related to African American civil rights.

"American Negroes will not shoulder a gun to fight for democracy abroad unless they get democracy at home.

A. Philip Randolph, 1948

▲ In 1942, General DeWitt issued Civilian Exclusion Order # 1, calling for the removal of persons of Japanese ancestry from Bainbridge Island, Washington.

◆ Arabella Martinez was confirmed as assistant secretary for human development under Health, Education and Welfare (HEW) Secretary Joseph Califano in 1977. Prior to her appointment with HEW, Martinez served as executive director of the Spanish-Speaking Unity Council of Oakland, California (1969-1974). She also was a social worker in the Spanish-speaking community.

■ In 1970, the first Convocation of American Indian Scholars met at the Woodrow Wilson School of Princeton University in New Jersey. The meeting was held from the 23rd to the 26th, and was chaired by San Juan Pueblo, Dr. Alfonso Ortiz.

◆ Patrick Henry delivered a speech before the Virginia Provincial Convention in 1775 and uttered his immortal words, "Give me liberty or give me death." Henry was proposing the arming of the Virginia militia to defend the colonies against England. Henry also served as governor of Virginia, a delegate to the First Continental Congress and commander-in-chief of Virginia's military forces. A great orator, Henry made another famous speech in 1765 against the British-imposed Stamp Act.

● African American inventor W.H. Phelps was awarded patent #579,242 for an apparatus for washing vehicles in 1897.

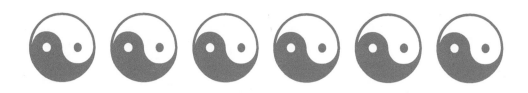

▲ The March 24, 1923, issue of the magazine, *Time*, reported that the number of aliens being smuggled into the US was increasing dramatically. The magazine cited that the aliens, many of whom were from China, were entering the country by posing as ship's crew members.

◆ Mexican golf pro Chi Chi Rodriguez won the *Vintage Arco International* in Palm Springs, California, in 1991. Rodriguez, with a final score of 206 (ten under par), won the tournament by two strokes.

M A R C H

■ Referring to Native Americans in the new Virginia "colony," King James I of England in 1617 required Anglican clergy to collect money for the "erecting of some churches and schools for ye education of ye children of these Barbarians in Virginia." A year later, 10,000 acres of land were set aside in the Virginia "colony" for the education of Native American boys.

◆ On this day in 1958, music superstar Elvis Presley, later called "The King," made national headlines when he traded his guitar for olive drab and a rifle. Presley, who was drafted into the US Army, reported to Local Draft Board 86 in Memphis, Tennessee. Said Presley of his future military service, "I'm looking forward to serving in the Army. I think it will be a great experience for me."

● The antislavery novel, *Uncle Tom's Cabin*, by Harriet Beecher Stowe was published in two volumes in 1852. The book analyzed the issue of slavery during the days of the Fugitive Slave Law (1850s) and portrayed the horror of enslaved people in an emotional, melodramatic and sentimental style. The book further drove a wedge between the free North and the slave-holding Southern states, causing Stowe's name to be cursed in the South. Some of the more famous characters in the book include Uncle Tom, Topsy, Little Eva and Simon Legree. During its first year of publication, the book sold more than 300,000 copies. Stowe became very popular with abolitionist organizations in the US and England.

▲ In 1985 in Los Angeles, California, Dr. Haing S. Ngor was awarded an Oscar for Best Supporting Actor in the movie *The Killing Fields*. With the award, Dr. Ngor achieved two firsts: he was the first person to win an Oscar for a first acting performance and the first Cambodian actor to win an Academy Award. In the movie, Ngor played the role of Cambodian journalist Dith Pran, who developed a friendship with a US journalist amid the death and destruction in war-torn Cambodia.

◆ The play *Zoot Suit* opened on Broadway in 1979. Written and directed by Luis Valdez, the play was the first written by a Mexican American to open on Broadway. The play was based on a real-life incident, the "Sleepy Lagoon" murder case in 1942.

*Whoopi Goldberg*

■ In 1899, the Colonial Dames of America in Savannah, Georgia, erected a monument in memory of Tomochichi. Tomochichi was a renown Creek chief who helped establish the Georgia colony.

❖ Italian American civil rights volunteer Viola Gregg Liuzzo was killed by members of the Klu Klux Klan (KKK) while transporting participants of the Selma-to-Montgomery civil rights march of 1965.

● In 1991, actor Whoopi Goldberg became the second African American woman to win an Oscar. Goldberg won the Oscar in the Best Supporting Actress category for her performance in *Ghost*. The first African American woman to win the same award was Hattie McDaniel, who won the award in 1939 for her performance in *Gone With the Wind*.

**Fiesta del Arbol,**
**(Arbor Day)**
**Spain**

▲ Today marks the last day of the first Filipino National Conference. The three-day conference was held in Sacramento, California, in 1938.

◆ President Reagan awarded Dr. Hector Perez Garcia the *Presidential Medal of Freedom* in 1984 for his work in protecting the rights of Hispanics in the United States. A World War II veteran and recipient of the *Bronze Star*, Garcia saw and experienced the problems facing Hispanic veterans returning home from war and Hispanics in general, when he returned to his home in Corpus Christi, Texas. To alleviate these problems, he founded the American GI Forum in 1946, which sought, through grass-roots politics, to get better medical care for Hispanic veterans, better living conditions and schools for Hispanic families.

■ Washington Matthews, a Navaho, first recorded sand paintings and songs of the Navaho in 1885. These were published in an ethnological report during that year.

❖ Poet Robert Frost was born in 1874 in San Francisco, California. He won the *Pulitzer Prize for Poetry* four times and was given a gold medal by Congress in 1960 as a tribute to his life's work, including poems such as "Mending Wall," "Stopping by Woods on a Snowy Evening" and "The Witch of Coos." In 1961, Frost read his poem, "The Gift Outright," at the inauguration of President John F. Kennedy.

● On this day, a patent was awarded to J. Hawkins for a gridiron in 1845, and William H. Hastie was confirmed as a federal district court judge for the Virgin Islands in 1937.

▲ In the case of *Hawaii v Consumer Product Safety Commission,* the US Supreme Court in 1943 refused to review a lower court decision and upheld the ban on the sale of firecrackers that had more than 50 mg of explosive. The Consumer Product Safety Commission put the ban into effect as a safety precaution; however, Chinese Americans opposed the ban, claiming that more powerful firecrackers were needed for their cultural and religious celebrations.

◆ The exhibition *Mexican Painting Today* was shown at the Philadelphia Museum of Art in 1943, featuring artists Alfara Siqueiros and Rufino Tamayo.

■ When Native American Javier Pereira died at Montaria, Colombia, in 1956, he was believed to be the world's oldest man. The four-foot-four Pereira claimed to be 168 years old. Experts said there was no way to verify or refute Pereira's claim.

❖ The American Academy of Arts and Letters announced that its *Award of Merit* and its $1,000 prize would go to Theodore Dreiser in 1944.

● Arthur Mitchell, founder of the Dance Theater of Harlem, was born in New York City in 1934. Mitchell joined the New York City Ballet Company in 1957. The following year, the company's choreographer, George Balanchine, created a special role for Mitchell in the ballet, *Agon,* thereby making him the first great African American classical dancer in the United States. Mitchell taught ballet and opened the Dance Theater of Harlem in 1968.

## 27 MARCH

## 28 MARCH

▲ The Chinese Woman's Association was organized during this week in New York City in 1932. In 1936, it became the first Chinese American women's club to incorporate. Theodora Chang Wang served as the organization's first president.

◆ Slightly more than one year after an accident in which her back was broken, singer Gloria Estefan was not only on her way to a complete recovery, but also had a best-selling single called *Coming Out of the Dark* on this day in 1991 (as reported by *Billboard* magazine).

> "Starting again is part of the plan. I'll be much stronger, holding your hand. Day by day I'll make it through, I know I can."
>
> "Coming Out of the Dark,"
> Written by Gloria and Emile Estefan,
> 1991

■ Phillip J. Stevens of Irvine, California, was named a special chief of the Rosebud Sioux Nation in Mission, South Dakota, in 1988. Stevens, a businessman, and great-grandson of Sioux warrior and chief, Standing Bear, pledged to help unite the Sioux Nation and retrieve land lost to whites after gold was discovered on it.

❖ In 1834, 234 Polish immigrants arrived in New York Harbor. The Poles, who were exiled from Austria following uprisings there, formed the Polish Committee in America while en route to their new home. The committee was the first Polish American organization in the United States.

● African American poet Countee Cullen received an honorary *Phi Beta Kappa key* from New York University in 1925. The "key" is given only to those college students who have displayed the highest academic achievement. Cullen was a well-known US poet. His first volume of poems, entitled *Color,* was published in 1925. *The Ballad of the Brown Girl* and *Copper Sun* as well as the anthology *Carding Dusk* were published in 1927.

**29**

M A R C **H**

**Youth and Martyr's Day**
Taiwan

"This means more to me than an honor to an actor. I consider it a vote of confidence and an act of faith, and believe me, I'll not let you down."

José Ferrer,
Academy Award acceptance speech,
1951

▲ In 1987, *The Last Emperor,* a historic epic movie dealing with the time leading up to and during the communist takeover of China, won 9 *Academy Awards,* including *Best Picture of the Year.*

◆ José Ferrer, a Puerto Rican American actor, won the *Academy Award* in the Best Actor category for the title role in the movie *Cyrano de Bergerac* in 1951.

■ PFC Joseph Michael Mermejo of the Picuris Pueblo, New Mexico, was killed near Que Nam in 1969. Mermejo became the first member of his pueblo to be killed in action during the Vietnam War.

❖ The first Swedish expedition to the "New World" landed in New Castle County, Delaware, on this day in 1638. Peter Minuit, formerly of New Netherland, headed the expedition. Today, the site of the landing is marked by Fort Christina.

● During this week in 1966, Bill Russell was named head coach of the Boston Celtics, a National Basketball Association team. He was the first African American to be named an NBA coach.

**30**

M A R C **H**

▲ The California Legislature passed an act to provide for the protection of foreigners and to define their liabilities and privileges in 1853. The act caused taxes to be imposed on foreign miners. This, together with the discovery of gold in Australia, reduced the number of Chinese emigrants to the United States.

◆ At a Holiday Inn in San Jose, California, the first annual National Hispanic Feminist Conference got underway in 1980. Issues discussed included discrimination in employment and education, support for families and community and support for the proposed Equal Rights Amendment. The conference was funded by the Women's Educational Equity Act program of the US Federal Office of Education.

■ On this day in 1967, the US Post Office issued an air-mail stamp commemorating the purchase of the state of Alaska. The stamp featured line art of a totem, a symbol in many Native American cultures.

❖ Joan M. Davenport was appointed to serve as assistant secretary for energy and minerals by President Carter in 1977. Before working in this position, Davenport had the distinction of being the first woman to serve as assistant secretary of the Interior.

● In 1886, African American inventor J. Ricke was granted a patent for his invention, an improved version of the horseshoe. Ricke also holds the patent for an overshoe for horses.

▲ In 1854, the *Treaty of Kanagawa* was signed by Commodore Matthew C. Perry of the United States and the government of Japan. The United States was permitted to have a consulate in Japan and US ships were permitted into Japanese ports for limited trade.

◆ Sometime in 1963, social worker Augustino Gonzales created the Puerto Rican Family Institute. With the help of volunteers, the institute, which operated in New York City, had as its goal assistance to Puerto Rican families that had recently emigrated to New York. The families were to be assisted in acquiring the skills needed to cope with the problems of setting up life in New York City.

■ People born between March 21 and April 19 have the red hawk as their totem, according to Sun Bear's Earth Astrology.

◆ Mabel Gilmore Reinike worked her last day on the job as a collector for the Internal Revenue Service in the First District of Illinois in 1929. Reinike, who was appointed to the position by President Harding, was the first female to serve as an IRS collector.

● Novelist Toni Morrison was awarded the *Pulitzer Prize in Fiction* in 1988 for her fifth novel, *Beloved*. The novel is set in post-Civil War Ohio, Morrison's home state. The subject is a freed African woman dealing with the painful life of enslavement she has known. When *Beloved* failed to win the *National Book Award* in the fall of 1987, 48 African American writers wrote an open letter to *The New York Times Book Review* in protest.

**31**

M A R C H

"But my daddy said, 'if you can't count, they can cheat you. If you can't read, they can beat you.' "

Toni Morrison,
*Beloved,*
1987

# MY PERSONAL LIST

On the 26th of this month in 1979, a nationwide boycott of iceberg lettuce was called by the United Farm Workers of America (UFWA). The leader of the boycott and the union was César Chávez. Chávez, of Mexican heritage, had been active in the concerns of migrant farm workers in the US, many of whom were Mexicans working in the West and Midwest.

Chávez knew from firsthand experience that life as a migrant farm worker was hard. Living conditions were often overcrowded, dirty and without electricity or running water. Moving from field to field made it difficult to go to school.

In 1944, at the age of 17, Chávez joined the navy. When his tour of duty was over, he returned to California and resumed his work in the fields. This time however, his goal was to help his people. Chávez taught many of his fellow workers to read and write so that they could pass the US citizenship test and become voters. Chávez later took a job with a local farm-worker advocacy group.

In 1962, Chávez began the task of organizing the farm workers into a union. During the sixties and seventies, Chávez organized strikes. He led national boycotts of crops such as grapes and lettuce. Chávez went without solid food for days at a time to protest the violence that would sometimes erupt between the growers and the pickers. After 1985, the California labor laws were changed to be more favorable to the workers. Chávez and his union continued to work for better treatment of farm workers and for fair contracts between the growers and the workers. At his funeral in 1993, among the thousands who came to pay tribute to César Chávez were many dignitaries who took turns every few minutes to bear his coffin as a sign of their deep respect for him and his life's work.

> "Fighting for social justice...is one of the profoundest ways in which man can say yes to man's dignity, and that really means sacrifice."
>
> César Chávez,
> April 1979

◀ *César Chávez*

◆ During this month in 1959, the New York City Board of Education published *The Puerto Rican Study*. The document included information collected through a four-year study (1953-1957) about teaching English as a Second Language (ESL) to Puerto Rican students. It also identified teaching methods and techniques that were thought to promote more expedient and effective transition of Puerto Rican parents and children into the community.

■ One of the first treaties between whites and Native Americans was made on this day in 1621 at what is now Strawberry Hill in Plymouth, Massachusetts. The treaty was between the war chief of the Wampanoag Massasoit and the Pilgrims. The agreement, a defensive action on the part of the Pilgrims, was honored by both parties for more than half a century.

❖ German American Frederick Augustus Micklenberg began service as speaker of the House in 1789. Micklenberg was the first person to hold this position in the newly formed House of Representatives. Several years later, Micklenberg regained the position and became the third speaker of the House for the United States.

● Bill White, a six-time all-star first baseman who played for the St. Louis Cardinals, the Philadelphia Phillies, and both the New York and San Francisco Giants over a 13-year playing career was elected president of the National League in 1989. White became the first African American to head a major professional American sports league. His election followed a campaign to promote qualified African Americans to leadership positions in sports. The campaign was largely fueled by remarks made by Los Angeles Dodgers's Vice President Al Campanis in 1987 that questioned whether African Americans had the qualifications needed to hold leadership positions in baseball.

▲ Tennis player Michael Chang won the Volvo Chicago tennis tournament in 1990 when he defeated Jim Grabb in two out of three sets.

1 APRIL

2 APRIL

◆ On this day in 1513, Juan Ponce de Leon discovered Florida. The land was claimed by Ponce de Leon for the king of Spain.

■ The allotment of land to be provided to Native Americans under the Dawes Act began with the Creek Nation during this week in 1899.

❖ During this month in 1874, Ann Eliza Young, the last wife of Mormon leader Brigham Young and the only one of his wives to file for divorce from him, held a lecture in Washington, DC, that was attended by many members of Congress as well as President and Mrs. Grant. The topic of the lecture was polygamy, a common practice among Mormons. A few weeks after the lecture, Congress passed the Poland Bill--the first piece of national legislation against polygamy. Several years later, Congress passed a second antipolygamy bill that had even stiffer penalties than the earlier bill.

● Dakar, Senegal, served as the site for the first World Festival of Black Arts. The festival, which is held from the 1st through the 24th of this month, took place in 1966.

▲ In 1986, curators of the New Orleans Museum of Art discovered Chinese manuscripts that dated back to the twelfth century. The rare manuscripts were discovered inside a Buddhist sculpture that had recently been donated to the museum. Estimates indicated that the manuscripts had been hidden inside the sculpture for about 800 years.

◆ On this day in 1971, members of the Chicano political group known as the *La Raza Unida* (The United People) party won seats on the Crystal City, Texas, school board. With the win, Chicanos gained a five-to-two majority on the board.

■ Former AIM activist and leader Russell Means reported that he was seeking the presidential nomination of the Libertarian party in 1987. Means, a member of the Oglala Sioux, lost the nomination on September 5th to former Texas Republican Ron Pearl in a 196-120 vote.

## 3

## A P R I L

◆ In 1979, Jane Byrne was elected as Chicago's first female mayor. Mayor Byrne won the election with the largest majority in a mayoral election since 1901.

● During this week in 1953, the first Phi Beta Kappa chapter to be established at an African American university became active at Fisk University in Nashville, Tennessee.

▲ During this month in 1854, the San Francisco-based newspaper *Kim-Shan Jit San-Luk* (*Gold Hill News*) was published. The newspaper was the first Chinese newspaper to be published in the United States.

## 4

## A P R I L

◆ Henry G. Cisneros beat eight candidates in the mayoral election of San Antonio, Texas, in 1981. Cisneros became the first Mexican American mayor of a major US city. Before being elected mayor, Cisnero served as a member of the San Antonio city council.

■ Lloyd Eagle Bull of the Oglala Sioux addressed a House Subcommittee on Indian Affairs in 1973 regarding the need for jobs for persons living on reservations. The address helped lead to the Indian Economic Development and Employment Act of 1973.

◆ The first female mayor in the United States was Susanna Medora Salter. Without her knowledge, Salter was nominated for the position by the Women's Christian Temperance Union. Salter discovered she was running as mayor when she went to the polls to vote in Argonia, Kansas in 1887.

● The Reverend Dr. Martin Luther King, Jr., was killed in Memphis, Tennessee on this day in 1968. While standing on a balcony at the Lorraine Motel, Dr. King was struck in the neck by a bullet fired by a gunman in an alley. King was in Memphis to join forces with striking sanitation workers as part of his "Poor People's Campaign." In the opinion of some, the Civil Rights Movement, as it was known during the 1960s, ended with King's life.

▲ On this day in 1975, 100 Vietnamese orphans who were being brought to the US as refugees were killed when the US Air Force plane carrying them crashed. This was the first flight in a program that was to bring about 2,000 Vietnamese orphans to the US for adoption by American parents.

> *"I want to tell you that there is nothing more important that you can do for my people than to get a job program for us....Get us jobs and there won't be an Indian problem anymore."*
>
> Lloyd Eagle Bull, Address to Congressional Indian Affairs Committee, 1973

**5**

**A P R I L**

**Arbor Day**
(Korea)

> *"Why do you take by force what you could obtain by love?"*
>
> Chief Powhatan, 1614

◆ In 1898, members of the US Consul in Cuba were recalled by President McKinley. A week later, he requested Congressional authorization to use armed force to end the civil war in Cuba.

■ During this month in 1614, Pocahontas, daughter of Chief Powhatan, married John Rolfe. Rolfe, who came from England, turned tobacco into a cash crop in Virginia. Rolfe later took Pocahontas to England, where she gave birth to a son.

◆ Swimmer Johnny Weismuller set three world records on this day in 1927 when he became the only person to hold every freestyle mark from 100-yards to one-half mile. Weismuller won the 100-meter swimming event at the 1924 Olympics with a record time of 59 seconds. Later, Weismuller became an actor and is best known for his role as "Tarzan of the apes."

● The Macmillan Publishing Company published Floyd McKissick's *Three-Fifths of Man* during this month in 1969. The book was an account of the past, present and future of the African American movement in the United States.

▲ Sadao S. Munemori was posthumously awarded the *Congressional Medal of Honor* in 1945. Munemori served in the US Army in Italy during World War II. While his unit was pinned down by enemy fire near Seravezza, Italy, Private Munemori knocked out two machine guns with grenades. However, when he saw an enemy grenade rolling toward two of his comrades, he threw himself upon the grenade, smothering its blast and saving the lives of his fellow soldiers. This heroic act also made it possible for his unit's victorious advance.

**6**

**A P R I L**

◆ The late sixties and seventies saw increasing political power among Hispanic Americans with the formation of the *LaRaza Unida* party (founded in Crystal City, Texas). On this day in 1971, three seats on the city council were won by LaRaza Unida candidates. This gave the party control of all five council seats. Three days earlier, LaRaza candidates won seats on the school board. This gave the Chicanos a five-to-two majority on the board.

■ This date marks the beginning of the Black Hawk "Indian War" in 1832. Black Hawk, leader of the Sauk Nation, agreed with the US federal government to move his people to what is now Iowa. However, once in Iowa, the Sauk nearly starved due to a lack of fertile growing soil. Black Hawk moved his people back to Illinois to plant a new corn crop and start fresh, but conflicts with whites moving westward arose. Nervous whites killed two Sauk carrying white surrender flags and seeking a conference to ease the tensions. When Black Hawk heard of this, he began to kill whites at random.

◆ Joseph Smith established the Church of Jesus Christ of Latter-Day Saints (the Mormons) in 1830 at Fayette, New York. Smith claimed to have received instructions from an angel named Moroni telling him to receive "golden plates" upon which the history of the people of the Western Hemisphere was written. After receiving and translating the plates, he published them as *The Book of Mormon*. After its first year of existence, the church claimed 1,000 members.

● African American explorer Matthew Henson arrived at the North Pole with Admiral Peary in 1909. This was the first group to reach the North Pole. Accompanying the explorers were 50 Eskimo who helped reach the destination by dogsled from Ellesmere Island. When they arrived, Henson planted the US flag at the North Pole.

▲ The April 6, 1942, issue of *Time* magazine included a feature story about the removal by train of Japanese aliens and Nisei (US-born Japanese) to a detention camp in Manazar, California. In the detention camps, the emigrants earned between $50 and $94 per month working on government projects. From this monthly wage, $15 was deducted for living expenses.

◆ Sailing on behalf of Spain, Portuguese explorer Ferdinand Magellan landed on the island of Cebu in the Philippines on this day in 1521. Magellan formed an alliance with the king of the island and converted him to Christianity.

■ In 1805, with the help of a Shoshone guide named Sacagawea, Lewis and Clark continued their expedition down the Missouri River and across the Rocky Mountains. Sacagawea's husband, Toussant Charbonneau, also traveled with the group. When Lewis and Clark met up with members of the Shoshone Nation, Sacagawea served as an interpreter to help them trade gifts for horses and supplies. During the expedition, Sacagawea gave birth to a son.

◆ German Americans, long opposed to slavery in the US, became outraged when the Kansas-Nebraska Act was passed in 1854. The act permitted people of those territories to be "perfectly free to form and regulate their institutions in their own way," including the enlavement of people. To show their rage, a group of German Americans in Chicago marched down Michigan Avenue on this day in 1854 and burned, in effigy, the author of the Kansas-Nebraska bill, Stephen A. Douglas.

*Sacagawea*

● Lorraine Hansberry became the first African American playwright to win the *New York Drama Critics Award* in 1959 for her play, *A Raisin in the Sun*.

▲ Sgt. Rodney Yano of Hilo, Hawaii, was posthumously awarded the *Congressional Medal of Honor* by President Richard Nixon in 1970. When helicopter crew chief Yano and his men were fired upon, Yano returned fire and marked the enemy's position using phosphorus grenades. A grenade exploded prematurely, burning Yano. Although injured, Yano threw the burning ammunition from the helicopter until the danger had passed.

A P R I L

**Hana Matsuri**
(the flower festival)
Japan

**Buddha's Birthday**
Japan & Korea

◆ Mexican American rights groups ended their 19-year boycott against the Joseph Coors Company in 1977. The boycott was initiated by Mexican Americans to protest job discrimination allegedly practiced against Chicanos by the Coors Company. Part of the reason for the end to the boycott was a promise by Coors to develop economic, education and employment programs that would benefit Mexican Americans.

■ US Army Second Lieutenant Ernest Childers of the 45th Infantry Division was awarded the *Congressional Medal of Honor* in 1944. Lieutenant Childers of the Creek Nation (Oklahoma) received his award "for conspicuous gallantry and intrepidity at risk of life above and beyond the call of duty in action on September 22, 1943, at Oliveto, Italy, during World War II." Despite a fractured instep, Childers advanced up a hill toward enemy machine gun nests with eight soldiers, eventually killing two enemy snipers firing at him. He and the eight comrades then killed all the occupants of the machine-gun placements. Childers then single-handedly captured an enemy mortar observer.

❖ In 1940, the US Post Office issued a stamp commemorating John James Audubon. Audubon was a Haitian American naturalist and artist. He has been honored two other times in stamps issued on December 7, 1963, and on April 26, 1967.

● Henry Aaron of the Atlanta Braves hit the 715th home run of his career in a game against the Los Angeles Dodgers in 1974. With that home run, Aaron became major league baseball's all-time career home-run leader, breaking the record of George Herman "Babe" Ruth of the New York Yankees.

▲ Korean and Japanese Americans celebrate Buddha's birthday.

> *"There's a place for us,*
> *somewhere a place for us."*
>
> Maria and Tony,
> Characters singing lovers' duet
> from *West Side Story*

◆ At the *Academy Awards* presentation in 1962, *West Side Story* was the recipient of many awards. The film dealt with the problems of an Hispanic American and a European American who fell in love. Among those taking awards home from *West Side Story* was Puerto Rican actor Rita Moreno with a *Best Supporting Actress Award* for her role as Anita.

# 9

## A P R I L

■ In 1977 several land claims were made by Native American nations in an attempt to have more internal control of their affairs. One claim made early this month was by the Catawba Nation of South Carolina. The Catawba voted 101-to-2 to ask Congress to help them obtain possession of 144,000 acres of land in York and Lancaster counties, South Carolina, that had been given to them in a 1763 treaty. The Catawba said that failure to receive a "fair and honorable settlement" from Congress would result in a lawsuit against those who were then living on the land.

❖ The US Civil War came to an end in 1865 when Confederate General Robert E. Lee agreed to terms of surrender for his defeated forces. The surrender commenced in Virginia when Lee turned over his sword to Union General Ulysses S. Grant in the Appomattox Court House.

● Coretta Scott King, widow of Dr. Martin Luther King, Jr., was elected to the board of directors of the Southern Christian Leadership Conference (SCLC) in 1968. On the same date, Dr. Ralph D. Abernathy was elected president of the organization.

▲ During this month in 1966, William D. Soo Hoo was elected mayor of Oxnard, California. Hoo is believed to be the first Chinese American to be elected to the position of mayor.

# 10

## A P R I L

◆ Congress passed the Foraker Act in 1900. The act established a civil government for the island of Puerto Rico and introduced free trade with the United States to the region.

■ A stamp honoring the 260th anniversary of the founding of the Province of Carolina along with the 250th anniversary of the original settlement near what is presently Charleston, South Carolina, was issued by the US Postal Service in 1930. The two-cent stamp was designed to show a "friendly" Native American (the original inhabitants of the region) and a colonial governor looking from the beach at two ships anchored in the bay.

❖ American newspaper publishing giant, Joseph Pulitzer, was born in Mako, Hungary, in 1847. After leaving home at the age of 17, Pulitzer tried to become a mercenary soldier but was rejected by three countries. While in Germany, a US Army recruiter enlisted Pulitzer to come to the United States to fight for the Union Army in the Civil War. After the war, Pulitzer settled in St. Louis and became a US citizen. He worked his way up to managing editor and part owner of a St. Louis-based German-language newspaper. After selling his interest in the newspaper, Pulitzer moved to Washington, DC, as a correspondent for the *New York Sun*. In 1877, he bought two newspapers, the *St. Louis Dispatch* and the *Evening Post*, which he merged into the *St. Louis Post-Dispatch* in 1878. Pulitzer used his money to buy *The World* (New York City). This newspaper, too, became a success. The prize which now bears Pulitzer's name was established at Columbia University, a school to whom Pulitzer left $2 million for the development of a School of Journalism.

● While watching the preparations for the attack on Fort Sumter in 1861, Robert Smalls, a Union Navy pilot, described his view of significance of the coming event to the members of his troop. Smalls told the troops, "This, boys, is the dawn of freedom for our race."

▲ A Korean delegation headed by Prime Minister Choi Tu Son attended the funeral services for US war hero General Douglas MacArthur (1964). MacArthur was the supreme commander of the UN forces during the Korean Conflict.

▲ In 1966, 12-year-old Gloria Rodriguez was killed while saving another 12-year-old girl, Julietta Sanchez, from being struck by a moving car. The heroic act took place in Los Angeles, California. The young Rodriguez was later posthumously awarded a *Carnegie Medal* for her heroic actions. The *Carnegie Medal* is awarded to individuals who risk their own lives while trying to save the lives of others.

# A  P R I L

■ During this month in 1808, the first play in the US about a Native American, *The Indian Princess*, was performed at the Chestnut Street Theater in Philadelphia, Pennsylvania. The play was an operatic melodrama written by James Nelson Barber.

◆ The Department of Health, Education and Welfare was established on this date in 1953. Oveta Culp Hobby was sworn in as its first secretary. Hobby became the second woman in US history to become a member of a president's cabinet.

● Roy Wilkins was elected executive secretary of the National Association for the Advancement of Colored People (NAACP) at its New York convention in 1955. He succeeded the late Walter White.

▲ In 1990, President Bush issued an executive order that protected Chinese students studying in the Unites States from being deported back to China when their visas expired. The executive order, which deferred deportation until January 1, 1994, was in response to the Tiananmen Square uprising that took place in 1989 and resulted in the deaths of scores of Chinese student protesters.

◆ Oscar Hijuelos won the 1990 *Pulitzer Prize for Literature* in the fiction category for his novel, *The Mambo Kings Play Songs of Love*. The novel told of the relationship of two Cuban brothers, both musicians, who traveled to New York City in the 1940s.

■ During the spring of 1970, Della Lowe, a dancer at the Stand Rock Ceremonial, organized the formation of a union for Native American ceremonial performers in Wisconsin Dells, Wisconsin. Lowe served on the negotiating committee when the union's first contract was drawn up.

# A  P R I L

◆ On this date in 1945, President Franklin Roosevelt suffered a massive cerebral hemorrhage in Warm Springs, Georgia, and died, ending the longest presidential period ever served, before or since. Vice president Harry S Truman was sworn in as the new president. It was Truman's job to complete the Allied victory in World War II and to decide the use of the atomic bomb to end the war with Japan.

● Emmett Ashford became the first African American to umpire a regular season major league baseball game when he worked an American League game between the Cleveland Indians of Ohio and the Washington Senators in 1966. Ashford was 51 years old when he got his assignment, four years before the mandatory retirement age.

▲ In 1847, the Reverend Samuel Brown, head of the first English school in China, arrived in New York City with three Chinese students whom he enrolled at an academy in Monson, Massachusetts. One of the students, Yung Wing, later earned a bachelor's degree from Yale, becoming the first Chinese college graduate in the United States.

◆ During this week in 1947, a United States appeals court in San Francisco ruled that segregation of Mexican American children in Southern California schools was unconstitutional.

■ The newly organized Citizens party in 1980 chose Comanche LaDonna Harris as their vice-presidential running mate for Barry Commoner. Harris was the wife of former senator Fred Harris of Oklahoma. The convention of the Citizens party was held in Cleveland, Ohio, and boasted an attendance of 500 delegates and alternates.

**13**

**A P R I L**

❖ Ruth Bryan Owen, daughter of three-time presidential candidate William Jennings Bryan, was appointed as US minister to Denmark by President Franklin Delano Roosevelt in 1933. With the appointment, Owen became the first female minister from the US to a foreign country.

● In 1963, Sidney Poitier became the first African American to win the *Academy Award for Best Actor*. Poitier won the award for his role as a handyman in the movie, *Lilies of the Field*.

▲ Japanese American insurance underwriter, Norman Y. Mineta, was elected as mayor of San Jose, California, on this date in 1971. Mineta, who had spent two years in relocation camps during World War II, became the first Japanese American government head of a major United States city located on the mainland.

**14**

**A P R I L**

◆ Franciscan Fray Suarez arrived in Florida on Holy Thursday in 1528. Suarez was the first Catholic bishop of the diocese within the territorial limits of the United States. He was nominated bishop of Florida and Rios de la Palmas by Papal Bull of Julius II.

■ The National Congress of American Indians held an "emergency conference" in Santa Fe, New Mexico, from April 13 -April 15, 1966, coinciding with a meeting of the Bureau of Indian Affairs in the same city. The emergency conference was called because Native Americans were being prohibited from attending the opening session of the BIA conference. As a result of the protests made by Native Americans, the BIA decided to allow a Native American delegation to attend their final session on April 15.

❖ Abraham Lincoln became the first president to be assassinated when he was shot while in the presidential box at Ford's Theater in Washington, DC, in 1865. Lincoln's assassin, a mentally unstable actor and former Confederate soldier named John Wilkes Booth, escaped during the confusion. Only five days earlier, Lincoln had seen the end of the Civil War.

● The Oxford University Press in 1988 published 30 volumes of texts in a series called *The Schomberg Library of Nineteenth-Century Black Women Writers*. The series, which was edited by Henry Louis Gates, Jr., includes biographies of the writers as well as fiction, poetry and essays that serve as examples of their work.

▲ Koreans attended the First Korean Liberty Congress in Philadelphia, Pennsylvania, in 1919. The Congress was organized in order to draw the world's attention to the plight of Koreans still living in Korea.

◆ In 1895, Cuban revolutionaries José Martí and Maximo Gomez arrived in Playitas, Cuba, from the United States to assist Cuba in its fight for independence from Spain. Four days later, Martí and Gomez were killed in battle near Dos Rios.

■ In 1966, Secretary of the Interior Steward Udall announced that legislation would be submitted in one year to bring a "new approach" to the problems facing Native Americans. The plans were to include reorganization of the BIA, a larger voice for Native Americans in managing their affairs, a greater emphasis on education and encouragement of Native Americans to develop their lands and resources.

## A P R I L

◆ In 1912, the *HMS Titanic* struck an iceberg and began to sink during its maiden voyage. Margaret Brown, who came to be known as the "unsinkable Molly Brown," became a heroine as she helped rescue women and children who were aboard the sinking ship. The lifeboat that Brown was in was rescued more than seven hours after the *Titanic* began to sink.

● During this week in 1984, author Louis R. Harlan won a *Pulitzer Prize* for his biography of Booker T. Washington.

▲ During this month in 1950, a group of people were called to testify before the Committee on Un-American Activities of the US House of Representatives. The committee had come to Hawaii to investigate allegations that top leadership positions in the Longshoremen's and Warehousemen's Union were being infiltrated by communists. The committee called a total of 66 people; of these, 39 refused to testify. This group became known as "The Reluctant 39." They were found to be in contempt of Congress but were later acquitted.

◆ Puerto Rican novelist Rita Dove won a *Pulitzer Prize* in 1987 for her work *Beulah and Thomas*.

■ Maria "Maria the Potter" Martinez, a native of the San Ildefonso Pueblo in New Mexico, was honored for her outstanding achievements in the field of pottery in 1954 when she received the *AIA* (American Institute of Architecture) *Craftsmanship Medal*. She was the only Native American to receive an award from the AIA. Martinez was called a "unique craftsman" who "not only revived the ancient forms and skills of their [her] forebears but added to them."

## A P R I L

◆ Former first lady Eleanor Roosevelt was awarded the *Woman of the Year Award* by the Women's National Press Club in 1949 for her work with the United Nations Human Rights Commission. Much of the work done by Roosevelt was on behalf of underprivileged people, especially children living in the United States, Latin America, Africa and Europe. In 1946, Roosevelt was elected to head the Human Rights Commission. At the same time, she maintained her duties as a delegate to the General Assembly.

● In 1869, Ebeneezer Carlos Bennet became the first African American to receive a diplomatic appointment. With his appointment, Bennet became Minister of Haiti.

▲ On the last day of a three day conference held in the 1940s by the Korean Independence movement, the Korean Bureau of Information was established in Philadelphia, Pennsylvania, under the leadership of Syngman Rhee and So Jae-p'il. The goal of this organization was to inform the Western World, particularly the United States, of the victimization of Koreans by their Japanese rulers.

> *"You gain strength, courage, and confidence by every experience in which you really stop to look fear in the face....You must do the thing you think you cannot do."*
>
> Eleanor Roosevelt,
> *You Learn by Living,*
> 1960

◆ Cuban exiles who received military training by the CIA in the United States attacked Cuba in the Bay of Pigs invasion (1961).

■ In a six-to-three decision, the US Supreme Court ruled in 1990 that the government could ban the use of drugs as part of religious rituals. The ruling resulted from a suit filed in Oregon in which Native Americans contended that the ban of the drug, peyote, from their rituals was a violation of their First Amendment freedom-of-religion right. The case originated in Oregon as *Oregon v Smith*.

A P R I L

❖ Italian explorer Giovanni da Verrazano sailed into what is now called New York Harbor on this day in 1524. The Verrazano-Narrows Bridge, a suspension bridge connecting New York's Staten Island with Brooklyn, is named for da Verrazano.

● The first college graduate of African descent in the Western Hemisphere, Francis Williams, became a published poet in 1758. Williams wrote his poems in Latin.

▲ On this day in 1925, the case of *Chan Chang et al v John D. Nagle* began its hearings before the Supreme Court. The case concerned itself with four US citizens of Chinese ancestry who had attempted to bring their wives to the US from China. The women were detained and not allowed to enter the country because they were not US citizens. The Supreme Court ruled in May that the Chinese wives of these US citizens could not become citizens by marriage and, therefore, were not allowed to enter the United States.

◆ A 26-year-old Cuban communist, accused of having collaborated with the Batista regime, was executed by a firing squad in 1964. Marcos Rodriguez was sentenced by a revolutionary tribunal and then by the Cuban Supreme Court.

■ Opechancanough, chief of the Powhatan, was carried into battle in Jamestown on a litter on this day in 1644. He was later captured and killed by one of the men who guarded him. Opechancanough was responsible for Captain John Smith's capture on an earlier occasion.

A P R I L

> "Samuel...reminded us that there is one big advantage we have. We are not white...We are black like the Africans themselves...And that we and the Africans will be working for a common goal, the uplifting of black people everywhere."
>
> Alice Walker,
> *The Color Purple*

❖ Early American patriot and silversmith Paul Revere made his famous ride from Boston to Lexington, Massachusetts, in 1775 to warn patriot forces that the British troops were on their way.

● Alex Haley was awarded a special *Pulitzer Prize* in 1977 for his semi-autobiographical book, *Roots*. The best-selling book told the story of an enslaved African's life in the US and was called "an important contribution to the literature of slavery." Five years later on the same day, Alice Walker was awarded a *Pulitzer Prize* in for her book, *The Color Purple*. The book is the story of the life of an African American woman and her struggle against loneliness, racism and male domination in the racially charged atmosphere of the South. .

▲ In 1973, the first Japanese-style hotel, the Kitano Hotel, opened on Park Avenue in New York City.

◆ José Martí, Cuban poet, journalist, lawyer, diplomat and one of the leaders in his country's independence movement, was killed in battle on this day in 1895.

■ The civil rights case of *Standing Bear v Crook* began during this week in 1879. Standing Bear, a Ponca Chief, argued that an "Indian" was a person just the same as any "white man" and should have the full rights and freedom guaranteed by the Constitution. The case began when Standing Bear and a group of Ponca were put in an army jail by General George Crook for leaving the "Indian Territory" (reservation) to return to their native land in what is now Nebraska. The judge ordered Crook to bring Standing Bear and his men before his court to show by what authority he held them. However, the US district attorney refused to put the judge's order into effect, stating that the "Indians" were "not persons within the meaning of the law." Standing Bear and his men received a few hundred acres of land near the Niobrara River in Nebraska.

◆ Medical researcher Joseph Goldberger of the US Public Health Service announced in 1905 that he had proved that a once-common disease, pellagra, was caused by a nutritional deficiency. Using prison inmates from a Mississippi jail as test cases, Goldberger showed that an insufficient amount of vitamin B in the diet caused the disease.

● Jill Brown became the first African American woman to qualify as a pilot for a major US airline in 1978.

▲ Because of anti-Japanese feeling in California, the *Webb Act*, or *Alien Land Law,* was passed in 1913. The act forbade aliens not eligible for citizenship from owning or leasing farmland in the state for a period of more than three years. The measures applied to all aliens but targeted the Japanese. The act was adopted despite protests by President Wilson.

# 19

## A P R I L

**Declaration of
Independence
Day**
Venezuela

> "If I pierce [my hand] I shall feel pain. The blood...will be the same color as yours. The Great Spirit made us both."
> Standing Bear, 1879

# 20

## A P R I L

◆ During this week in 1959, Fidel Castro, premier of Cuba, made an unofficial goodwill tour of the US and Canada. The tour, which began on April 15, lasted 11 days.

■ The beaver is the totem for people born between April 20 and May 20, according to Sun Bear's Earth Astrology.

◆ On this day in 1657, an appeal granted equal privilege to Jewish Americans Asser Levy and Jacob Barsimon. The council of New Amsterdam had passed a law denying people of Jewish faith the privilege of standing guard and keeping watch at a time when this service was required of all others. Levy and Barsimon objected to the discrimination and filed suit against New Amsterdam.

● The New Orleans Citizen's Council, a segregationist group in Louisiana, in 1962 initiated a plan to provide free one-way transportation to African Americans who wished to move to cities in the North. The trips, called "reverse freedom rides," were made by 96 people during a six-month period.

◆ ▲ A unit of Puerto Rican American and Asian American students at Yale University, calling themselves the United Front for Black Panther Defense in 1970, announced that they would support a "stoppage of all normal activities" on the Yale campus in support of 14 Black Panther members who were on trial in a New Haven, Connecticut, court.

◆ In 1519, Hernan Cortes landed in a place he called *Villa Rica De la Vera Cruz*, meaning "the rich village of the true cross." Today, the region where Cortes landed is the state of Veracruz.

■ President Ulysses S. Grant appointed Brigadier General Ely Samuel Parker, a chief from the Tonowanda-Seneca Nation, as commissioner of Indian Affairs (later known as the BIA) in 1869. Parker, whose Native American name is Do-Ne-Ho-Geh-Weh, became the first Native American to hold this position. He held the position until his term expired in December 1871.

**21 APRIL**

◆ With the assistance of five African American women, Clara Barton administered first aid to Civil War wounded during passage through Baltimore in 1861. Barton later won national recognition as the founder of the American Red Cross.

● In Washington, DC, the Reverend Walter Fauntroy, a disciple of Martin Luther King, Jr., was sworn in as a nonvoting member of Congress for the District of Columbia during this week in 1971. Fauntroy was a graduate of Yale University.

▲ The *Frederic Bancroft Prize* for a book on history was awarded in 1966 to Professor Theodore W. Friend, III of the State University of New York, Buffalo. Friend won the award for his book, *Between Two Empires: The Ordeal of the Philippines 1926-1946*. The book focused on US-Philippine relations during those years.

**22 APRIL**

◆ In 1969, Mexican American member of Congress Henry B. Gonzales of Texas addressed the House in an attack against the militant actions of several Chicano groups. Gonzalez denounced tactics of such groups as MAYO (Mexican American Youth Organization) and the Mexican American Unity Council of San Antonio, Texas. Gonzales suggested that what these groups, as well as all Mexican Americans, wanted was justice from the US government in the form of "decent jobs at fair wages."

■ On this day in 1889, the Creek and the Seminole made an unconditional sale of their lands to the US federal government.

◆ Dr. Jonas Salk was honored at a special White House ceremony in 1955 for his development of a successful polio vaccine. Before the vaccine was developed, polio, a potentially fatal disease, confined thousands of people to wheelchairs or beds for life. President Dwight D. Eisenhower called Dr. Salk a "benefactor of mankind" and called his work the "highest tradition of selfless and dedicated medical research." At the ceremony, Dr. Salk also received special Congressional recognition. While receiving the award, Salk said, "I hope that we may have the opportunity to see again in our lifetime the beginning of the end of other fears that plague mankind." The ceremony, which was held in the White House Rose Garden, also gave a special award to the National Foundation of Infantile Paralysis for their research.

● The first recorded slave revolt in the United States took place on this day in 1526 in an area that is today part of the state of South Carolina. The revolt took place in the first European American settlement that used enslaved people as laborers.

*Dr. Jonas Salk*

▲ The first commercial all-Chinese radio program was broadcast from San Francisco in 1940. The broadcast, carried by KSAN, was sponsored by Thomas Tong, the director of the Golden Hills Radio Company.

◆ During this month in 1979, César Chávez, president of the United Farm Workers Union (UFW), announced a national boycott of iceberg lettuce. Chávez asked for the boycott to support the UFW's strike against California lettuce growers.

■ During this month in 1966, Secretary of the Interior Stewart L. Udall called for "foundation legislation" during a conference about Native American needs. The legislation was to give more elasticity to the trusteeship for Native American lands and, hopefully, to help Native Americans experience a more rapid economic growth in the development of their resources.

❖ In 1896, Thomas Edison presented the first showing of motion pictures on a public screen at Koster and Bial's Music Hall in New York City. The program included footage of two blonde dancers, a comic boxing exhibition and a short comic allegory entitled *The Monroe Doctrine*. A *New York Times* review of the motion pictures described the exhibition as "all wonderfully real and singularly exhilarating."

● Leontyne Price, African American opera soprano, was one of 12 artists to receive the first *National Medal of Arts* award in Washington, DC, in 1985. President Ronald Reagan presided over the ceremony in which the 12 artists and one corporation were given sterling silver medals. Price kissed her medal when she received it. Price is best known for leading roles in the three operas *Aida, Tosca* and *Porgy and Bess*.

▲ In 1852, Governor John Bigler requested that the California legislature use the state's power of taxation to restrain Asian immigration. Bigler also suggested that the state petition Congress to pass legislation prohibiting the importation of "coolies" (Chinese indentured servants) as mine laborers.

**23**

**A P R I L**

**24**

**A P R I L**

◆ President John F. Kennedy formally accepted responsibility for the failure of the Bay of Pigs invasion of Cuba in 1961. The previous week, a small force of anti-Castro Cubans, with the support of US CIA officials, landed in Cuba. Within days of their invasion, Castro's troops had defeated the rebels and captured 743 men. The US action was condemned worldwide.

■ Joan Tower became the winner of the *Grawemeyer Award* for her musical composition *Silver Ladders* in 1990. The composition was an orchestral piece composed by Tower in 1985 for the St. Louis Symphony Orchestra. Tower, a music professor at Bard College in New York became both the first female and the first Native American to win the award, which was given by the University of Louisville, Kentucky, and carried a $150,000 prize.

❖ During this week in 1968, Eric Starvo Galt was indicted for the assassination of the Rev. Dr. Martin Luther King, Jr. On May 7, the name on the indictment was formally changed to James Earl Ray when the government learned the true identity of the alleged assassin.

● In 1814, African American Elijah McCoy applied for and later received a patent for a locomotive lubricator. From the time when people wanted to be certain they had a true version of his device, the popular phrase, "the real McCoy," came into use.

▲ In 1951, Corporal Hiroshi H. Miyamura became a distinguished combat soldier. While fighting in Korea, Miyamura's company was attacked. Miyamura, a machine-gun-squad leader, killed about ten members of attacking enemy forces with his bayonet. After returning to his unit, Miyamura administered first aid to soldiers in his company and then evacuated the unit. Miyamura performed similar feats in two other enemy attacks. Miyamura was promoted to the position of sergeant. Three years later, in 1954, President Eisenhower awarded Miyamura the *Congressional Medal of Honor*.

◆ Following the destruction of the *USS Maine* in Havana Harbor and other events, the United States officially declared war against Spain on this date in 1898.

**25**
**A P R I L**

■ Seventy-two-year-old Mae Chee Castillo, a Navaho, was honored in a ceremony held on the White House lawn by President Reagan in 1985. Castillo was honored for her heroic efforts in the rescue of children from a burning school bus. During the celebration, Castillo took the opportunity to explain to President Reagan, through an interpreter, the need for social security benefits for the elderly because many had nothing else to rely on for support. Later, the White House expressed its displeasure with Castillo's use of the ceremony to voice her concerns.

❖ During this week in 1894, a group of men who called themselves "Coxey's Army" arrived in Washington, DC. The "army" was actually a group of unemployed men who were led by Jacob Coxey. Coxey wanted the federal government to create jobs through a massive road-improvement program to help those who had lost their jobs during the Depression in the 1890s. Coxey left Massillon, Ohio, with a group of 100 men. He expected to have 100,000 by the time he reached the nation's capital. However, he had fewer than 500 men with him when he arrived. When Coxey was arrested for walking on the lawn of the US Capitol, the army broke up.

● The Johnson Publishing Company became the first large African American company to enter the publishing industry in 1962.

▲ In 1861, the US clipper ship, the *Bald Eagle,* sailed through the Golden Gate in California after a 41-day journey from Hong Kong. The ship was carrying 400 Chinese into the states.

**26**
**A P R I L**

◆ In 1977, Vilma S. Martinez, a Mexican American civil rights activist from California, was granted the *John D. Rockefeller III Youth Award* in 1976. Martinez was given the award for her effective defense of the civil rights of Mexican Americans (Chicanos) living throughout the country and, specifically, in the Southwest.

■ During this month in 1969, Native Americans of the Cochiti Pueblo of New Mexico entered into a business arrangement with the Great Western United Corporation. The arrangement called for the leasing of 7,500 acres of Cochiti land by Great Western for a period of 99 years. The land was to be used for the construction of housing. In addition, Native Americans were to be trained and employed by Great Western in any fields in which they could be used.

❖ After a relentless search, the hiding place of John Wilkes Booth was discovered by federal troops in 1865. Booth had been hiding out on the farm of Richard Garrett near Port Royal, Virginia. When the assassin of Lincoln refused to come out of a barn and surrender, a US soldier shot and killed Booth, despite orders to capture Booth alive.

● Supreme Court Justice Felix Frankfurter named William T. Coleman to serve as his law clerk in 1948. Coleman was the first African American to serve in this capacity.

▲ Following a student uprising on April 19, Korean President Syngman Rhee resigned on this day in 1960. Korean Foreign Minister Huh Chong became head of a caretaker government until the new president was elected.

◆ The US Post Office placed a stamp honoring the first Puerto Rican gubernatorial election on sale in San Juan, Puerto Rico in 1949.

**27 APRIL**

■ Robert L. Bennett was sworn in as Commissioner of Indian Affairs by President Johnson in 1966. During the ceremonies, Johnson stated that the "time has come to put the first Americans first on our agenda. . . ." Johnson also stated that he wanted ". . . to begin work today on the most comprehensive program for the advancement of Indians that the government of the United States has ever considered. . . ."

◆ The largest monetary literary award, the $15,000 *Christophers Prize*, was given to writer George Howe in 1949 for his novel, *Call It Treason*. The story, which is set in World War II, tells of three German prisoners of war employed by US Army Intelligence. The soldiers are dropped behind enemy lines to carry out acts of espionage within Germany.

● Director of the A. Philip Randolph Institute, Bayard Rustin, accepted the *Stanley M. Isaacs Human Relations Award* from the New York chapter of the American Jewish Committee in 1969 for contributions toward community understanding. Rustin addressed the members of the committee about his views on the problems facing the educational quality of African Americans. In his address, Rustin urged that college officials "stop capitulating to the stupid demands of Negro students.... and see that they get the education they need." Rustin criticized many programs offered by colleges, saying that African American students "suffering from the shock of integration" demanded "soul courses [as] an easy way out of their problems."

▲ During this week in 1941, the American Oriental Society issued a report concluding that Chinese characters are written up-and-down instead of across the page because ancient Chinese books were written on bamboo slats.

**28 APRIL**

◆ The Cuban American film *El Super* opened on this day in 1979 at movie theaters in New York City. The story dealt with a Cuban exile living in New York City with his wife and daughter and their adjustments to life in the US. The movie starred Elizabeth Pena and was directed by Leon Ichaso and Orlando Jimenez Leal.

■ Richard Wilson, Sr., president of the Oglala Sioux of Pine Ridge, South Dakota, was indicted along with his son and several other Sioux tribal members in 1975 for the alleged beating of four non-Native American members of the American Indian Movement. The beatings allegedly occurred while the AIM members were visiting the Sioux reservation. Wilson was later acquitted of the charges.

◆ Leonard Bernstein was awarded the *Boston Symphony Merit Award* in 1949 for his symphony entitled *The Age of Innocence*. Bernstein was best known for his work with the New York Philharmonic and for his televised *Concerts for Young People* held during the fifties and sixties. Through his televised concerts, Bernstein tried to expose children to classical music.

● Because of his refusal to be drafted into the US Army, Muhammad Ali, claiming the status of conscientious objector as required by his Islamic faith, was stripped of his heavyweight championship belt in 1967. Ali also objected to the war in Vietnam because he viewed the goals of the war as being imperialistic and racist.

▲ The city of San Francisco, California, played host in 1981 to the Thirteenth Session of the Korea-US Security Councilitative Meeting (SCM). A follow-up meeting was held in Seoul, Korea, three months later to expand economic and trade cooperation between the two nations.

*Muhammad Ali*

◆ *Public Law 45* was passed in 1943. One aspect of this law included the spending of public monies to implement an agreement with Mexico about the treatment of "braceros" (Mexican laborers brought to the US under contract). The law called for an assumption of responsibility by the United States Department of Agriculture for the contracting, recruiting and transporting of all braceros.

■ Shortly after midnight on this day in 1860, Navaho, under the leadership of Manuelita and Barbonicito, attacked Fort Defiance in what is now northwest Ohio. The Navaho warriors almost succeeded in completely destroying the fort; however, feeling that they had adequately frightened the troops within the fort, they ceased their attack at dawn.

❖ In 1964, a stamp commemorating European American John Muir went on sale in Martinez, California. Muir, who was born in Scotland, moved with his family to Wisconsin while he was young. Muir later moved to California and earned a reputation as a naturalist and environmentalist while leading a crusade to save California's giant redwoods.

● In 1992, a California jury acquitted four Los Angeles officers in the beating of African American Rodney King. In response to the verdict, which was believed unfair by many US citizens of all races because of a videotape of the beating incident, four days of intense rioting ensued in Los Angeles. The rioting resulted in numerous injuries and deaths, and property damage exceeding $100 million. Riots also occurred in San Francisco, Atlanta and Seattle. In other cities that had large African American populations, such as Philadelphia and New York, many peaceful demonstrations of protest were held.

▲ In 1900, Congress passed an act approving appropriations for a variety of civil expenses of the government for the fiscal year ending June 13, 1901. One of the results of this act was to empower the immigration commissioner to take charge of the Chinese Exclusion Law.

**A P R I L**

**Emperor's Birthday**
Japan

**A P R I L**

◆ A Spanish comedy dealing with an expedition of soldiers was performed on the Rio Grande near what is now El Paso, Texas, in 1598. The play was the first theatrical performance given in North America.

■ On this day in 1966, the Senate confirmed the nomination of Robert LaFollette Bennet as Indian Affairs Commissioner. Bennet, who was 53 at the time of the appointment, was a member of the Oneida Nation.

❖ A conservative Republican Dutch newspaper called *De Grondwelt* began publication in the US in 1860. The newspaper, which was published by Dutch American Jan Roost, was meant to compete against the Democratic Dutch newspaper *De Hollander*.

● After a successful eight-year run, the final episode of *The Cosby Show* aired on NBC (1992). The show, which won many awards during its broadcast, featured the daily life of an upper-middle class African American family named the Huxtables. Actor Bill Cosby was the main character and also the producer of the show. Phylicia Rashad, sister of choreagrapher Debbie Allen, played the mother on the show.

▲ Author Maxine Hong Kingston won a *National Book Award* 1981 in the general nonfiction category for her book, *China Men*.

"He took her to see the Statue of Liberty....She said, "I have seen everything....everything's possible on the Gold Mountain."

Maxine Hong Kingston,
*China Men*

# MY PERSONAL LIST

When many of us think about Native American history, the names that come to mind are usually men, such as Geronimo, Sitting Bull and Osceola. In contrast, images of Native American women are often of the anonymous squaw, exemplified in Longfellow's poem "Hiawatha." However, after the "Indian War" period ended around 1890, Native American women leaders came into prominence.

In 1985, the role of Native American women as leaders expanded dramatically. In this year, Wilma P. Mankiller was officially installed as chief of the Cherokee Nation. As the first woman to lead a "major" Native American nation, Mankiller accepted her role in the spotlight confidently and was reelected in 1991.

As chief, Mankiller sees economic growth and development as the key elements to the progress of the Cherokee. "Responsible business" with "good environmental records" are what she has pledged to work toward.

Mankiller uses her training in social work to help heal internal Cherokee differences. Aside from tensions brought on by high unemployment, bad health care and poor quality education, there have been hard feelings between "full blood" and "mixed-blood" Cherokees. She and former chief Ross Swimmer spent a lot of time working to resolve these problems. With her social-activist, educational and common sense background, Mankiller holds the promise of a successful term as chief.

> "The Cherokee are worried about jobs and education, not whether the tribe is run by a woman or not."
>
> Chief Wilma Mankiller,
> 1985

◀ *President Ronald Reagan and Chief Wilma P. Mankiller*

**MAY**

**Beginning of
Asian American
Heritage Month**

■ During the Revolutionary War, American "colonists" celebrated a holiday known as Tammany Day on the first of May. This holiday was in honor of Chief Tammany of the Lenni-Lenape (Delaware) Nation, who greeted William Penn on his arrival from England and signed two treaties with him. Tammany was named by some colonists as their patron saint to separate their new identity from England.

❖ In 1975, fifty-three-year-old Lila Cockrell became mayor of San Antonio, Texas--the nation's largest city to be governed by a woman. At the time, San Antonio was ranked as the tenth-largest city in the United States.

● In 1950, Gwendolyn Brooks was the first African American to receive the *Pulitzer Prize for Poetry* for *Annie Allen,* a collection of poems that follows an African American woman from childhood through adulthood. Brooks was also named poet laureate of Illinois (1969) and poetry consultant to the Library of Congress.

▲ President Reagan visited China in 1984 to formalize agreements on economic development, cultural and scientific exchanges and the development of nuclear energy.

The 1961 *Pulitzer Prize for Editorial Writing* in the journalism category went to William J. Doreviller of the San Juan, Puerto Rico, newspaper, *San Juan Star*. Doreviller wrote a series of 19 editorials beginning in 1960 criticizing the Puerto Rican Roman Catholic bishops for their opposition to government policies on birth control, and for telling Puerto Rican Roman Catholics not to vote for the Popular Democratic party in upcoming elections. Doreviller, a Roman Catholic, is also editor and publisher of the *San Juan Star,* which was started one and one-half years before he won the award.

**MAY**

■ In May of 1965, Peter MacDonald became director of the Office of Navaho Economic Opportunity, a government program established under President Lyndon B. Johnson to help wage the "war on poverty."

❖ In 1970, jockey Diane Crump of Oldsman, Florida, became the first woman to ride in the Kentucky Derby. Crump, who rode a horse named *Fathom*, finished fifteenth out of seventeen.

● The New York City Ballet presented the first performance of George Balanchine's *Requiem Canticles* in memory of the Rev. Dr. Martin Luther King, Jr., on this day in 1968. The ballet was performed at Lincoln Center, New York, and was set to Stravinsky's 1966 score of the same title.

▲ The world renown cellist, Chinese American Yo Yo Ma was awarded the *Avery Fisher Prize* at the Lincoln Center in New York City, New York, 1978.

◆ In 1960, the *Pulitzer Prize for Journalism/Photography* was awarded to Andrew Lopez of United Press International (UPI). He won the award for a series of photographs of a Cuban army corporal facing a firing squad in Cuba.

■ As part of the Jamestown Commemorative Stamps--Issue of 1907 Series, the US Postal Service produced a five-cent stamp featuring Pocahontas of the Powhatan tribe. Pocahontas is most known for her marriage to John Rolfe as part of a peace treaty between Jamestown colonists and the Powhatan. Pocahontas is also featured in the one-cent stamp that is also part of this series.

❖ During this week in 1957, Irish American Senator John Fitzgerald Kennedy of Massachusetts was awarded the *Pulitzer Prize* for *Profiles in Courage,* a book dealing with the decisive actions of famous US statespersons. The 39-year-old Massachusetts senator would later become president of the United States in the 1960 election.

● The May 1992 issue of *Working Woman* magazine reported that African American Linda Johnson Rice was one of the 25 most successful women in business. Rice, the daughter of publisher John H. Johnson, currently serves as the president of Johnson Publishing, which produces *Jet* and *Ebony* magazines.

▲ *The New York Times* correspondent Sydney Schanberg was awarded a *Pulitzer Prize in Journalism* for his coverage of the communist takeover in Cambodia. His series of articles describing the mass killings in Cambodia were the inspiration of the *Academy Award*-nominated film, *The Killing Fields* (1984). The communist takeover of Cambodia was an outgrowth of the Vietnam War. When the North Vietnamese soldiers took refuge in Cambodia, the US began to bomb the area to force the soldiers to leave. This expanded the war outside of Vietnam, and competing groups began to fight within Cambodia for control of the country.

❖ In May 1968 Aspira, the Puerto Rican-based education organization, sponsored a nationwide conference addressing special-educational needs of Puerto Rican youth. The conference, which was held in New York City, resulted in the publication of *Hemos Trabajado Bien* (We Have Worked Well).

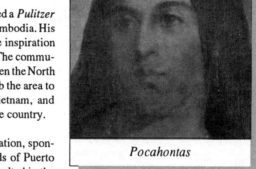

*Pocahontas*

■ A photograph of Hollow Horn Bear, a chief of the Brule Sioux, was used as the basis for a 14-cent stamp issued by the US Post Office in May of 1923. The stamp was first placed on sale in Washington, DC. It was also released in Muskogee, Oklahoma, the location of the headquarters of the Five Civilized Native American tribes.

❖ A Dutch ship called the *de Eendracht* arrived in New Amsterdam carrying the first Norwegian settlers to the US in 1630. Among those aboard the ship were Roelf Jansen, his wife Anneke, and his mother-in-law, Tryn Jones.

● Charles Gordone was the winner of the 1970 *Pulitzer Prize in Drama* for his long-running off-Broadway play, *No Place to be Somebody.* The first off-Broadway play to win a *Pulitzer Prize,* the play, which was described as a "Black black comedy," examines the African American search for a place in a racially antagonistic society and is set in an African American-owned bar in the West Greenwich Village of New York City.

▲ Mrs. Toy-Len Goon, owner of a laundry service in Portland, Maine, was chosen as the US "Mother of the Year" in 1952. Goon, a widow since 1940, brought up eight children, supporting them with her laundry service. All of her children, five sons and three daughters, received higher education and pursued successful careers.

❖ During this week in 1970, the Reverend Patrick Fernandez Flores was consecrated as auxiliary bishop of San Antonio, Texas. Flores was the first Mexican American ever to be raised to episcopal rank.

■ Dr. N. Scott Momaday, an associate professor of English at the University of California, Santa Barbara, and a Kiowa, became the first Native American to win the *Pulitzer Prize* in 1969. Dr. Momaday won in the literary-fiction category for his book, *House Made of Dawn*. The book tells the story of a young Native American veteran of World War II who returns to his reservation and of the problems and frustrations he encounters.

◆ Nicola Sacco and Bartolomeo Vanzetti, two Italian immigrants considered political radicals, were arrested on this day in 1920. The two men were charged with the murders of a paymaster and a payroll guard in South Braintree, Massachusetts. There were many who believed the subsequent trials and executions to be discriminatory, leading to a great deal of public controversy at the time.

● Moneta Sleet, Jr., a photographer for *Ebony* magazine was awarded the *Pulitzer Prize for Photography* in 1969. The prize-winning photograph was taken of Martin Luther King's widow Coretta and her daughter Bernice at Dr. King's funeral service in Atlanta, Georgia, in 1968. The photograph was widely used in newspapers and magazines around the country.

▲ Korean and Japanese Americans celebrate Children's Day.

◆ Mexican Americans celebrate *Cinco de Mayo*. The celebration commemorates the victory of the Mexican army over the French in Pueblo, Mexico, in 1862.

## MAY

**Cinco de Mayo**
(Fifth of May)
Mexico

**Children's Day**
Korea & Japan

## MAY

■ Manhattan Island, part of what is today New York City, was sold to the Dutch by the Shinnecocks on this day in 1626. The island was sold for a price of what today would be between $20 and $30. Peter Minuit, governor of the Dutch, was responsible for the purchase.

◆ On this day in 1929, 30-year-old Robert Maynard Hutchins was named president of the University of Chicago. Hutchins, who previously served as dean of the Law School for Yale University, became the youngest president of a major US college.

● Loretta Glickman was elected mayor of Pasadena, California, by the city board of directors in 1982. Glickman became the first African American woman to become mayor of a major United States city.

▲ President Chester Arthur signed the Chinese Exclusion Act in 1882, which prevented both skilled and unskilled Chinese laborers from entering the United States for a period of 10 years. This act is also considered to be a factor leading to the quota system of the 1920s.

◆ Mexican artist Diego Rivera was featured in an article in the May 6, 1929, issue of *Time* magazine. The previous week, Rivera won the annual *Fine Arts Medal* of the American Institute of Architects (AIA). Rivera was born in Mexico to parents of Mexican and Aztec descent. As an adult, he spent part of his time living in Paris, France, before returning to Mexico with his Russian wife. Rivera built a reputation as being a "communist" painter.

*"The Mexican artists, such as Diego Rivera, understood and represented in their art the hardships, concerns and contributions of the common man."*

■ During this month in 1836, nine-year-old Cynthia Ann Parker was taken prisoner by the Quahada of the Staked Plains (a group belonging to the Comanche nation) in Limestone County, Texas. Parker, who was raised by the Comanche group, learned to speak their language and eventually married Nacona, the tribe's chief. They had a daughter, Topsannah, and two sons, Quanah and Pecos. Quanah eventually became the tribe's chief and was responsible for the movement of the Comanche to a reservation near Fort Sill in Oklahoma.

**7**

**MAY**

◆ During this week in 1939, John Steinbeck's novel about a family of Oklahoma farmers fleeing the "Dust Bowl" and heading west during the Great Depression of the 1930s, *The Grapes of Wrath*, won the *Pulitzer Prize*.

● In 1800, 21 years after building the first home on the Chicago River, Jean Baptiste Pointe DuSable, an African American credited as being the "Father of Chicago," sold his land and personal property for $1,200 and moved with his family to Missouri. His wife, Atherine, a Native American woman, was given to DuSable as a gift from the Potawaton.

▲ The first Japanese person on record to come to the United States was Manjiro Nakohama. Nakohama, who was also known as John Mung, was rescued at sea by Captain William H. Whitfield of the whaling ship *John Howard* in 1843.

◆ The United States-Puerto Rico Commission on the Status of Puerto Rico convened during this month in 1965 to hear testimony on the status of legal and constitutional issues affecting Puerto Rico. The commission, which met in San Juan, Puerto Rico, published its findings in 1966 in an official report.

**8**

**MAY**

■ The Reverend Donald E. Pelotte, son of an Algonquin laborer, became the first Native American ordained bishop in the Roman Catholic Church during this week in 1986. Pelotte was 41-years old when he was ordained.

◆ In 1879, George B. Seldon, an inventor and lawyer from Rochester, New York, filed the first patent application for a gasoline-powered automobile. The vehicle developed by Selden had four wheels, a carriage body, a two-cycle engine, running gear, a shift and a clutch.

● African American agricultural scientist George Washington Carver, through his experiments with various plants, especially the peanut, revitalized the future of Southern agriculture. His impact was so great that the peanut business honored Dr. Carver with a full-page tribute in their trade magazine, *The Peanut World*, during this month in 1921. Among his other honors were a 1923 *Springarn Medal* from the NAACP and election to the New York University Hall of Fame.

▲ On this day in 1955, Mrs. Miten Ishida, the president of the Japanese Federation of Women Societies of San Francisco, greeted Michiko Sako of Japan with a bouquet of flowers at Travis Air Force Base. Sako was accompanied by a group of 24 Japanese women who were coming to the US for plastic surgery to repair scars from the Hiroshima bombing.

◆ Hernando de Soto and a company of Spanish explorers sailed into the Mississippi River in 1541 near what is today Memphis, Tennessee.

> *"It is important to have a vision that is not clouded with fear."*
>
> Cherokee leader

**9**

**MAY**

■ In 1845, news of the death of Cherokee leader Sequoya was published in *The Cherokee Phoenix,* using the Cherokee alphabet which Sequoya had created.

✦ The first trial of Mary E. Surratt, the first woman hanged by the United States government, began on this day in 1865. Surratt, who was convicted by a military commission for conspiracy in the assassination of President Abraham Lincoln at Ford's Theater on April 14, 1865, was tried by nine army officers. She was found guilty and sentenced to death by hanging. She was hanged, along with three male conspirators, on July 7, 1865.

● The musical, *Ain't Misbehavin'*, which celebrated the music of Fats Waller, opened on Broadway in 1978. The show was conceived and directed by Richard Maltby, Jr. During its run, *Ain't Misbehavin'* won the *New York Drama Critics Circle Award for Best Musical* and the *Tony Award* in the same category.

▲ The Japanese American creed was published in the Congressional Record in 1941. It was written by Japanese American Citizen's League (JACL) member and International District Council Chairperson Mike Masaoka in 1940.

✦ Teresa McBride, at the age of 28, was honored by the Small Business Administration as the *National Minority Small Businessperson of the Year* in 1989. She was later named *Hispanic Businesswoman of the Year* by the US Hispanic Chamber of Commerce. McBride is the owner of a growing computer company called McBride and Associates in Albuquerque, New Mexico. Her goal is to foster the entrepreneurial spirit of young Hispanic Americans.

**10**

**MAY**

■ Betty Mae Jumper was elected chairman of the tribal council of the Seminole Nation of Florida in 1967. Jumper was the first woman to be elected to this position. She pledged to continue the "war" of the Seminole nation against the federal government of the US. The Seminole, who never signed a peace treaty with the US government, still considered themselves to be at war with the US.

✦ J. Edgar Hoover was appointed director of the Bureau of Investigation (later changed to the Federal Bureau of Investigation) in 1924. He remained in this post for 48 years until his death in 1972. During his reign, the bureau achieved several high points: the world's largest fingerprint file, its own crime laboratory and the FBI training academy. Many believe that Hoover also acquired scandalous information on many important officials which he then used to influence their actions.

● The Lewis H. Latimer Public School was dedicated in Bronx, New York, in 1968. Latimer, known most for his contributions and improvements in electric lighting, also devoted much of his time to teaching mechanical drawing and English to immigrants. Latimer was a civil rights activist.

▲ A criticism leveled by Korean American reporter Li-Yeon Mary Yuh at *Pulitzer Prize*-winning *New York Newsday* columnist Jimmy Breslin on May 4, 1990, was responded to by Breslin with racial slurs. As a result of his comments, Breslin was suspended from his job for two weeks during this month in 1990.

✦ In 1781, Bernardo de Galvez, Spanish governor of Louisiana, led an attack from Pensacola Bay that resulted in the British giving up the region.

■ St. Regis Seminary, the first Catholic school for Native Americans, opened its doors in Florissant, Missouri, on this day in 1824. The school, run by Father Van Quickenborne, had an enrollment of about 50 students.

**MAY**

◆ Margaret Brewer was sworn in as brigadier general in the US Marine Corps on this day in 1978. Brewer was nominated to the position by President Jimmy Carter. With her promotion, Brewer became the first woman magistrate to reach the rank of general in the US armed forces.

● The premier performance of *Pas de "Duke"* was presented in New York City in 1976. The performance in honor of jazz composer Duke Ellington was choreographed by Alvin Ailey. Featured dancers were Mikhail Baryshnikov and Judith Jamison.

▲ In May of 1817, the first class of the Foreign Mission School in Hawaii was held, with less than 20 students attending. The school was established by the American Board of Commissioners for Foreign Missions

◆ Access to the Plumbers Union Local 2 in New York was blocked on this day in 1964 as a protest against the union's refusal to accept Puerto Rican and African American members. The protest was initiated by CORE under the leadership of James Farmer. On May 15, New York Mayor Robert Wagner announced that a settlement had been reached between the union and the protesters. The union agreed to enroll three Puerto Rican and one African American if the workers could pass the qualification tests.

**MAY**

■ During this month in 1786, Creek and Seminole living in North Carolina and Florida signed a treaty with militia representing the US. The treaty, known as the *Treaty of Colerain*, called for a return by the Native Americans of any fugitive African "slaves" to their "owners." This treaty ultimately became the largest factor separating the Spanish Seminole tribe from the Creek tribe.

◆ Amy Eilberg was ordained as the first female Conservative rabbi on this day in 1985. Eilberg was 31. The graduation ceremonies took place at the Jewish Theological Seminary in New York City.

● In 1871, a young African American boy (name unknown) began his own personal sit-in on a racially segregated horse-drawn street car in Louisville, Kentucky. He was eventually dragged from the car by a band of white teenagers who screamed and cursed him. Soon after, other young African American men proceeded to sit in aboard Louisville streetcars, enduring threats and abuse from local whites. The Louisville Streetcar Company eventually agreed to integrate their streetcars, seeking to avoid more violence and opposition.

▲ During this month in 1872, the Alabama and Chattanooga Railroad went bankrupt. After the bankruptcy, the largest group of Chinese laborers ever gathered in the southern United States was dispersed. Many moved to Louisiana to work on plantations.

◆ The Mexican government in 1835 authorized the selection of available vacant lands in Texas for "peaceable and civilized Indians who may have been introduced into Texas."

■ This day was set aside as "Indian Day" in 1916 by the Society of American Indians. The purpose was to recognize and honor Native Americans and to focus on the need to improve their living conditions.

◆ The first "permanent" English colony on the North American continent was established in 1607 at what is now Jamestown, Virginia. More than 100 whites settled on the left bank of the James River, then called the River of Powhatan. Three ships, *Sarah Constant*, *Goodpeed* and *Discovery,* had brought the whites here from England. The London Company had organized and paid for the voyage.

**MAY**

● African American pilot Robert Smalls sailed the *Planter*, an armed Confederate steamship, out of Charleston, South Carolina, in 1862. Smalls presented the *Planter* to the US Navy, taking it out of Confederate hands.

▲ The Corps for the Advancement of Individuals was organized by Korean Americans in 1913. Ahn Cho-ho served as chairman of the board of the organization.

◆ The Society of Friends of Puerto Rico honored Senator Robert Kennedy of New York in 1966.

**MAY**

■ The Native American Rights Fund filed suit on behalf of 62 Native Americans of the Hopi Nation in 1976. The suit requested that strip mining of coal on the Hopi reservation in Arizona be halted. The coal was being used to supply a plant that produced power for the "Four Corners" region of the country. Two days earlier, five Navaho had filed a suit requesting a court order against the power plant. The Environmental Defense Fund and the Wildlife Federation both announced that they, too, had planned similar suits against the power plant on behalf of the Native Americans.

◆ When millionaire John D. Rockefeller donated $100 million to the Rockefeller Foundation in 1913, it was believed to be the largest single act of philanthropy in history.

● Linda Gainer, a scientist and member of the Chrysler Corporation *Saturn 1B* launch crew, in 1973 became the first woman and the first African American woman to "power up" a space vehicle.

▲ During this month in 1942, the Citizens Committee to Repeal the (Chinese) Exclusion Acts was formed as a result of the introduction of a bill titled *An Act to Repeal the Chinese Exclusion Acts, to Establish Quotas, and for other Purposes.* The chief goal of this bill was to raise immigration quotas for persons of Chinese descent. The bill finally passed in 1943, ending more than 60 years of discrimination by the US government against Chinese immigration.

◆ The 1975 Nielson television ratings were released on this day in *Variety* magazine. *Chico and the Man*, a situation comedy starring Puerto Rican comedian Freddy Prinze, was the third most popular television show of the 1975 season. The show focused on the interaction between a Hispanic American mechanic named Chico and his European American boss. The other four shows in the top five also dealt with the issues of ethnicity and racism in the US. These four shows were *All in the Family* (number one), *Sanford and Son* (number two), *The Jeffersons* (number 4) and *M\*A\*S\*H* (number five).

> "...I believe that every right implies a responsibility, every opportunity, an obligation, every possession a duty."
>
> John D. Rockefeller, *Ten Principles,* 1941

■ In 1934, the Indian Reorganization Act was passed to restore the "Indian" way of life. The act was designed to encourage tribal self-government and Native American-owned businesses and to provide scholarships for individuals.

❖ Ellen Church became the first "stewardess" (flight attendant) in airline history when she was hired by United Airlines in 1930. Church's first flight was from San Francisco, California, to Cheyenne, Wyoming.

**15**

**MAY**

● Internationally-famous entertainer, Josephine Baker, was honored by the NAACP in New York during this month in 1951 for her efforts in combatting racism. Baker had electrified audiences in Europe and the United States with her unique performances. She spent a great deal of time from the 1920s through the 1940s performing in France where she felt there was less discrimination.

▲ In 1893, the US Supreme Court declared the Geary Exclusion Act, an anti-Chinese immigration law, unconstitutional.

❖ During this month in 1961, Joseph Monserrat addressed the National Conference of Social Welfare in Minneapolis, Minnesota. The address, titled "Community Planning for Puerto Rican Integration in the United States," emphasized the need to help Puerto Ricans who emigrate to the United States to function effectively as a societal group. The address also stressed the contributions Puerto Rican emigrants could make to the economic development of the United States.

**MAY**

■ Mugg, a chief of the Arasaguntacock, was killed in 1677 during an attack on Black Point (now Scarboro, Maine). Mugg had led an earlier attack against the English in 1675 and had taken many English prisoners. Later, he was taken prisoner by the English and was brought to Boston. After his release, he attacked the English at Black Point in retaliation for the treatment he had received in prison.

❖ The five Ringling brothers founded their now famous circus in Baraboo, Wisconsin, during this week in 1884. The five Ringling brothers were Albert, Otto, Alfred, Charles and John. Along with 17 other workers, they did everything from sew and pitch the tent to selling tickets and performing in acts. This marked the beginning of a circus dynasty that continues today. In 1919, the Ringling Brothers bought and merged with the Barnum & Bailey Circus. With the purchase, the circus officially changed its name to the Ringling Brothers, Barnum & Bailey Circus.

● Rhythm-and-blues, pop- and gospel-singer Cissy Houston received the second annual *Lifetime Achievement Award* of the Jersey Shore Jazz and Blues Festival in 1992. Houston, a native of Newark, New Jersey, received the award after a career of more than 20 years in the music industry. In addition to her own successful career, Cissy Houston enjoyed watching her daughter Whitney build a successful career in the music industry.

▲ Junko Tabei, a 35-year-old woman from Japan, became the first woman to reach the 29,028-foot summit of Mount Everest on this day in 1975.

❖ Pittsburgh Pirate Roberto Clemente, a Puerto Rican American, got his 1,000th career hit in 1961. Clemente, who had a .351 batting average, was awarded the *Silver Bat Award* later in the year.

■ The Organic Act of May 17 was passed by Congress in 1884. The act provided for a civil government in the territory of Alaska and recognized the rights of the Innuit people (Eskimo) who inhabited the land. With the passage of the act, the Eskimo were permitted to keep their rights to Alaskan territorial lands.

❖ The Scandanavian newspaper *Nordisk Tidende* reported in 1948 that 10 members of Congress were of Norwegian descent. They included three senators--Warren Magnuson, Alexander Wiley and Edward J. Thye--and seven representatives--Leroy Johnson, Harold Hagen, Henry Jackson, Thor Tollefson, August Anchesson, Henry O. Talle and Harold Knutson. Together, the members of Congress represented five states--Washington, Minnesota, California, Wisconsin and Iowa.

● The US Supreme Court handed down its ruling in the landmark *Brown v Board of Education of Topeka, Kansas* case in 1954. In its unanimous ruling, the court declared that segregated education was illegal. School systems were instructed to move with "all deliberate speed" to integrate the schools.

▲ In 1882, the US and Korea signed a treaty establishing diplomatic relations (see May 22nd entry). In 1982, President Ronald Reagan proclaimed the 100th anniversary of this treaty "the week between May 16 and May 22, as a national observance of the centennial of diplomatic relations between the US and Korea, and the ties of friendship that bind our two peoples."

◆ On this day in 1961, Premier Fidel Castro of Cuba declared his willingness to exchange Cuban rebel prisoners taken in April for 500 American bulldozers. On May 22, a Tractors for Freedom Committee was set up in the United States. Negotiations broke down, however, over the total numbers.

**17 MAY**

**18 MAY**

■ In a class action lawsuit, members of the Northern Cheyenne Nation of Montana sued the Cheyenne tribal government in order to gain "vested property rights" of any mineral or other natural resources found underneath land that was allotted to them under a 1926 Congressional act. The tribal government claimed that the act gave the mineral rights to them as a governing body, not to the individual owner of a tract of land. The US Supreme Court denied the suit, ruling in favor of the Cheyenne tribal government.

❖ Margaret Kuhn, 67, of Philadelphia, Pennsylvania founded an organization known as the Gray Panthers in 1972. Kuhn said the Gray Panthers existed in order to fight various forms of discrimination against older people. She claimed that older people, when organized, would become a dynamic force, influencing social, political and economic areas in the US.

● In response to the acquittal of four Dade County police officers in the beating death of African American insurance salesperson, Arthur McDuffie, riots erupted in Miami in 1980. The riots resulted in the deaths of 9 people and injury to 160 others. In addition, stores were looted and businesses were burned. As protesters carried out their riotous activities, they chanted the name, "McDuffie."

▲ Asian American high-school student Ronald Kim of East Brunswick High School in New Jersey was recognized as the top scholar in the *Star-Ledger Scholar Awards* in 1992. Kim, a 16-year-old student, graduated high school in 1992. Kim planned to attend Princeton University to pursue a degree in physics.

◆ In 1992, Jackie Nespral was hired by the NBC television network to co-anchor the weekend slot on their *Today Show*. In taking this position, Nespral became the first Hispanic female to anchor on a major network news. Regarding her new position, Nespral said, "I think this is a door opener. I think the networks are looking at Hispanics for talent."

■ Kateri Tekakwitha, known as the "Lily of the Mohawk," was formally approved for beatification, or sainthood, in the Roman Catholic Church by Pope Pius XII on this day in 1939. Tekakwitha became the first Native American to be so honored. Tekakwitha, who was recommended for beatification by cardinals in Rome on the ninth of this month, was born in 1656 at Ossernenon near Auriesville, New York.

**19**

**MAY**

◆ The first law setting limitations on the number of Germans who could emigrate to the United States was passed on this day in 1921. The Quota Law permitted only 3 percent of the German population (based on the 1910 census) to emigrate to the United States.

● At the twentieth annual *Emmy* awards celebration in 1968, actor Bill Cosby won the award for *Best Actor in a Dramatic Series* for his leading role in *I Spy*.

▲ The Alien Land Act passed in the California Legislature and became law in 1913. The law affected not only Japanese but also Koreans living in the United States. According to the law, a person ineligible for US citizenship was forbidden to purchase land that was to be used for agricultural purposes.

◆ In 1822, Augustine de Iturbide, considered by many to be the liberator of Mexico, persuaded the Mexican Congress to elect him emperor. He was crowned Augustine I on July 25th.

**MAY**

■ Officials of the state of Wisconsin and of the Chippewa announced in 1991 that they had reached an agreement in a 17-year battle over treaty rights. The agreement was based on a ruling that prevented the Chippewa from collecting $325 million in damages for the loss of treaty rights. The ruling also set limits on the number of fish Chippewa could catch and prevented tribal members from harvesting timber on the reservation.

◆ In 1932, Amelia Earhart began her quest to become the first woman to fly solo across the Atlantic Ocean. She departed from Harbor Grace, Newfoundland, and landed in Ireland. Her other accomplishments include being the first woman to fly from Honolulu, Hawaii, to the US mainland, being the first woman to fly alone across the US in both directions and being the first woman to receive the *Distinguished Flying Cross*. In 1937, she attempted to become the first woman to fly around the world, but her plane disappeared near Howland Island in the South Pacific.

● Robert Nix, a Democrat, became the first African American elected to Congress from Pennsylvania when he defeated Cecil Moore in a special fourth-district election in 1958.

◆ The first administration of the Republic of Cuba, free from United States occupation, was established with Tomas Estrada Palma as president in 1902.

> "I, for one, hope for the day when women will know no restrictions because of sex, but will be individuals free to live their lives as men are free."
>
> Amelia Earhart, 1935

■ The deer is the totem for people born between May 21 and June 20, according to Sun Bear's Earth Astrology.

*Benjamin O. Davis*

◆ When Charles Lindberg landed on a Paris airfield on this date in 1927, he achieved international fame as the first person to fly solo across the Atlantic Ocean. His specially built plane, *The Spirit of St. Louis,* carried Lindberg 3,600 miles in 33 1/2 hours. A hero's welcome greeted Lindberg when he returned home to the US.

● Benjamin O. Davis, Jr., in 1959 became the first African American in the US Air Force to hold the rank of major general. Davis's father, Benjamin, Sr., held the honor of being the first African American general in the US Army.

▲ During this month in 1958, Dr. Chien Shiung Wu, a professor of physics at Columbia University in New York, was awarded an honorary doctorate in science by Princeton University of New Jersey. This was the first honorary doctorate ever granted to a woman by the prestigious ivy-league school.

# 21 MAY

◆ The *Treaty of Guadalupe Hidalgo* was ratified by the Mexican Congress at Queretaro on this day in 1848. The treaty permitted the United States to acquire the land that today makes up about half of Colorado, along with the states of Arizona, California, Utah and New Mexico. The treaty also established a clear border for the south of Texas. Under the treaty, the United States was to pay Mexico $15 million for the land.

# 22 MAY

■ In 1873, Kintpuash, along with 80 men of the Mondoc Nation, surrendered to the army of the US. Kintpuash was a subchief of the Mondoc, a group that lived on the West Coast between Oregon and California. Kintpuash is better known historically as "Captain Jack."

◆ On this day in 1922, Dr. Willis Carrier introduced a centrifugal refrigeration machine, or air conditioner, designed for use in large buildings, such as office buildings. The machine was later put on display in the Smithsonian Institution in Washington, DC.

● Judge Lawson Thomas was appointed to head Florida's first all-African American court in Miami in 1950. This was the first court of its kind since Reconstruction (1865-1877). The court tried only cases involving African Americans.

▲ On this day in 1882, the governments of the United States and the Kingdom of Korea concluded a treaty that called for peace, friendship, trade and navigation. The treaty provided for the establishment of diplomatic relations and the establishment of permanent missions in the capitals of each country. One hundred years later in 1982, the Republic of Korea presented the United States with a "plaque of friendship" commemorating the anniversary of friendly diplomatic relations between the two countries. The plaque was signed by Korean Speaker Jung Nae-Huk and was inscribed in both Korean and English.

◆ On this day in 1992, Felipé Alou was named manager of the Montreal Expos baseball team. Alou became the first native of the Dominican Republic to be named manager of a major league baseball team.

■ During this week in 1956, the US Senate voted to create a new Native American tribe to be known as the "Lumbee Indians." The tribe was to include about 4,000 Native Americans living in the Robeson County area, North Carolina. The Native Americans were descendants of the peoples who were in that area near Sir Walter Raleigh's "lost colony."

❖ Financier Bernard M. Baruch was awarded the 1944 *Churchman Award* for "promotion of good will and better understanding of all people."

● The first African American recipient of the *Congressional Medal of Honor*, Sergeant William H. Carney, was issued his medal in 1900. US Army Sgt. Carney served in C Company, 54th Massachusetts Colored Infantry during the Civil War. He was awarded the medal for his actions on June 18, 1863, during the Battle of Fort Wagner, South Carolina. When the standard bearer, or flag carrier, fell during the charge on the fort, Carney picked up the flag and resumed the charge toward the fort, planting the flag within the fort as the fort was being taken by the Union Army. Sgt. Carney was wounded twice during the battle.

▲ The Korean Women's Association was established in San Francisco, California, on this day in 1908.

◆ During this month in 1991, the last Cuban troops who had been sent to help fight a civil war in Angola between 1975 and 1978 were withdrawn.

## 23 MAY

## 24 MAY

■ The Haskell Institute of Lawrence, Kansas, which opened as a vocational educational facility for Native Americans in 1884, was dedicated as a registered national historic landmark on this day in 1968.

❖ On this date in 1844, Samuel Morse transmitted the first telegraph. Morse was very interested in the possibilities of the telegraph instrument and invented an alphabet or code for use in transmitting messages via the telegraph machine commonly known since then as the Morse Code. A member of the American Hall of Fame, a statue of Morse stands in Central Park, New York City.

● Nat "Sweetwater" Clifton joined the New York Knickerbockers of the National Basketball Association on this day in 1950. Clifton became the first African American professional basketball player.

▲ The independence of Korea, uncertain as it was in the face of manipulation by Japan, Russia and China, was recognized by the United States government in 1882. A commercial treaty between the US and Korea was also signed that year.

◆ On this day in 1846, an army under General Zachary Taylor took the tour of Monterey in what is today New Mexico. The tour was conducted during the Mexican American War.

*"Hurrah for old Kentuck! That's the way to do it. Give 'em hell, damn 'em!"*

Zachary Taylor,
Rallying battle cry,
1847

■ In 1804, a grant of land was obtained from the Seminole by attorney John Forbes of the law firm of Panton, Leslie and Company. The agreement was signed at Cheskatolfa, Florida, by 21 chiefs of the Seminole and Lower Creek Nations.

◆ In Oradell, New Jersey, on Memorial Day in 1992, a monument was dedicated to the first woman military officer to lead troops into battle, Major Marie Rossi. The monument was dedicated posthumously. Major Rossi was killed in a helicopter crash while returning from a reconnaissance mission in Saudi Arabia after a cease fire was called during the Persian Gulf War (Operation Desert Storm) in 1991. The monument, a bronze bust of Major Rossi that is attached to a 20-ton boulder, was dedicated by Italian American Governor James Florio, members of the Veterans of Foreign Wars (VFW) and members of the American Legion.

● Branford Marsalis, jazz musician from Louisiana, and his band became the new *Tonight Show* band when Jay Leno took over from Johnny Carson as the host of the show in 1992.

▲ On this day in 1925, the Supreme Court ruled against Toyota Hidemitsu, declaring that, although he served in the military of the United States, he was not eligible to become a US citizen. The court based its ruling on the fact that Hidemitsu was neither white nor black.

◆ Author Gary Soto was the winner of the 1985 *American Book Award* for his non-fiction book, *Living Up the Street: Narrative Recollections*. The book was praised for Soto's eloquently-told story of his own childhood experiences growing up poor as the son of a single parent farmworker.

MAY

MAY

■ Apache of Oklahoma and New Mexico sued the US for $8 million in 1948. The suit claimed that the Apache were imprisoned by the US Army in Florida, Alabama and Oklahoma from 1886 to 1913 and that Apache land in New Mexico was given to whites in 1877.

◆ Petty Officer First Class Beth Blevins was named "Sailor of the Year" by the US Navy in 1988. Blevins became the first woman in navy history to win the honor. In addition to the award, Blevins won a navy commendation and a promotion to the position of chief petty officer.

● Despite a US Supreme Court decision 20 days earlier (May 6, 1857) preventing his freedom, enslaved African Dred Scott won his freedom when he and his family were purchased by Taylor Blow. Blow then gave the Scotts their freedom.

▲ President Coolidge signed the Immigration Bill into law on this day in 1924. Upon the signing of the bill, Japanese immigrants became aliens ineligible for US citizenship. Chinese immigrants had been excluded from citizenship under earlier legislation.

◆ During this month in 1980, the Federation for American Immigration Reform requested of the Supreme Court that they enjoin, or stop, census taking. FAIR was formed to support changes in US immigration policy.

■ During this month in 1970, the women of the Isleta Native American Pueblo, a pueblo dating back to ancient times, were given the right to vote in pueblo elections. The pueblo approved a new constitution that included this right.

◆ The city of El Paso, Texas, elected Suzie Azar mayor in 1989. Azar became the fourth woman to hold a mayoral seat in a major city in Texas. At the time of the election, the state's three other major cities (Houston, Dallas and San Antonio) were also governed by women.

**27 MAY**

● Dorie Miller, a messman/attendant from the US battleship *West Virginia,* was awarded the *Navy Cross* in 1942. Miller received this honor for his heroic actions during the Japanese attack on Pearl Harbor, Hawaii, in December of the previous year. Miller was below deck when he heard explosions. He ran on deck and saw Japanese planes attacking the ship. Miller saved the life of his captain by dragging him to safety. He then grabbed a machine gun, never having used one before, and shot down four Japanese fighter planes.

▲ In 1869, the first group of Japanese immigrants arrived in the United States and settled in Gold Hill, California, where they set up the Wakamatsu Tea and Silk Farm Colony. The group arrived aboard the *SS China*.

◆ A bill establishing the Alliance for Progress was signed by President Kennedy on this day in 1961. The bill provided $600 million in special aid to Latin America.

**28 MAY**

■ In 1830, under the direction of President Andrew Jackson, Congress enacted legislation calling for the "removal" of Native Americans from the southeastern states of Georgia, Alabama and Mississippi. The first group to be moved was the Choctaw Nation, which was removed to Oklahoma.

◆ The cornerstone of Helga Trefaldighat Kyrcka (Holy Trinity Church) was laid in 1698. The church was built on the site of the burial grounds of the Swedish settlers who built Fort Christina in what is now New Castle, Delaware.

● During this week in 1963, 30 African nations formed the Organization of African Unity at a conference in Addis Abbaba.

▲ In 1898 largely in response to controversy about the Chinese Exclusion Act, the US Supreme Court declared in the *Wong Kim Ark v United States* case that native citizenship was without respect to race or color. A child born in the US was now a US citizen regardless of the parents' nationality.

◆ Cuban American ballerina Lourdes Lopez was one of many dancers who participated in two performances of the American School of Ballet's 40th anniversary celebration this month in 1974. The performances were held at the Juilliard Theater in New York City's Lincoln Center.

*Lourdes Lopez*

■ In 1873, an executive order was issued setting aside a reservation for the Mescalero, a subgroup of the Apache.

**MAY**

◆ Janet Guthrie became the first woman to qualify for the Indianapolis 500 auto race in 1977. She was forced to drop out during the race, however, because of a defective fuel pump.

● Vernon Jordan, Jr., executive director of the National Urban League, was hit in the back by gunfire as he returned to his motel room in Fort Wayne, Indiana, in 1980. Jordan was in town to address the local chapter of the Urban League. Despite an intensive search by FBI agents as late as 1982, the perpetrator of the crime was never found, and no specific reason for the crime was ever determined. Jordan continued his career in public service and, in 1992, was named to co-chair newly elected President Bill Clinton's transition team.

▲ Tensing Norgay of Nepal, along with Sir Edmund Hillary, reached the top of Mount Everest on this day in 1953. The two men were the first to completely scale the 29,028-foot Himalayan peak.

◆ In 1934, the Platt Amendment was abrogated by mutual agreement between the United States and Cuba. The two nations also signed a reciprocal-trade agreement.

**MAY**

■ Billy Cypress of the Seminole Nation graduated from Stetson University in Deland, Florida, with a bachelor of arts degree in English in 1965. Cypress was also commissioned as a second lieutenant in the US Army Reserves. Cypress was believed to be the first Seminole to graduate from a university and the first to become a US army officer. At the time of his graduation, he planned to go to graduate school and then return to the Seminole Nation to teach children.

◆ The first formal observance of Memorial Day took place in 1868 following the request of General John L. Logan, national commander of the Grand Army of the Republic, to "decorate the graves of comrades who died in defense of their country during the late rebellion."

● During this week in 1972, *Malcolm X*, a documentary about the life of the African American civil rights leader, was released in New York theaters. The documentary was an adaptation of the book *The Autobiography of Malcolm X*, written with Alex Haley. The film was produced by New York City journalist and talk-show host Gil Noble.

▲ At the San Francisco City Hall in 1892, Dennis Kearney delivered a speech intended to encourage discrimination against Japanese, similar to existing discrimination against the Chinese. Kearney encouraged white taxpayers to keep Japanese students from attending US public schools.

◆ Fernando de Soto arrived in Florida in 1539 with 600 men. De Soto was sent by the king of Spain to begin to consolidate Spain's domination in the area. Nine days earlier, the explorer had been on the island of Cuba.

■ The US Supreme Court handed down its ruling in *Hynes v Grimes Parking Company* in 1949. In this ruling, the court stated that reservations formed under the Reorganization Act were "subject to the unfettered will of Congress" and that the secretary of the Interior had no right to give the nations "any permanent title or authority" over their lands.

❖ On this day in 1692, John Alden of Boston, Massachusetts, was accused and convicted of being a warlock. The accusation against Alden took place during the witchcraft hysteria in the Salem, Massachusetts, area at the end of the 1690s. He was acquitted of the charge at a later date.

● Dr. Harvey A. Itano, an M.D. and Ph.D. , received the first *Rev. Dr. Martin Luther King, Jr., Medical Achievement Award* from the Philadelphia chapter of the Southern Christian Leadership Conference (SCLC) in 1972. The award was given to Dr. Itano for his outstanding contributions in sickle-cell anemia research.

▲ The *Reciprocity Treaty of 1875* was concluded between the Hawaiian Kingdom and the US government, allowing both nations to establish free trade of major goods across the Pacific. King Kalakoua ratified the treaty, and President Ulysses S. Grant gave it his approval on this day in 1875. The treaty did not take affect, however, until September 1876. As a result of this treaty, the Hawaiian economy revived, with a dramatic increase in sugar and rice exports.

▲ New Jersey's Garden State Arts Center hosted the second annual Hispanic Heritage Festival sponsored by New Jersey in 1992. The festival featured folklore, food and artwork from many countries. The festival also featured music by Latin musical performers. Three of the music performers at the festival were Edy Palmieri, Ismael Quintana and Willie Colon.

# MY PERSONAL LIST

# JUNE

**1** ● During this month in 1792, Benjamin Banneker published his first almanac.

■ In 1868, the Navaho signed a treaty with the US setting aside 3.5 million acres of land in NM and AZ for Navaho use.

**2** ● President Nixon invited 36 African American Republicans to a briefing in which he responded to complaints from the Congressional black caucus (1971).

■ The Seminole of Florida fled to the Everglades to avoid removal to the West (1837).

**3** ◆ The US government announced in 1980 that more than 100,000 Cuban refugees had emigrated to the US in the past three months.

◆ Alexander Graham Bell transmitted the first wireless telephone message (1880).

**4** ● In 1895, Rudolph Lee was awarded a patent for a bread-crumbing machine. Lee later sold his rights to a manufacturer in New Hampshire.

**9** ■ The first "dime" novel titled *Malaska, or the Indian Wife of a White Hunter* was published in 1860.

■ A Native American rodeo was held in White Swan, Washington, in 1969.

◆ Temperance agitator Carrie Nation died (1911).

**10** ◆ The first Dutch to land on Manhattan Island came in 1610.

■ In 1898, the Post Office issued a stamp called "Indian Hunting Buffalo." The stamp was made from an engraving in the *Schoolcraft History of Native American Tribes*.

**11** ● Inventors Purdy and Sadgwar were granted a patent for a folding chair in 1889.

◆ The Displaced Persons Act was passed in this month in 1948, admitting 205,000 refugees and homeless Europeans from 1948 to 1950.

**12** ▲ Independence Day in the Philippines

◆ The US applied for the extradition of James Earl Ray from London, England, after his arrest four days earlier (1968). Ray was wanted for the assassination of civil rights leader, Reverend Dr. Martin Luther King, Jr.

**17** ● P.B. Downing was granted a patent for an electric railroad switch (1890). Downing was also the recipient of patents for a letter box and a street letter box (1891).

**18** ◆ In 1975, Swedish American Margita White became the first woman to serve as director of the White House Office of Communications. White became a US citizen in 1955.

**19** ▲ During this week in 1868, 148 Japanese arrived in Honolulu as contract laborers.

● "Juneteenth" is observed by African Americans sometimes by staying home from work and not patronizing places of business in protest against discrimination.

**20** ◆ Flag Day in Argentina

● In 1990, South African nationalist leader Nelson Mandela began an eight-day tour of the US. Mandela met with heads of states and cities, strengthening US support of antiapartheid policies in South Africa.

**25** ■ Custer was defeated at the Battle of Little Big Horn (1876) by an alliance of Native Americans directed by Crazy Horse and Chief Sitting Bull (AKA Tatanka Yotanka, Sitting Buffalo). The battle was one of many in which US troops tried to take plains land from Native Americans forcefully.

**26** ● James Weldon Johnson, the first African American lawyer in the state of Florida and creator of the first African American daily newspaper, *The Daily American*, died when his car was struck by a train in 1938.

**27** ▲ In 1907, the Board of Police Commissioners in San Francisco refused licensing for an employment agency to six Japanese.

◆ Juan Rodriguez Cabrillo left Mexico to begin exploration of the west coast of California in 1542.

**28** ● In 1971, the US Supreme Court found in favor of Muhammad Ali by overturning the draft evasion decision.

● The Fugitive Slave Laws were repealed in 1864.

**5** ▲ David H. Wang's play M. Butterfly won the 1988 *Tony Award for Best Play*.

◆ Irish-Catholic Senator Robert Kennedy was shot in a hotel after winning the CA primary in 1968. Kennedy died early the next day.

**6** ● Harvey Gantt won the Democratic senatorial primary in North Carolina (1990).

▲ Korean Memorial Day

◆ Pope Pius XII excommunicated Juan Peron of Argentina in 1955. The excommunication lasted for eight years.

**7** ▲ Governor Reagan of CA led Japanese Americans in a dedication service commemorating the Gold Hill colony of the Sierra Nevadas in 1969.

◆ In 1971, Mayor John Lindsay of New York proclaimed the week beginning June 7 as Puerto Rican Cultural Week.

**8** ■ The Yakima Agency Boarding School, the first reservation boarding school for Native Americans, was created in 1855 as a result of a treaty made between the US and the Yakima Nation.

**13** ◆ The US Supreme Court handed down its *Miranda v Arizona* decision in 1966. Criminal suspects were now advised of their rights before interrogation.

● T. W. Stewart received a patent for a mop in 1883.

**14** ▲ In 1900, Hawaii became a US territory.

■ A meeting to unify members of the 19 Native American tribes living in Oklahoma was held at the University of Oklahoma (1965).

**15** ● New York City in 1964 came up with an acceptable desegregation plan for African Americans.

**16** ● Kenneth A. Gibson became mayor of Newark, NJ, in 1970.

■ Tenskwatawa, brother of Shawnee chief Tecumseh, won popularity as a prophet from Shawnee, Creek and Cherokee tribes after performing what is now called "the miracle of the eclipse."

**21** ● ◆ James Chaney, Andrew Goodman and Michael Schwerner disappeared in Philadelphia, Mississippi, in 1964 after being arrested for a traffic violation. The three men were conducting an African American voter-registration drive in Neshoba County.

**22** ● A Biloxi, Mississippi, grand jury returned indictments against 15 alleged Klu Klux Klan (KKK) members (1966) in connection with the murder of Vernon F. Dahmer. Dahmer was slain on January 10, 1966.

**23** ■ In 1683, Philadelphia founder William Penn signed a treaty of peace and friendship with Native Americans.

**24** ◆ Sally Ride in 1983 became the first woman from the US to complete a space mission. Ride made her trip aboard the space shuttle *Challenger*, which blasted off on June 18.

**29** ● R.B. Spikes received a patent for his combination milk-bottle opener and bottle cover in 1926.

◆ Hispanic Americans from Chile, Columbia, Peru, Spain and Venezuela celebrate the Feast of Sts. Peter and Paul.

**30** ● The mother of the Reverend Dr. Martin Luther King, Jr., was shot and killed while attending church in 1974.

■ The St. Regis Seminary, a Catholic school for Native Americans in Florissant, Missouri, closed its doors in 1831.

**KEY**

● African Americans
◆ Hispanic Americans
■ Native Americans
▲ Asian Americans
◆ European Americans

# JULY

**1** ▲ Chinese Americans from Hong Kong celebrate the Half-Year Holiday.

■ Emory S. Sekaquattawa, a Navaho, became the second Native American admitted to West Point in 1949.

**2** ● Congress passed the Federal Elections Bill (1890). The bill was designed to protect the voting rights of African Americans.

◆ James Garfield, 20th president of the United States, was shot in Washington, DC, in 1881. He died in September.

**3** ● The national convention of CORE met in 1966 and voted to adopt the "black power" concept.

◆ In July 1914, Victoriano Huerta resigned as leader of Mexico, bringing an end to the constitutionalist revolution phase of the Mexican Revolution.

**4** ● E.M. Bannister received first prize for his painting, *Under the Oaks*, at the Philadelphia Centennial Exposition (1876).

■ Delegates of the Cherokee Nation met to elect a successor to Chief Path Killer and to begin to write a tribal constitution (1827).

**9** ● Daniel Hale Williams performed the world's first successful heart operation in Chicago's Provident Hospital in 1893.

◆ Independence Day in Argentina

**10** ▲ Bon Day (Feast of Fortune) is celebrated by Japanese Americans.

● Educator Mary McLeod Bethune was born in Mayesville, South Carolina, in 1875.

**11** ● The Reverend Dr. Martin Luther King, Jr., was awarded the *Medal of Freedom* posthumously in 1977.

**12** ◆ In 1984, Italian American Geraldine Ferraro was chosen as Walter Mondale's vice-presidential running mate.

● F. M. Jones received a patent for an air-conditioning unit and a starter generator (1949).

**17** ● In 1862, the first "regular colored troops" were enlisted at Leavenworth, Kansas.

▲ Constitution Day is celebrated in Korea

**18** ◆ National Day in Spain

● Inventor C.J. Dorticus received a patent for a device called a leak stop in 1899. Dorticus also held patents for other devices used in photography.

**19** ◆ School teacher Christine McAuliffe was selected by NASA to take part in a space shuttle mission (1985). McAuliffe, the first teacher to be considered for a space mission, was killed in 1986 when the space shuttle *Challenger* exploded moments after liftoff.

**20** ◆ Independence Day in Colombia

◆ Astronaut Neil Armstrong in 1969 became the first person to walk on the moon.

■ Jay Silverheels, co-star of *The Lone Ranger* television show, received a star on Hollywood's Walk of Fame in 1979.

**25** ● In 1973, Barbara Jordan, the only African American Judiciary Committee member, spoke on television in favor of impeaching President Nixon for his cover-up of the Watergate Hotel break-in and the bugging of Democratic party headquarters.

**26** ● President Harry Truman issued an executive order in 1948 banning segregation in the armed forces.

◆ Fidel Castro's "26th of July Movement" (1953) led an attack on the Moncado Army Barracks in Santiago, Cuba, in an attempt to overthrow the Batista government.

**27** ● William Henry Hastie was unanimously confirmed by the Senate as the first African American judge of the circuit court of appeals. Hastie was appointed to the Third Judicial Circuit.

**28** ◆ Independence Day in Peru

■ A battle between the Sartee Sioux and the US Cavalry took place at Story Lake, Minnesota in 1862.

● In 1868, the Fourteenth Amendment became part of the Constitution.

**5** ● In 1947, Larry Doby became the first African American in baseball's American League.

■ Satanta and Big Tree were sentenced to death by hanging in Texas in 1874. The death sentences were later changed to life sentences by the governor of Texas.

**6** ◆ Inventor B.H. Taylor received a patent for a slide valve in 1897. Taylor also held a patent for a rotary engine.

▲ The last essay written by Sui Sin Far, "Chinese Women in America," was published during this month in 1913. The essay dealt with issues of sexism and racism.

**7** ■ Chee Doge was elected chairman at the first Navaho Tribal Council meeting in 1923.

◆ In 1946, Mother Frances Xavier Cabrini was canonized, becoming the first American saint.

● In 1864, Maryland amended its constitution to abolish slavery.

**8** ◆ In 1881, Sandra Day O'Connor was nominated as a US Supreme Court justice by President Reagan.

● CORE director Floyd McKissick announced that he would take a leave of absence from the organization (1981). McKissick was replaced by Roy Innis.

**13** ● An international rock concert called *Live Aid* was held simultaneously in the cities of London, Philadelphia, Sydney and Moscow in 1985. The *Live Aid* concert raised money for people in Africa who had fallen victim to severe drought conditions and poverty.

**14** ◆ In 1972, Jean Westwood, descendant of the earliest pioneers of Utah, became the first woman in US history to be elected chairperson of a major political party. In this role, Westwood served as manager of George McGovern's presidential campaign.

**15** ◆ Hispanic Americans from Spain celebrate St. James Day.

● In 1929, Consul to Liberia W. T. Francis died in Africa. Francis was appointed consul to Liberia by President Coolidge.

**16** ◆ Neil Armstrong and Buzz Aldrin landed on the moon (1969). This became the first of five US moon-landing missions.

**21** ● African American S.C. Shank received a patent for a sleeping-car berth in 1897.

◆ Jesus T. Pinero was named by President Truman as the first governor of Puerto Rico (1946).

**22** ◆ Journalist Wiley Post landed his airplane at New York's Bennett Field after completing the first solo around-the-world flight in 1933.

● M. W. Birga received a patent for a street sprinkling apparatus in 1879.

**23** ● Citizenship for African Americans is granted in 1868 with the ratification of the Fourteenth Amendment.

**24** ◆ Hispanic Americans from Ecuador and Venezuela celebrate Simon Bolivar's birthday.

● Charles V. Bush became the first African American page in the US Supreme Court (1954) and the first in Capitol Page School.

**29** ◆ After a five-year fight, the UFWOC, a union made up largely of Mexican American migrant farmers, signed a contract with 26 Delano grape growers in California (1970).

**30** ■ In 1609, the Iroquois were defeated for the first time at Ticonderoga, NY.

■ In 1684, the Iroquois agreed to be ruled by the king of England.

**31** ● S.E. Thomas was awarded a patent for a casting device in 1888. Thomas held other plumbing patents (pipe connection, waste trap, waste trap for basin and closet).

■ In 1763, the British defeated the Ottawa at Bloody Run, Michigan.

## KEY

● **African Americans**
◆ **Hispanic Americans**
■ **Native Americans**
▲ **Asian Americans**
◆ **European Americans**

# AUGUST

**1** ● In 1955, the Georgia Board of Education ordered teachers who were members of the NAACP to resign from that organization or have their teaching licenses revoked for life.

● Jesse Jackson condemned the apartheid government of South Africa in 1979.

**2** ● William Still started the underground railroad in 1850.

◆ Ms. Robbins became the first female cantor at a Jewish synagogue in New York City (1955).

**3** ◆ President Dwight D. Eisenhower signed a bill changing the name of Bedloe's Island, home of the Statue of Liberty, to Liberty Island in 1956.

◆ Columbus left Spain in search of the "New World" and arrived in the Bahamas on October 12, 1492.

**4** ◆ President Truman in 1947 signed the Crawford Butler Act, permitting Puerto Rico to elect its own government.

**9** ● Jesse Owens won four gold medals at the 1936 Olympics in Germany.

◆ Richard Nixon resigned from the presidency in 1974.

**10** ◆ The Pan American games were held in Cuba during this month in 1991.

◆ Herbert Hoover, 31st president of the US, was born in 1874.

◆ Independence Day in Ecuador

**11** ● *Roots* author Alex Haley was born in 1921.

▲ Physicist Hsue-Shen Tsien stated in 1954 that thermonuclear reactors produce 5 times more electricity than fossil fuels.

■ Cherokee Chief John Ross forced Elias Boudinot to resign his job as editor of the tribal newspaper in 1832.

**12** ■ The New York Power Authority paid the Tuscarora Indians $850,000 in 1960 for use of the land near Niagara Falls for a reservoir.

◆ Baseball Hall of Famer, Stan Musial announced his retirement in 1963.

**17** ● ◆ A three-day music festival called Woodstock ended on this day in 1969. The musical event became one of the most significant events in rock 'n' roll history. Among featured performers were African American guitarist Jimi Hendrix and Hispanic performer Carlos Santana.

**18** ● Labor Secretary James Wilkins in 1954 became the first African American to attend a weekly presidential cabinet meeting.

◆ Virginia Dare, the first child of English parents in the United States, was born in Virginia in 1587.

**19** ■ Santee Sioux Chief Little Crow and other chiefs assembled a war party to attack Ft. Ridgely, MN, as a result of a dispute with white traders in 1862.

**20** ● The first National Negro Convention was held in 1830 in Philadelphia, PA, with Richard Allen as chairman.

**25** ● In 1925, A. Philip Randolph organized the Brotherhood of Sleeping Car Porters Union.

**26** ◆ World-famous US pilot Charles Lindbergh died on the Hawaiian island of Maui in 1974.

**27** ● W.E.B. Dubois, civil rights leader, died in 1963.

● About this day in 1955, African American Emmett Louis Till was murdered for speaking to a white woman in Money, Mississippi.

**28** ● Reverend Dr. Martin Luther King, Jr., delivered his "I have a dream" speech in Washington, DC, in 1963.

◆ Noted publisher and columnist Bennett Cerf died in 1971.

| | | | |
|---|---|---|---|
| **5** ● Althea Gibson became the first African American to win in women's tennis singles at Wimbledon, England, in 1957. | **6** ● The Voting Rights Act was passed in 1965. This act made it easier for African Americans to vote, especially in the South.<br><br>▲ In 1945, the United States dropped an atomic bomb on Hiroshima, Japan, in an attempt to end World War II. | **7** ● Joyce Alexander was sworn in as the first African American woman magistrate in 1979.<br><br>■ The Oklahomans for Indian Opportunity (OIO) was formed as an educational, nonprofit organization in 1965. LaDonna Harris was elected president of the organization. | **8** ● Five African Americans were elected to the ten-member city council of Selma, Alabama, for the first time in 1972.<br><br>■ Sioux Mary Louise Defender was named Miss Indian America 1954 in a Minnesota fair. |
| **13** ● Muhammed Ali was marshall of an integrated parade through the Watts section of Los Angeles in 1967.<br><br>■ Chief Manteo of the Hatteras in 1587 became the first Native American baptized into the Church of England and into the Protestant faith. | **14** ● Mississippi public schools in 1964 were integrated for the first time.<br><br>▲ Chinese newspapers in the US praised the Atlantic Charter signed by FDR and Winston Churchill in 1941. | **15** ◆ Baseball legend Roberto Clemente of the Pittsburgh Pirates was born in 1934.<br><br>▲ Independence Day in Korea. In 1948, the Republic of South Korea was created with Syngman Rhee as its leader. | **16** ❖ National Restoration Day in the Dominican Republic<br><br>❖ Elvis Presley, 1950s and 1960s rock n' roll singer, died in 1977. |
| **21** ▲ Following a self-imposed exile in the U.S., Philippine opposition leader Benino Aquino, Jr., returned to his homeland (1983). He was shot to death moments after his plane landed. | **22** ◆ Argentine author Jose Luis Borges won the $25,000 *Pulitzer Prize in Literature* in 1970.<br><br>■ Two Native American Nations, Saginaw-Chippewa and Stockbridge Munsee, were given full control over their own affairs in 1949. | **23** ● Nat Turner's slave revolt ended in Virginia in 1831.<br><br>■ During this month, soldiers with US representatives James Calhoun and Colonel John Washington shot and killed Navaho leader, Narbona in 1849. | **24** ● Edith Sampson was first African American named as alternate delegate to the United Nations in 1950. |
| **29** ● In 1950 Althea Gibson became the first African American to play in a national tennis tournament.<br><br>❖ Oliver Wendell Holmes, doctor and Supreme Court justice, was born in 1809. | **30** ● Roy Wilkins, civil rights leader and head of NAACP, was born in 1901. | **31** ● Fannie Lou Hamer demanded her right to register to vote in 1962. As a result, Hamer and her family were forced to leave their home. Two years later, Hamer cofounded the Council of Federated Organizations, a group that recruited Northern students to protest for African American rights. | **KEY**<br><br>● **African Americans**<br>◆ **Hispanic Americans**<br>■ **Native Americans**<br>▲ **Asian Americans**<br>❖ **European Americans** |